Strategic Business Alliances

NEW HORIZONS IN INTERNATIONAL BUSINESS

Series Editor: Peter J. Buckley
Centre for International Business,
University of Leeds (CIBUL), UK

The New Horizons in International Business series has established itself as the world's leading forum for the presentation of new ideas in international business research. It offers pre-eminent contributions in the areas of multinational enterprise – including foreign direct investment, business strategy and corporate alliances, global competitive strategies, and entrepreneurship. In short, this series constitutes essential reading for academics, business strategists and policy makers alike.

Titles in the series include:

Alliance Capitalism and Corporate Management
Entrepreneurial Cooperation in Knowledge Based Economies
Edited by John H. Dunning and Gavin Boyd

The New Economic Analysis of Multinationals
An Agenda for Management, Policy and Research
Edited by Thomas L. Brewer, Stephen Young and Stephen E. Guisinger

Transnational Corporations, Technology and Economic Development
Backward Linkages and Knowledge Transfer in South East Asia
Axèle Giroud

Alliance Capitalism for the New American Economy
Edited by Alan M. Rugman and Gavin Boyd

The Structural Foundations of International Finance
Problems of Growth and Stability
Edited by Pier Carlo Padoan, Paul A. Brenton and Gavin Boyd

The New Competition for Inward Investment
Companies, Institutions and Territorial Development
Edited by Nicholas Phelps and Philip Raines

Multinational Enterprises, Innovative Strategies and Systems of Innovation
Edited by John Cantwell and José Molero

Multinational Firms' Location and the New Economic Geography
Edited by Jean-Louis Mucchielli and Thierry Mayer

Free Trade in the Americas
Economic and Political Issues for Governments and Firms
Edited by Sidney Weintraub, Alan M. Rugman and Gavin Boyd

Economic Integration and Multinational Investment Behaviour
European and East Asian Experiences
Edited by Pierre-Bruno Ruffini

Strategic Business Alliances
An Examination of the Core Dimensions
Keith W. Glaister, Rumy Husan and Peter J. Buckley

Investment Strategies in Emerging Markets
Edited by Saul Estrin and Klaus E. Meyer

Strategic Business Alliances
An Examination of the Core Dimensions

Keith W. Glaister,

Professor of International Strategic Management, Centre for International Business, Leeds University Business School, University of Leeds, UK

Rumy Husan,

Senior Lecturer in the Business Development of Emerging Markets, Centre for International Business, Leeds University Business School, University of Leeds, UK

and

Peter J. Buckley,

Professor of International Business and Director of the Centre for International Business, Leeds University Business School, University of Leeds (CIBUL), UK

NEW HORIZONS IN INTERNATIONAL BUSINESS

Edward Elgar
Cheltenham, UK • Northampton, MA, USA

© Keith W. Glaister, Rumy Husan and Peter J. Buckley 2004

All rights reserved. No part of this publication may be reproduced, stored in a retrieval system or transmitted in any form or by any means, electronic, mechanical or photocopying, recording, or otherwise without the prior permission of the publisher.

Published by
Edward Elgar Publishing Limited
Glensanda House
Montpellier Parade
Cheltenham
Glos GL50 1UA
UK

Edward Elgar Publishing, Inc.
136 West Street
Suite 202
Northampton
Massachusetts 01060
USA

A catalogue record for this book
is available from the British Library

Library of Congress Cataloguing in Publication Data
Strategic business alliances: an examination of the core dimensions / edited by Keith W. Glaister, Rumy Husan, and Peter J. Buckley.
    p. cm.
Includes bibliographical references and index.
    1. Strategic alliances (Business)–Management. 2. Joint ventures–Management. 3. Investments, Foreign–Management. I. Glaister, Keith W. II. Husan, Rumy. III. Buckley, Peter J., 1949–

HD69.S8S78 2004
658'.044–dc22

2003069119

Printed on elemental chlorine free (ECF)
recycled paper containing 30% Post-Consumer Waste

ISBN 978 1 84376 177 8

Typeset by Cambrian Typesetters, Frimley, Surrey

Printed and bound in the USA

Contents

Acknowledgements	vi
List of figures	viii
List of tables	ix
1. Introduction: What do we know about international joint ventures?	1
2. Strategic motives and performance	18
3. The nature of partner selection	31
4. Management control	53
5. Decision-making autonomy	77
6. Learning to manage international joint ventures	100
7. Partnering skills and cross-cultural issues	120
8. Performance assessment in IJVs: The relationship between subjective and objective methods and the influence of culture	138
9. Culture and the management of IJVs	157
10. Summary and conclusions	175
Appendix 1 Research methods and sample characteristics	179
Appendix 2 Case vignettes: outlines of the sample IJVs	185
References	195
Index	207

Acknowledgements

The authors and publisher gratefully acknowledge permission for use of the following material:

Chapter 1: A large part of this chapter is based on P.J. Buckley and K.W. Glaister, 'What do we know about international joint ventures?', in F. Contractor and P. Lorange (eds.) (2002), *Co-operative Strategies and Alliances*, Elsevier Science: UK. Ch. 3, 49–69, with permisison from Elsevier.

Chapter 2: An earlier version of this chapter was presented at the *Australia–New Zealand Academy of International Business Annual Conference*, University of New South Wales, Sydney, October 1999.

Chapter 3: An earlier version of this chapter was presented at the *Academy of Management Annual Meeting*, Toronto, August 2000.

Chapter 4: An earlier version of this chapter was presented at the *British Academy of Management Annual Conference*, Manchester Metropolitan University, September 1999.

Chapter 5: This chapter is based on K.W. Glaister, R. Husan and P.J. Buckley (2003), 'Decision making autonomy in UK international joint ventures', *British Journal of Management*, Vol. 14, with permission from Blackwell Publishing.

Chapter 6: This chapter is based on K.W. Glaister, R. Husan and P.J. Buckley (2003), 'Learning to manage international joint ventures', *International Business Review*, Vol. 12, No. 1, pp. 83–108, with permission from Elsevier.

Chapter 7: This chapter is based on P.J. Buckley, K.W. Glaister and R. Husan (2002), 'Partnering skills and cross-cultural issues', *Long Range Planning*, Vol. 35, No. 2, pp. 113–134, with permission from Elsevier.

Chapter 8: An earlier version of this chapter was presented at the *European International Business Academy (EIBA) Annual Conference*, ESCP-EAP, Paris, December 2001.

Acknowledgements

The work in this book forms part of an ESRC project *An Investigation of the Core Dimensions of UK International Joint Venture Activity with European Partners* (R000236676).

Every effort has been made to trace all the copyright holders but if any have been inadvertently overlooked the publishers will be pleased to make the necessary arrangements at the first opportunity.

Figures

1.1	IJVs: the time window of observation	14
5.1	Dimensions of IJV decision making	96
6.1	Lessons in the management of IJVs	109
7.1	IJV skills set	123

Tables

1.1	Relevance of received theory	4
1.2	Special theories of IJVs	6
1.3	Key issues in IJV research	7
1.4	Control	12
2.1	Market entry motives: questionnaire data	23
2.2	Non-market entry motives: questionnaire data	24
2.3	IJV satisfaction by strategic motivation: interview data	26
2.4	IJV performance measures: questionnaire data	26
2.5	IJV satisfaction by strategic motivation: questionnaire data	27
3.1	Task-related selection criteria: questionnaire data (1)	39
3.2	Task-related selection criteria: questionnaire data (2)	43
3.3	Prior relationships and favourable past association as a partner selection criterion: interview data	45
3.4	Importance of partner selection criteria: questionnaire data	46
3.5	Status indicators – quantitative summary: interview data	49
4.1	Control mechanisms	56
4.2	Mechanisms of control used by partners to influence IJV management: interview data	60
4.3	Mechanisms of control used by partners to influence IJV management: questionnaire data	64
4.4	Extent of partner control: interview data	66
4.5	IJV partners' extent of control: questionnaire data	69
4.6	Partner involvement in functional areas: interview data	71
4.7	More active partner in regard to the functional management of the IJV: questionnaire data	73
5.1	Perceptions of IJV autonomy	83
5.2	IJV decision-making autonomy: questionnaire data	84
5.3	Extent of joint decision-making: questionnaire data	85
5.4	Nature of IJV decision-making: interview data	87
5.5	Correlation between satisfaction and autonomy: questionnaire data (Spearman's rho)	91
5.6	Correlation between (i) Satisfaction with performance and perception of IJV autonomy (ii) Age of JV and perception of IJV autonomy: interview data (Spearman's rho)	93

5.7	Correlation between age and autonomy: questionnaire data (Spearman's rho)	95
6.1	Categories of lessons learned from interview data	106
6.2	Categories of lessons learned from questionnaire data	107
7.1	Categories of partnering skills from interview data	124
7.2	IJV skills set matrix	125
8.1	Means and standard deviations for hypothesized variables	145
8.2	Spearman rank order correlations for hypothesized variables: all partners	146
8.3	Regression analysis for variable sets	148
8.4	Spearman rank order correlations between assessments of performance	149
8.5	Spearman rank order correlations between perception of performance satisfaction and reported performance satisfaction	151
8.6	Spearman rank order correlations between parent firms' assessments of specific aspects of IJV performance by (i) culture clusters and (ii) Kogut–Singh index of cultural distance	152
8.7	Spearman rank order correlations between UK parent firms and IJV managements' assessments of specific aspects of IJV performance by (i) culture clusters and (ii) Kogut–Singh index of cultural distance	154
9.1a	Problems in managing the IJV due to cultural differences	164
9.1b	Problems in managing the IJV due to cultural differences: summary table	165
9.2a	Relative importance of national culture and corporate culture differences for managing the IJV	168 169
9.2b	Relative importance of national culture and corporate culture differences for managing the IJV: summary table	169
9.3	Problems experienced in managing the IJV	
9.4	Differences in culture contributing to differing views on management of the IJV	170
9.5	Spearman correlations between the extent culture differences contribute to different views on IJV management and problems experienced in managing the IJV	171
A1	Characteristics of the sample	183
A2	JV number by partner nationality and industry	184

1. Introduction: What do we know about international joint ventures?

INTRODUCTION

The proliferation of inter-firm collaboration has been well documented (e.g. Hergert and Morris, 1988; Hagedoorn, 1996; Gomes-Casseres, 1996; Beamish and Delios, 1997a; Glaister and Buckley, 1994; Glaister et al. 1998), with alliance activity now a crucial part of the strategy of many firms (Harrigan, 1985, 1988a; Bleeke and Ernst 1993a,b). Competitive advantage increasingly depends not only on a company's internal capabilities but also on the types of alliances and the scope of its relationships with other companies (Parkhe, 1991). These trends signal the need to understand the nature of inter-firm collaborative activity, not least because it has a profound effect on the practising managers (Buckley and Young, 1993: 215).

The focus of this book is a subset of strategic alliance activity – that of international equity joint ventures (JVs). These involve two or more legally distinct organizations (the parents), each of which invests in the venture (the child) and actively participates in the decision-making activities of the jointly owned entity. A JV is considered to be international if at least one partner has its headquarters outside the venture's country of operation or if the JV has a significant level of operation in more than one country.

International joint ventures (IJVs) have been described as 'a logical and timely response to intense and rapid changes in economic activity, technology, and globalisation' (Doz and Hamel, 1998: xiv). Doz and Hamel argue that globalization has opened the 'race for the world' as firms enter once-closed markets and pursue untapped opportunities. At the same time the 'race for the future' compels firms to discover new market opportunities, new solutions for customers, and new answers to poorly met needs. Moreover, few firms can now create and deliver products and services on their own, let alone control leading-edge technologies: technologies are seldom controlled by single firms; significant technological development depends on collaborative activity.

IJVs do not occur by chance; rather they are the outcome of a company decision, hence certain goals and motives must be present to justify creating an IJV. It cannot be assumed that IJVs are always prompted by a single aim, however, they are more likely to be the result of a number of different motives. Furthermore, the expectations and goals that led to the creation of the IJV constitute the rational measures for evaluating the success or failure of the IJV (Buchel et al., 1998: 15–16).

The major dimensions of JV investigation identified in the prior literature (summarized by Parkhe, 1993) are: motives for JV formation, partner selection, management control and JV performance. These four research dimensions are adopted as the core elements of this study. While these four dimensions constitute discrete aspects of JV activity they also represent a set of integrated relationships. The empirical research reported in this book considers each of the discrete dimensions and also investigates a set of interrelationships among these dimensions.

There is a vast amount of literature on joint ventures and alliances, although this literature has been criticized for being non-cumulative and unsynthesized (Parkhe, 1993). In the following sections we set out the context for the rest of the book by examining the core dimensions of IJVs. We then set out the domain of the study.

WHAT DO WE KNOW ABOUT INTERNATIONAL JOINT VENTURES?

The first point to note is that IJVs are simply one business arrangement among many. The choice of an IJV is made against the competing alternatives of licensing arrangements, mergers, wholly owned subsidiaries, foreign direct investment and looser 'non equity' collaborations (Buckley and Casson, 1998a). Consequently, it is essential to remember that the normal issues of business practice apply to IJVs as to all forms of business institutions and practices. The following section makes this point in detail. Thereafter, we examine the unique or unusual issues involved in IJVs and the extent to which special explanations are required for their existence. We then produce a matrix of 'issues by explanation'. This matrix is capable of further refinement as we shall see.

IJVs AS BUSINESS PRACTICE AND BUSINESS INSTITUTIONS

This section seeks to show that many of the features of IJVs are amenable to standard analysis using regular business theories and approaches – economics, finance and organization theory. Standard techniques of analysis are

Introduction

as applicable to IJVs as to other business arrangements. Intrinsic to this argument is the view that standard microeconomic analysis is relevant to IJVs. It can be shown that the search for economies of scale and market power provide the underpinning for the suggestion that IJVs provide increasing returns to scale analogous to any business expansion programme. In addition IJVs are a powerful technique for reducing transaction costs in situations where there are barriers to other forms of expansion (such as mergers) (Buckley and Casson, 1998a). The Resource Based Theory of the firm is also relevant and many attempts have been made to integrate this approach with transactions cost economics.

The rules of finance also apply to IJVs. IJVs are sought, just like other real options, because the risk/return trade-off is thought to be favourable. Here, as elsewhere, the flexibility of IJVs allows them to be converted either to a fully owned investment or liquidated (by sale to the partner, perhaps) (Buckley and Casson, 1998b). Valuation problems arise in IJVs, both as a partner selection issue, as a management problem and as an issue in liquidation, sale or conversion to a wholly owned operation.

Organization theory, too, has an important bearing on IJVs. The role of learning is critical in many IJVs (Gomes-Casseres, 1996) and life-cycle concepts are useful in many situations.

In terms of the techniques needed to analyse IJVs, in addition to those deriving from economics, finance and organization theory, it will be particularly appropriate to examine game theory and agency theory. Game theory lends itself to IJVs because of the crucial notion that IJVs involve at least two players – the parents – with possibly a third player if the IJV can be considered an independent player. Agency theory is relevant because of the remoteness of the decision-makers (the managers of the IJV) from the owners (the parents).

It is therefore essential that, before considering the 'special issues' involved in IJVs and the need for unique theories, techniques and explanations, we delimit the area of 'specialness' by utilizing extant methods of analysis. These are summarized in Table 1.1.

SPECIAL ISSUES IN IJVs

IJVs involve managing across the borders of the unitary firm. They therefore raise a number of special issues, in particular motives for formation, partner selection, management, control and performance.

The question of *motives* for establishing IJVs requires special attention insofar as the choice of form of joint venture can be contrasted with other means of achieving corporate objectives. IJVs thus can be analysed by

Table 1.1 Relevance of received theory

Economics	Economies of scale and scope
	Increasing/consolidating market power
	Increasing returns
TCE (Transaction Cost Economics)	Reducing transaction costs (versus agency costs)
Resource Based Theory of the firm	Accessing competencies
Finance	Return
	Risk
	Valuation
	IJVs as real options
Organization theory	Learning
	Reduce resource dependence
	Life cycle models

reference to the alternatives forgone – takeover, greenfield (wholly owned venture), licensing. Each of these forms will have advantages and disadvantages as compared to IJVs and these need to be carefully clarified and quantified. Essentially, these forms are horizontal, market access alternatives. Similar analyses can be performed for vertical IJVs. Other motives may need more extensive analysis.

The choice of *partner* is clearly a major issue in IJVs. Partner selection will be a key factor determining the success (performance) of the IJV. This is analogous to, but not congruent with, a takeover. In a takeover, complementarities may be vital, but a takeover may be effected in order to close down or remove the victim. The key issue in takeovers is valuation, in IJVs it is negotiation. In a takeover, management becomes unitary (hierarchical) whereas in an IJV, it is perforce co-operative.

This leads to the view that *management* is (or needs to be) different from that in the unitary firm. IJVs are to some degree exceptional in the context of a stereotyped hierarchically organized firm. Directives from top-down are clearly not a viable way of managing beyond the firm's boundaries, and some modification of management practice and style are necessary.

This is closely related to the notions around '*control*' in the IJV. Work has focused on the *extent* of control, the *mechanisms* by which it has been exercised and the *focus* of such control. It may be suggested that control of an IJV is more difficult than in a normal ownership situation and thus the decisions of the IJV are to some extent outside the determination of the (any) parent. Thus the parent has to design mechanisms into the structure and management of the

IJV and, maybe, has to focus its control on a subset of these decisions. The subset chosen will reveal a great deal about the objectives and strategic direction that the parent wishes to achieve. There may, too, be a trade-off between extent of control and the degree of risk assumed by the parent.

Finally, the *performance* of IJVs may be difficult to evaluate. If the motive for establishment differs from straight profit – maximization, then perhaps the IJV should be judged against these objectives rather than a calculus of profits. Moreover, it may well be difficult to evaluate the profitability of an IJV in that it is not a free-standing entity and indivisibilities exist between its profits and those of its parents. The termination of an IJV may not be an indicator of failure – indeed it may connote success in that the objectives set for it have been achieved. If IJVs are judged as 'real options' (Buckley and Casson, 1998b; Kogut, 1991), then the taking up of the option by internalization may be entirely congruent with the parent's initial goals. IJVs, paradoxically, may be most successful when they are relatively short-lived! Given this, how can performance, at a given point of time, be meaningfully measured? Again, perhaps the only true measure is against an alternative business form. Table 1.2 examines special theories of IJVs correlating 'issues' with 'concepts'.

Table 1.2 can be collapsed into a more comprehensible two-by-two matrix examining the twin issues of entry and management and the two conceptual structures of 'international business' and 'international management', as shown in Table 1.3. International business is the set of concepts from transaction cost economics (Williamson, 1975, 1985) and internalization theory (Buckley and Casson, 1976; 1998a; 1998b). International management is the applied area of resource based theories of the firm (Grant, 1996). This simple division highlights the differences between the two most important explanatory approaches to IJVs.[1]

It will be noted that this is set up as a process in fixed stages and in a definite time sequence – motives, choice of partner/partnering, management, control (operation), performance (outcome). This framework can be a straitjacket for analysis. It has some similarities with the 'Uppsala' analysis of 'stages of international involvement' which was mistakenly taken by some as a determinate process. And here we go back to an old issue, that of models versus frameworks (Buckley, 1996). The analytic modelling of joint ventures and alliances focuses on isolation of a few key variables, particularly environmental variables, and predicting from the model the way in which the firm will behave (Buckley and Casson, 1996). This contrasts with the approach based on synthesis (for example Parkhe, 1993) which leaves the assumptions implicit and derives propositions from an extensive literature review.

The comparative perspective is particularly important in respect of JVs. In answering questions on why firms choose JVs or how successful they have been, it is essential to compare JVs with other institutional arrangements. In

Table 1.2 Special theories of IJVs

Issues	Internalization	TCE	Resource based theory of firm	Strategic management	Organization theory
1. Motives	i. Benefits of internalizing intermediate goods ii. Indivisibilities iii. Barriers to merger.	Opportunism Bounded rationality Small numbers Asset specificity	Leverage Internal resources (capabilities)	Speed to market Risk reduction Scale economies	Reduce resource dependency
2. Partnering – choice of partner	Potential benefits of internalization and indivisibilities	Partner choice mitigates effects of (i) above	Compatible management possession of complementary capabilities	Compatibility of goals Task related complementarity Similar goals	Key is reduction of dependency (trade-off with management problems)
3. Management	Co-operation: Mutual forbearance Commitment Trust	Trust as TC reducing element	Transmit and receive capabilities		Network management
4. Control – Bases Extent Focus Mechanisms	Comparative perspective	Trade off control versus market elements	Choose optimum means of accessing resources	Strategic dissonance between partners	Variety of means of control power structure
5. Performance duration	'Flexibility' necessarily limited	Inherently unstable?	Access to resource is key Lasts so long as effective means of access	Strategic choice changes over time	

Table 1.3 Key issues in IJV research

	International business	International management
Entry	Benefits of internalizing intermediate goods versus barriers to merger	Complementarity of capabilities and compatibility of goals
Operation and management	Reduce co-ordination costs through increasing trust and growth in commitment	Transmit and receive capabilities

practice, this introduces difficulties, because JVs are an intermediate state, between wholly owned subsidiaries and looser market based arrangements like licensing. Analytical techniques are much better at examining extreme solutions or outliers, rather than intermediate, moderate, middling outcomes.

There is a further, related problem in the analysis of IJVs and alliances which directly relates to issues of time, and that is longevity. This is not new. Alfred Marshall himself said 'For the element of time, which is the centre of the chief difficulty of almost every economic problem' (preface to first edition of *Principles of Economics* 1890 (p. vii in 8th edition 1930)). As mentioned above, the most successful joint ventures and alliances may be the most short-lived. Flexibility in strategy may require rapid and frequent moves into and out of a series of joint ventures.

A successful analysis of JVs must not then fall victim to the tyranny of time. But we must acknowledge that time is a crucial element in the approach to JVs. Should we then split up the above process into separate pieces? Or is there a more subtle way of encompassing the time dimension?

There are techniques to compress time – notions of sunk costs, stocks rather than flows, discounting future benefits and real options are all attempts to capture the shadow of the future. Perhaps it is dissatisfaction with these techniques which leads management theorists to despair of 'models' and turn to 'frameworks'?

A related difficulty is that of 'learning'. This needs to be encompassed both *within* a single joint venture and *across* multiple joint ventures (leading to the notion of 'joint venture sophisticated firms'). Feedback mechanisms may, again, be regarded as an inadequate response to learning, but if we can more carefully specify what precisely the learning is about, then maybe progress can be made (Casson, 1994).

Perhaps time-dependent processes require new forms of analysis, such as notions of irreversibility and path dependence which need to be fully integrated into JV theory.

A further philosophical issue arises in assessing joint ventures, which is not unique to them. This is the appropriateness of a 'Platonic' method versus an 'Aristotelian' method. Platonists prefer to compare situations and institutions with the (Platonic) ideal. An example of this is the standard of 'perfect competition' in economics. Aristotelians prefer a concrete comparison. This is raised in Williamson's (1996) idea of 'remediableness'. A situation is 'remediable' in the following terms: 'Within the feasible subset, the relevant test [for remediableness] is whether (1) an alternative can be described that (2) can be implemented with (3) expected net gains.' (Williamson 1996: 210).

This has strong parallels with Hirschman's (1970) notion of *repairable* lapses of economic actors. We should beware of comparing JVs with a Platonic ideal, unless we use this criterion everywhere. There is at least a suggestion in the literature that IJVs are often compared against an ideal institutional alternative rather than applying the remediableness criterion.

CONCEPTUAL INNOVATIONS IN ANALYSING IJVs

Because of the argument that joint ventures are special and require special explanations, several relatively new concepts have been developed to tackle the above issues. (Perhaps it is more accurate to state that more weight has been put on several extant concepts felt to be particularly relevant to IJVs.) With Ockham's razor in mind, we should beware the proliferation of concepts and introduce new ones only when absolutely necessary.

Among the new concepts are co-operation (variously defined), trust, culture, learning and networks.

One further issue arises which leads us into the realm of research method. This is the question of whether 'objective' or 'subjective' explanation is necessary for IJVs. Is it possible to have a satisfactory explanation of the structure, motives, management and performance of IJVs from secondary data alone? *Or* is there something inherent in IJVs which requires knowledge of the motivations, outlook and 'native categories' (Buckley and Chapman, 1998) of the individual manager?

Managers are important in international business theory (Buckley, 1996). They make judgements in the face of uncertainty and therefore, sometimes, they make mistakes. The information on which they work and the conceptual frameworks within which they operate are currently subject to intense analysis (Buckley and Carter, 1999; Buckley and Chapman, 1996; 1997).

Buckley and Casson (1988) see joint ventures as an institutional arrangement to mitigate the worst consequences of mistrust. They represent a compromise contractual arrangement for minimizing the transactions costs of a complex sequence of interactions between the firms. The JV allows the interaction of a mutually positive kind based on the exercise of 'mutual forbearance'. The JV is, however, only the formal structure which permits this behaviour. It is the behaviour (mutual forbearance) which brings the benefit, not the structure (JV) per se. On this reading, JVs are a *permissory* institution. The research agenda arising from this goes on to identify the types of environmental conditions that lead to JVs. These key variables are not purely economic, but include technological and cultural elements. Key determinants include obstacles to licensing (lack of patent rights, uncertainty about technological competence), obstacles to IJVs (cultural distance) and obstacles to merger (protection of the firm's independence, scope economies in technology) – all of which are clearly institutional comparators (Buckley and Casson, 1996). Buckley and Casson simplify the institutional choice by showing that joint ventures are likely to be chosen in intermediate market conditions (large volatile market or small stable market). These are precisely the areas where managerial judgement (or perception) of the relevant comparative costs are likely to be at their most critical.

- IJVs as 'compromise' (between market modes e.g. licensing and takeover); 'intermediate state'
- Use in large but volatile markets and stable but small markets
- IJVs as a 'real option'; cultural benefits of IJVs (versus hostile takeover)
- Extreme values *do not* capture IJVs

MOTIVES

Following Gomes-Casseres (1996) we can identify three major motives for the formation of alliances and joint ventures. These are: (1) supply based alliances, which function along the supply line and involve resource transfers beyond simple exchange relationship (finance, design, management skills and technology may flow between the partners) in order to reduce transaction costs and to enhance innovatory relationships. (2) Alliances based on corporate learning which enable the transfer of tacit knowledge and the creation of cross-company terms, perhaps across a technological frontier. (3) Market based reasons. This may include the traditional cartel and reducing the speed to market (Lei and Slocum, 1991). Motives for IJV formation are summarized as follows:

- Foreign Market Entry v Non-Market Entry
- IJVs as Entry Choice: – Learning
  – Reducing competition
  – Diversification
  – Cost sharing
  – Regulatory restrictions
  – Vertical IJVs (reduce TCs)

A crucial distinction in motives for IJVs arises between market entry and non-market entry motives. Buckley and Casson (1998a) analyse market entry motives where markets are differentiated by size and volatility. IJVs are found to be an 'intermediate mode' used where markets are growing but not overwhelmingly large (where FDI and merger are preferred) or small (where licensing is optimal). They are also useful in large but volatile markets, where their role as an 'option' on deeper involvement or withdrawal is at a premium. However, a number of other key motives have been identified in the literature. These include learning, reducing competition, diversification, cost sharing (including R & D costs) and regulatory restrictions. At least a modification of the standard market entry analysis is required where such motives are important.

In addition, we must not ignore vertically linked IJVs. The spectrum of choice runs through full integration, through quasi vertical integration (Blois, 1972), IJVs and alliances, long-term contracting (relational contracting) to simple buyer–seller relationships. These issues are well explored in the literature.

PARTNERING

The standard transaction cost/internalization theory argument on choosing joint venture partners is that internalizing one or more markets in intermediate goods provides benefits for the IJV, but that there must also be significant barriers to merger (Buckley and Casson, 1988). The resource based theory of the firm suggests similarities in management strategy combined with complementarities (differences) in capabilities. In the language of strategic management, this represents compatibility of goals and task-related complementarities. Both vertical and horizontal complementarity may produce an IJV. Horizontal IJVs pose competition issues and raise strategic questions arising from competitors in one area co-operating in another. Cartels rather than IJVs may be the appropriate nomenclature for JVs which have market-based rationales.

- 'Differences' versus 'similarities'
- Complementary capabilities and similarities in management strategy
- Impact of competitors (alliance capitalism); cultural influences
- Dynamic aspects – management and trust

Collapsing the arguments (particularly of Porter and Fuller, 1986), we can suggest that four key elements may be involved in partner choice.

1. The firms must have complementary capabilities.
2. The firms must have compatible (international) strategies.
3. At least in their current operating area, there must be a low risk of the partner becoming a competitor (although, of course, firms will compete and collaborate with firms in different products, segments and markets). There are issues here of 'reciprocal dependency' and 'hostages'.
4. The partnership may have a pre-emptive value in relation to competitors.

MANAGEMENT

It is clear that joint ventures need a different management approach from the unitary firm. Almost all works on IJV attribute immense importance to the growth of trust between partners – so much so that the study of trust and the mechanisms of inculcating trust have become a subject in their own right. Buckley and Casson (1988) take a theoretical approach and look for 'mutual forbearance' between the partners to produce a commitment to the joint venture, which then produces trust as an output. Trust can be an input too, as the transactions cost literature makes clear and surrogates for this may be involvement with previous IJVs (and JVs), and a declared similarity of goals. The dynamics of generating trust can be examined by deliberate looseness of contract to allow for growth in co-operation, by 'taking the easy decisions first' or by deliberate forgoing of the use of bargaining power (as exemplified by the initial shareholding – perhaps 50:50 rather than 60:40).

CONTROL

Issues on control are the bases of control, its extent, focus and the mechanisms by which it is exercised. The notion of parental control is to some extent a contradiction of co-operation but it must be recognized that both can co-exist and can be seen as separate domains by the managers involved (see Table 1.4).

Initial research on the *extent* of control as Child and Faulkner (1998) point out, saw control as a single, continuous variable. Consequently it could be plotted on a single continuum (for example dominant – shared – independent control). It was often taken as being dependent on centralization or on the location of decision making. This rather simplistic approach was replaced by a more differentiated view of control, examining the focus, mechanisms and bases of control.

A differentiated view of control sees parents as exercising control over a relatively wide or narrow range of the joint venture's activities (Geringer

Table 1.4 Control

Extent	Control as single continuous variable?
	Differentiated view – focus of control
Focus Wide or Narrow?	Technology
	Finance
	Quality
	Marketing issues
	Management
Mechanisms	Equity share
	Key managers/directors
	Formal contracts
	Key inputs (e.g. technology)
	Financial control
	Control of communications
Bases	Capabilities
	Strategies
	Reciprocal dependencies

and Hebert, 1989). Parents may focus on financial control, control over technology, over quality or marketing issues or over the choice of senior management.

The mechanisms of control are varied, and also suggest the areas that the parents feel to be most important. They include:

- equity shareholding;
- appointment of the IJV's Board of Directors;
- appointment of key managers;
- control of key inputs, including technology;
- financial reporting, budgeting and rationing;
- control over communications.

The fundamental basis of control may be reduced to three:

1. In equity joint ventures, the (majority) equity share.
2. Willingness or ability to commit key resources to the IJV, including continuing operational support, and
3. Bargaining power.

The first two have a direct managerial and economic basis, the third takes on a socio-political dimension.

PERFORMANCE

There are clearly difficult and unusual elements in assessing the performance of IJVs. The first is the obvious point that the goals of the partner can, and do, differ. Second, objective data on performance are difficult to gather. Ideally, the analysis should be conducted on a with IJV/without IJV comparison, but this is impossible. Third, a subjective analysis of how far the IJV has met its goals, is just that – subjective; and from whose point of view – the partners or the IJV management? In addition, studies of IJV performance have been obsessed with the relationship of performance with control.

The performance of IJVs should be compared with the results of acquisition or non-equity means of achieving the same goals.

It we take IJVs as a method of achieving market access – as one choice among several; then we can explain a great deal about them. Where motives are non-market access, we need to adopt a similar method to achieve further understanding. That is, we need to see IJVs as one choice among several in learning, reducing competition, diversification and cost sharing.

This list does *not* include vertical alliances as the key factors in the spectrum between full internalization, quasi-internalization (Blois, 1972), alliances, long-term contracting and simple market relations are well known.

METHODOLOGY AND INTERRELATIONSHIPS

Two further issues require clarification. The first is the appropriate methodology with which to tackle these issues. Here it is possible to fall into an arid debate between 'positivistic' approaches versus others. The 'native category' problem also bedevils the investigation of terms which may be imperfectly understood by the respondents (Buckley and Chapman, 1998). Interviews and even more so, questionnaires, need to be constructed so as to minimize the cultural distance between academic perception and participant understanding.

Research methods also need to comprehend interrelatedness. Bilateral relationships between variables (control and performance, for instance) are embedded in a nexus of causality which need careful investigation. A fruitful approach is the use of network theory, but often this can obfuscate rather than illuminate. Joint ventures frequently can only be understood in a wider picture of inter-firm relationships and untangling these is often a challenge in itself.

Many studies of IJVs suffer from problems with regard to the window of observation. As Figure 1.1 shows, many studies are a mix of observations of IJVs that (1) began during the observation period, (2) ended during the period, (3) both began and ended during the period and (4) persisted throughout the observation period and beyond. As Marshall noted, time often is the chief

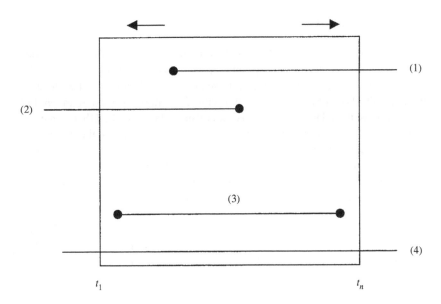

Figure 1.1   IJVs: the time window of observation

difficulty of analysis, particularly when performance issues are being investigated. A promising avenue here is to pay more attention to 'sunk costs' (Sutton, 1991), particularly as entry-deterrence mechanisms. This has the effect of producing a snapshot in time of a dynamic strategic process.

CONCLUSIONS

What do we know about joint ventures? The answer clearly is quite a lot. However, IJVs are not one phenomenon and there is not one single question which needs to be answered. One stance which is not justified is the 'Gee whiz, these things are *so* different' approach which cuts off JVs from the scope of conventional analysis. JVs and IJVs are institutional choices to achieve company goals just like any other form of business activity. They need to be evaluated in exactly the same way as more conventional modes of operation – comparatively over time, over space (different countries) and against the counterfactual. Issues of time and time related variables *do* impact on the analysis, but not in ways that cannot be imaginatively handled.

There is not one simple overarching theoretical perspective designed for, and exclusively dealing with, IJVs. There has been some 'rush to empiricism' without a fully thought out theoretical structure in many cases.

However, many issues centred on IJVs are explicable via conventional analysis.

We need to know far more about certain (interrelated) key variables (trust, opportunism, reciprocity, forbearance). Work on IJVs represents a research agenda, not yet fully accomplished. Concentration on the special areas of IJVs (motives, partnering, management, control and performance), perhaps sequentially, will lead us out of the morass which justifies the criticism that much of the work is 'non-cumulative'.

DOMAIN OF THE STUDY

This study focuses on a subset of strategic alliance activity – that of international equity joint ventures. As noted in the introduction, these involve two or more legally distinct organizations (the parents), each of which invests in the venture (the child) and actively participates in the decision-making activities of the jointly owned entity. The study examines two partner IJVs because of difficulties associated with analysing multiple partner IJVs, which may demonstrate significant differences from IJVs with two partners (Geringer, 1991). A distinct focus of the study is concentration on partners from developed industrial economies (compared to a focus on partners in developing countries found in other studies).

The main objective of the study is to examine the core dimensions of joint venture activity – strategic motives, partner selection criteria, management control and performance outcomes. The background literature, definition and operationalization of variables, and research questions of the study are detailed in each of the respective chapters that follow. Essentially, the study is of an empirical nature and broadly comprises an analysis of primary data obtained from senior managers in each element of the IJV system – both parents and IJV management – by means of personal interviews and self-administered questionnaires. The research methods of the study and sample characteristics are set out in Appendix 1. Outlines of the sample IJVs are in Appendix 2.

Chapter 2 examines motives and performance. The motives for IJV formation are identified, making a broad distinction between market entry motives and non-market entry motives. Contrary to the propositions advanced, the study finds that (i) measures of performance of the sample of IJVs are not based on a broad set of criteria but are based largely on financial criteria, and (ii) partners which have broadly different motives for the formation of the IJV do not adopt different performance criteria. In line with expectations, the study finds that the level of satisfaction of IJV performance tends not to vary with underlying motives for IJV formation.

Chapter 3 builds on prior research by investigating partner selection in IJVs through an examination of the nature of task-related and partner-related selection criteria. Findings indicate that task-related selection criteria reflect resource complementarity, with partners displaying a greater awareness of resource complementarity than the IJV managers. The relative importance of the degree of favourable past association between partners appears to be a function of the number of prior ties between partners. Trust between top management teams is the most important element of partner-related selection criteria. The status indicators of reputation, financial stability and to a lesser extent the partner company's size are also important elements of partner-related selection criteria. There is some support for the view that there is greater consensus between partner groups on the importance of the set of partner-related selection criteria than on the different factors of task-related selection criteria.

Chapter 4 investigates the form of management control exercised by parent firms over their international joint ventures. The main goal of the chapter is to identify the dimensions of control for a sample of UK–Western European IJVs in terms of the mechanisms of control, the extent of control and the focus of control. The main findings are: (1) that IJV partner firms seek to use an array of mechanisms to ensure control; (2) that different partners to an IJV will seek to influence IJV management through different mechanisms of control; (3) the extent of partner control is independent of the equity share of the partner, however, this finding may be largely conditioned by having a sample where in the majority of cases the equity share is equally split or nearly so; (4) partner firms will seek to concentrate on particular aspects of IJV control associated with their key skills and competencies.

Chapter 5 investigates approaches to decision making in international joint ventures from the perspectives of the transactions cost and resource based theories of the firm. In particular, the concept of autonomy in decision making is examined. The findings show that there are differences in the perception of autonomy between each of the parent firms, and between the parent firms and the IJV management. When we unpack the nature of autonomy in detail, it is found that IJV managers have greater degrees of operational autonomy than strategic autonomy and that decision making by IJV managers takes place within the context of constraints set within the IJV's business plan. This confirms the transaction cost theory which posits that key internal markets (for management, technology and capital) will be under parent control and also supports the resource based view that key capabilities are protected under the business plan established by the parent firms. The influence on IJV autonomy of the moderating variables IJV performance and IJV duration are also examined.

Chapter 6 identifies the key lessons of managing IJVs from the perspectives of IJV experienced partners and managers. Broadly, the response categories are grouped into three distinct areas of learning: the management of the IJV formation process, management of the boundary relationship between partners, and the management of the operation of the IJV. The chapter elucidates the lessons regarding these three areas of IJV management and provides a set of propositions for future research.

Chapter 7 provides new perspectives on the partnering skills needed for success in IJVs. Four categories of skills are analysed: inter-partner skills, managing the IJV managers, the 'upward management' skills of IJV managers managing the 'parent' partners, and those of managing the IJV itself. The chapter presents a matrix to examine the four categories of skill in the context in which each is used. Serving both as an analytical device and a diagnostic tool, this matrix offers results that have important implications for the management of IJVs with regard to the selection and training of managers and the inculcation of the skills required for each level of operation.

Chapter 8 replicates and extends a number of findings regarding performance assessment of IJVs. Findings support the growing evidence that while IJV objective performance measures and IJV subjective performance measures are positively correlated, they actually measure different phenomena. Findings show that the subjective performance assessment of one element of the IJV (partners or IJV management) matches that of the other elements, and that each element of the IJV has a good perception of the performance evaluation of the other elements. Correlations between partners' assessments of IJV performance are stronger in IJVs involving parents with similar national cultures when culture difference is measured by way of culture clusters, but not when cultural difference is measured by the Kogut–Singh index of cultural distance. Similarly, correlations between UK partners' assessment of IJV performance and the IJV management's assessment of performance are stronger in IJVs involving parents with similar national cultures when culture difference is measured by way of culture clusters, but less so when measuring cultural difference by the Kogut–Singh index of cultural distance.

Chapter 9 examines the extent to which differences in culture pose a problem to the management of IJVs and in particular whether national cultural differences or corporate cultural differences are more important in contributing to different views on the management of the IJV. The findings show that while cultural differences do exist they are not severe enough to cause significant problems for the management of the IJVs. Where problems do exist it was not firmly established whether national culture differences or corporate cultural differences were the chief cause of problems in managing the IJV.

A summary and conclusions from the whole study are provided in Chapter 10.

NOTE

1. We are grateful to Alan Rugman for the original insight into this issue.

2. Strategic motives and performance

INTRODUCTION

This chapter provides an empirical examination of the motives for IJV formation and performance outcomes. The following section briefly reviews the literature relating to motives for IJV formation and issues associated with IJV performance, and identifies a set of research questions. The findings are presented in the third section and discussion in the fourth section. Conclusions are in the final section.

MOTIVES AND PERFORMANCE IN IJVs

The Strategic Motives for IJV Formation

An explanation for the use of IJVs stems from theories on how strategic behaviour influences the competitive positioning of the firm (Kogut, 1988: 321). The literature clearly indicates a number of overlapping perspectives on the strategic motives for IJV formation, with the various authors arriving at a broadly similar set of motivating forces, for example, Mariti and Smiley (1983), Harrigan (1985), Porter and Fuller (1986), Contractor and Lorange (1988).

Young et al. (1989: 19) have noted that it is necessary to distinguish between the role of IJVs in establishing corporate linkages, such as sharing investment risks, attainment of economies of scale, exchange of complementary technology, and so on, as opposed to their role in corporate entry strategies, principally entry to new geographical markets. This suggests greater difficulties and possibly greater risks involved in market entry IJVs and highlights the importance attributed to a close knowledge of national cultural factors when a new market is being envisaged.

An important purpose for IJV formation is to facilitate market entry (Hill et al., 1990; Glaister and Buckley, 1996). This may encompass both entry to a new product market and entry to a new geographical market, whereby the IJV facilitates international expansion and entry to a foreign market. A firm may, for example, have the production capability but lack knowledge of foreign markets for which it depends on its partners. In general it is an expensive, difficult and time-consuming business to establish a global organization and a significant international competitive presence (Contractor and Lorange, 1988: 15). In this respect an IJV offers considerable time savings. The speed of internationalization may be critical given the benefits that may accrue to early entrants such as the ability to command premium prices and the possibility of gaining significant market share (Gannon, 1993). The choice of an IJV as an entry strategy may be influenced by external or internal reasons (Buchel et al., 1998: 45). External reasons may include government policy requiring foreign companies to join with local companies to do business in the host country. Internal reasons may include lack of experience in foreign markets or high entry barriers in the form of investments or market complexities.

The strategic motives for a sample of UK IJVs with partners in western Europe, the United States and Japan were analysed by Glaister and Buckley (1996). With data from a questionnaire survey they identified the main strategic motives for formation by UK firms as intrinsically linked to the market and geographical expansion of the firm. Glaister and Buckley concluded that the main strategic motives were underpinned by the theories of strategic positioning and organizational learning.

Doz and Hamel (1998) have summarized the primary purposes for IJV formation. Pointing out that few companies have everything they need to succeed on their own, IJVs play a key role in three areas. IJVs through 'co-option' are able to turn potential competitors into allies and providers of the complementary goods and services that allow new businesses to develop. 'Co-specialization' involves the process of combining previously separate resources, positions, skills and knowledge sources to generate synergistic value creation. In this process partners contribute unique and differentiated resources – skills, brands, relationships, positions and tangible assets – to the success of the IJV, and the IJV creates value when those resources are co-specialized. In other words they become substantially more valuable when bundled together in a joint effort than when kept separate. IJVs may also be the vehicle for learning and internalizing new skills, in particular those that are tacit, collective and embedded, and thus hard to obtain and internalize by other means. It is not possible to purchase core competencies through the market system; however, these skills can be learned from a partner, internalized, and exploited beyond the boundaries of the IJV itself. So the learning to be gained from an IJV partner can often be leveraged broadly into other activities and businesses beyond those covered by the IJV (Hamel, 1991). The strategic significance of these purposes makes IJVs much more central to corporate strategy.

IJV Performance

Proceeding from their own respective goals, it is usually assumed that partners agree on a set of objectives and activities for the IJV. The IJV is then given the task of realizing the aims upon which the partners have decided, using agreed resources. The IJV must show clear benefits for both partners (Buchel et al., 1998: 30). Success and failure are thus vital issues for IJVs so it is not surprising that performance has been an important theme in the IJV literature. However, the measurement of IJV performance is a controversial area (Geringer and Hebert, 1991; Glaister and Buckley, 1998a, 1998b; Geringer, 1998). A major issue of considerable debate is the appropriate yardstick(s) to be used when assessing IJV performance. More fundamentally, controversy surrounds the lack of clarity between indicators of performance and determinants of performance (Anderson, 1990).

Traditional measures of success are often based on financial criteria such as profit, productivity, turnover or other short-term criteria that relate to the past. These statistics are relatively easy to determine and to compare. Several authors (see, for example, Buchel et al., 1998: 190) question whether these provide an adequate basis on which to evaluate an IJV, arguing that such measures cover only a small part of what is needed for a comprehensive assessment of the IJV system. A full assessment must take into account a variety of aspects. Financial and objective measures often inadequately reflect the extent to which an IJV has achieved its aims: despite poor financial results, liquidation or instability, an IJV may have met or exceeded the parents' objectives and so be considered successful by one or all of the parents (Geringer and Hebert, 1991). Conversely an IJV may be viewed as unsuccessful despite good financial results or continued stability. Concerns over the ability of financial and objective measures to effectively gauge IJV performance led several researchers to use perceptual measures of a parent's satisfaction with IJV performance (Killing, 1983; Schaan, 1983; Beamish, 1985), which are able to provide information regarding the extent to which the IJV has achieved its overall objectives.

Success is often regarded as an absolute, but success and failure are relative matters and can only be evaluated according to specific criteria and measures. Success from one point of view may appear to be a failure from another. Two partner companies using different measures to evaluate their IJV may reach totally different conclusions regarding its performance (Buchel et al., 1998: 188). Evaluations may also differ depending on whether they are made by the partners or by the managers of the IJV itself. It may be the case that an IJV appears successful in its own right, but the partners are not satisfied with it. Or the partners may be more satisfied than they believe the IJV management to be. Assessing the IJV for the partners' viewpoint involves, first, evaluating performance against the objectives with which the partner entered the co-operation. Secondly, more general benefits which the IJV brings to that partner need to be examined; for instance, additional contributions or benefits which the partner had not foreseen and therefore could not expect (Buchel et al., 1998: 204).

Following from this discussion, the chapter seeks to answer the following research questions:

- What are the motives for IJV formation?
- Do these motives coincide between partners to an IJV?
- How is IJV performance measured?
- Do the adopted performance measures reflect success in terms of the motives for IJV formation?
- What is the level of success measured in a subjective manner?
- Does the subjective measure of success vary with the motives for IJV formation?

From the prior literature (for example Glaister and Buckley, 1996) and the pilot interviews, a list of strategic motives was derived. These basically distinguished between market entry motives and non-market entry motives. In the self-administered questionnaire the questions relating to motives were *ex post* measures of managers' perceptions of the relative importance of the motives at the time of IJV formation. Responses were assessed using five-point Likert-type scales (that is 1 = 'of no importance'; 5 = of major importance').

Subjective performance measures were broadly derived in the manner followed by Geringer and Hebert (1991). Each IJV parent and management's *subjective level of satisfaction* with the IJV's overall performance was assessed using a five-point Likert-type scale (from 1 = 'very dissatisfied' to 5 = 'very satisfied').

FINDINGS

Motives

Interview data
The broad distinction has been made between market entry motives and non-market entry motives. Market entry may be entry to a new business or product segment and/or entry to a new international market. The IJV may facilitate market entry in several ways: by enabling faster entry to the market, enabling a presence in new markets, facilitating international expansion and helping overcome regulatory restrictions. Other motives are classified as non-market entry motives and cover a spectrum of motives ranging from enabling the partner to maintain a position in existing markets, through cost and risk sharing to obtaining inputs. Of the 20 UK partners, half considered the major motive to be market entry with half considering it to be non-market entry. For European partners nine considered the major motive market entry and 11 non-market entry.

The data shows that for six of the IJVs the motives of the parents differ in that one parent views the main motive as being market entry while the other parent does not. This lack of conformity between parents as to motive while potentially representing a problem in terms of the IJV fulfilling the ambitions of the parents is perhaps better viewed as a reflection of the reciprocal dependencies between the partners. Examination of the data indicates that a market entry motive for one partner is entirely consistent with a non-market entry motive for the other partner. In the case of IJV 1, for example, the motive for the UK partner was market entry to a new business. The IJV allowed the UK partner to access a market sector where it did not possess a product. The new product fitted into an existing product range in a sector where if a full product range was not on offer to customers this would have been detrimental to long-term export hopes. The UK partner viewed the IJV as enabling faster entry to the market and as a stepping stone towards a broader consolidation of the European industry. For the European partner the key strategic motive was to increase volume and make an existing business bigger, so enhancing their position in an existing market. This would allow them to more effectively compete against other competitors as well as facilitating the sharing of R&D and other costs and an exchange of technology. The IJV thus provides a number of synergistic links, which serves the motives of both partners while the motives for each are fundamentally different.

There was a high degree of conformity between the opinion of the IJV management and that of the respective partner as to the basic motive driving formation of the joint venture. Where data is available from the IJV management in all cases there is agreement between the IJV management and the UK partner's view as to the motive of the UK partner for forming the IJV. Although there is not full conformity between the views of the IJV management and the European partner as to the European partner's motives for the formation of the IJV, in 16 cases where data is available there is conformity of view. It would appear therefore that there is a high degree of conformity in terms of the IJV management's understanding of the parents' motives for the formation of the IJV. This has positive implications for the management of the venture in that an understanding of the parents' motive on the part of the IJV management should lead the latter to manage the venture in order to achieve the goals underpinning these motives.

Questionnaire data

Market entry was reported as the most important motive by 22 (35.5 per cent) of questionnaire respondents and other motives by 40 respondents (64.5 per cent). The nature of market entry as a motive is reported in Table 2.1, which shows that in terms of rank order the IJV was formed in order to enable faster entry to the market, to enable presence in new markets, and to facilitate international expansion.

Table 2.1   Market entry motives: questionnaire data

Motive	Rank	Mean	SD
Enable faster entry to the market	1	4.41	0.67
Enable presence in new markets	2	3.82	1.33
Facilitate international expansion	3	3.59	1.53
Overcome regulatory restrictions	4	2.72	1.49

Note: N = 22. The mean for the market entry motives is the average on a scale of 1 (= no importance) to 5 (= very important).

Where market entry was not the most important motive, the motives for IJV formation are shown in Table 2.2. By rank order the main non-market entry motives are to maintain position in existing markets, to compete more effectively, and to share investment costs. This set of motives may be compared with the findings of Glaister and Buckley (1996) who examined a sample of 94 UK alliances formed in the 1980s. The latter study did not clearly differentiate between market entry and non-market entry motives and found that the motive to gain presence in new markets was first ranked from a list of 16 motives. The present study supports the earlier findings in terms of the importance given to market entry as a motivating force for IJV formation. But the present study in considering the non-market entry motives separately finds that the non-market entry motivation for IJV formation is dominated by the need to maintain the partner's position in existing markets and to compete more effectively against common competitors. Table 2.2 also indicates that cost sharing and competition-reducing motives are important non-market entry motives.

Performance

Interview data

Analysis of the nature of the performance measures used to evaluate the IJVs shows that in almost all cases performance is measured by standard financial criteria. The financial measures reported most often were profit rates and cash flow. Notwithstanding the espoused motives for the formation of the IJVs, their *raison d'être* is to produce profit, as this is what they are largely judged by. The IJVs are commercial organizations, which were formed by profit-seeking commercial organizations, so it is perhaps not surprising that IJV performance should be viewed in terms of financial criteria. What is rather surprising, however, is the lack of reference in the measures of performance to the motives for forming the IJV. The performance of the IJV is principally viewed in terms of commercial criteria and not by way of the outcomes of the

Table 2.2 Non-market entry motives: questionnaire data

Motives	Rank	Mean	SD
Maintain position in existing markets	1	3.80	1.02
Compete more effectively against a common competitor	2	3.53	1.45
Share investment costs	3	3.48	1.11
Formed with existing or potential competitor to reduce competition	4	3.15	1.57
Exchange of complementary technology	5=	3.00	1.32
Economies of scale: joint operations lower unit costs	5=	3.00	1.45
Enabling product diversification	7=	2.93	1.46
Share R&D costs	7=	2.93	1.51
To concentrate on higher margin business	9	2.83	1.34
Spreading the risk of a large project over more than one firm	10	2.78	1.37
Enabling faster payback on the investment	11	2.75	1.26
Production transferred to lowest cost location	12	2.55	1.11
Exchange of patents or territories	13	2.13	1.22
Obtain raw materials	14	1.80	1.07
Conform to foreign government policy	15	1.39	0.78

Note: N = 38. The mean for the non-market entry motives is the average on a scale of 1 (= no importance) to 5 (= very important).

strategic motives for the formation of the IJV. We found in the interview data that only occasionally are non-financial performance measures stressed. In these instances a greater emphasis is given to the motives driving the formation of the IJV. For instance in IJV 14, formed between a UK dairy products company and a French dairy products company for the distribution in the UK of the French company's yoghurt brand, the UK partner's motives for the IJV formation are faster market entry to a high value added product area, which provides product diversity and a cost effective and less risky entry. The UK partner reported that it was conscious of the need to measure growing awareness of the product and positive attitudes towards the brand by UK consumers. As the distributor, these are obviously important criteria for the UK partner. As the supplier of the product, the French partner's motives for formation were to gain fast and low-cost entry to the UK market. The only performance measures stressed by the French partner, however, were the standard financial criteria.

Investigation of the data reveals that generally the partners to an IJV have very similar views as to how the performance of the IJVs should be measured. Also, the managers of an IJV have a very similar set of criteria for performance to the IJV partners. One clear conclusion from this data is that there is a high degree of congruence between the partners, and the partners and the IJV managers, as to the performance criteria of the IJVs. Considering performance criteria from an agency theory perspective, it might be expected that there would be a divergence of opinion between the IJV partners and the IJV managers, regarding the salient performance measures. This view does not appear to be supported by this sample of IJVs.

The overall level of satisfaction with IJV performance by strategic motivation for the IJV is shown in Table 2.3. The non-parametric Mann–Whitney test of differences in means shows that there is no significant difference in the overall level of satisfaction between those IJVs formed for market entry motives compared with those formed for non-market entry motives. This finding applies both to UK partners and European partners.

Questionnaire data
The criteria used to measure the performance of the IJVs according to the questionnaire respondents are shown in Table 2.4. About 95 per cent of the respondents report that the IJV is measured according to financial criteria. Far fewer respondents (about 45 per cent) report that the IJV is measured by non-financial criteria. The questionnaire data reported in Table 2.4 accords with the findings of the interview data and adds to the view that the IJVs are principally measured in terms of financial performance.

The overall level of satisfaction with IJV performance by strategic motivation for the IJV is shown in Table 2.5. As with the interview data the non-parametric

Table 2.3 IJV satisfaction by strategic motivation: interview data

Performance measure	Motivation	n	Mean	SD	Mean rank	Mann–Whitney U
Overall satisfaction: UK partners	Market entry	10	2.9	1.37	10.1	46.00
	Non-market entry	10	3.0	1.63	10.9	
Overall satisfaction: European partners	Market entry	9	3.22	1.39	9.06	36.50
	Non-market entry	11	3.81	1.07	11.68	

Table 2.4 IJV performance measures: questionnaire data[1]

	Financial criteria				Non-financial criteria			
	Yes		No		Yes		No	
	No.	%	No.	%	No.	%	No.	%
UK partner	14	93.3	1	6.7	7	46.7	8	53.3
European partner	12	85.7	2	14.3	6	42.9	8	57.1
IJV management	25	100.0	0	0.0	11	44.0	14	56.0
Total	51	94.4	3	5.6	24	44.4	30	55.6

Note: 1. Totals less than 63 due to missing data.

Table 2.5 IJV satisfaction by strategic motivation: questionnaire data

Performance measure	motivation	n	Mean	SD	Mean rank	Mann–Whitney U
Overall satisfaction: UK partners	Market entry	4	3.75	1.25	10.00	
	Non-market entry	11	3.00	1.27	7.27	14.00
Overall satisfaction: European partners	Market entry	5	3.40	0.89	7.10	
	Non-market entry	9	3.67	0.86	7.72	20.50
Overall satisfaction: IJV managers	Market entry	13	3.61	1.12	17.38	
	Non-market entry	18	3.33	0.97	15.00	99.00

Mann–Whitney test of differences in means shows that there is no significant difference in the overall level of satisfaction between those IJVs formed for market entry reasons compared with those formed for non-market entry reasons. This applies across both partner groups and the IJV mangers. Based on both the interview data and the questionnaire data, it is clear that for this sample of IJVs overall satisfaction with performance does not vary with the broad difference in motives for IJV formation.

DISCUSSION

It would appear reasonable to expect that a broad set of criteria would be used to evaluate the performance of IJVs and that performance measures would not be based unduly on financial criteria. This expectation is confounded by the findings of this study. The interview data unambiguously shows that respondents from all three elements of the IJV system usually emphasize financial measures when evaluating IJV performance. This finding is supported by the questionnaire data. The reliance by partners and managers on financial criteria to evaluate IJV performance may be due to the carrying over to IJV appraisal the conventions which managers apply to standard organizational forms. Reliance on customary financial criteria may also be because the objectives for the IJV may not be well defined. Where this is the case it is easier to rely on financial performance measures than to articulate other measures which may more closely measure the extent to which the objectives have been reached.

The findings of this study show that the measurement of IJV success by the parents does not vary with the underlying motives of the parents for the JV formation. The interview data indicates that the IJVs are basically assessed on financial criteria without overt reference to the motives of the parents. This finding is consistent across the IJV parents and the IJV managers. The questionnaire data supports the finding that financial criteria dominate IJV performance measures with no overt reference to motives in the performance criteria. Viewing IJVs as an option for such things as gaining market access and carrying out basic research, in other words as an instrument for providing future options and reducing the risk of missing important market or technological developments, obviously reduces the meaning and validity of short-term, quantitative indices of success. This problem of relying on financial criteria as the main measure of IJV success does not seem to have occurred to the majority of IJV partners or managers in the sample.

In considering IJV performance Doz and Hamel (1998: 84–85) point to the danger of measuring the wrong things, noting that it is all too easy for the partners to lose sight of the value creation logic of the IJV and to fall back on purely financial measures of performance. For Doz and Hamel this practice is both misleading and dangerous. The manner in which financial benefits are to be generated and over what scope of activities and time frame will vary greatly according to the IJV's value creation logic. While recognizing that ultimately financial performance will be a yardstick in all IJVs, Doz and Hamel argue that managers need to develop a balanced and comprehensive scorecard to assess the performance of an IJV, one that is consistent with the value creation logic that it pursues. It is apparent that such a balanced scorecard approach to IJV performance evaluation is not widely adopted in this sample of IJVs, where there is heavy reliance on standard financial criteria to measure IJV performance. One recommendation for practitioners arising out of this study is to try to develop a more broad based approach to IJV performance evaluation and in particular to relate this evaluation to the logic for the formation of the IJV.

Findings from the study indicate that the subjective level of satisfaction of IJV performance outcome tends not to vary with underlying motive for IJV formation. The evidence both from the interview data and the questionnaire data indicates no significant difference in the mean level of satisfaction of overall IJV performance in terms of market entry and non-market entry motives. As far as satisfaction with performance is concerned, this indicates that IJVs are not to be preferred for one type of motive over another. Traditionally, IJVs have been established to facilitate foreign market entry for multinational enterprises (MNEs) in developing countries. This motive remains important for the establishment of IJVs between firms from advanced industrial economies, as data from this study confirms. However, a broader range of motives also exists whereby partners gain the benefit of reciprocal dependencies. The findings from this study indicate that both broad types of IJV provide an approximately equivalent level of overall satisfaction with IJV performance. In this sense the use of the IJV organizational form should not be viewed as superior for one set of motives compared to another.

CONCLUSIONS

This chapter examines the strategic motives for IJV formation between UK and western European partners and considers IJV performance in the context of these motives. The study adopts a mixed methods approach, first, by obtaining data from each of the IJV elements and, second, from attempting to obtain multiple responses from each IJV element by way of self-administered questionnaires. Each data source supports the findings of the other, providing confidence in the reliability of the evidence reported. The study finds that IJV formation to facilitate foreign market entry is important for many firms in the sample. For other firms, however, a broader range of motives applies whereby partners gain the benefit of reciprocal dependencies. The study finds that for the sample of IJVs, measures of performance are not based on a range of criteria related to motive for formation, but are based largely on specific financial criteria. Furthermore, partners which have different motives for the formation of the IJV do not adopt different performance criteria. The study also finds that the level of subjective satisfaction of IJV performance tends not to vary with the underlying motive for formation – market entry compared to other motives. This study indicates that both broad types of IJV provide an approximately equivalent level of overall satisfaction with IJV performance. In this sense the use of the IJV organizational form should not be viewed as superior for one set of motives compared to another.

A number of caveats associated with the findings of the study should be noted. The sample is composed of IJVs formed by western European firms with one of the partners from the UK. The findings therefore may not be generalizable to IJVs formed in other parts of the Triad, particularly IJVs with partner firms from the USA and Japan, or to IJVs involving partners from developing countries. In the main the IJVs reported in the chapter are drawn from the manufacturing sector. Consequently, the findings may not apply to IJVs in other industry sectors.

There are several future research possibilities. Investigation of the extent to which there is agreement between the partners, and the partners and the IJV managers, over the subjective performance measures would be worthwhile. Where motives differ between partners, examination of the manner in which this is reconciled in IJV performance measures would be valuable. It would also be beneficial to know the extent to which performance measures vary over the life-cycle of IJVs, and the manner in which IJV performance measures differ from those of other organizational modes, such as wholly owned subsidiaries.

3. The nature of partner selection

INTRODUCTION

While the expected gains of inter-firm collaboration are well known, it is also the case that such collaboration is often short-lived and prone to failure (Bleeke and Ernst, 1993a; Lei and Slocum, 1991; Beamish and Delios, 1997b). It is clear that central to the international joint venture formation process is the quest for a suitable partner (Parkhe, 1993; Blodgett, 1991a; 1991b; Brown et al., 1989; Burton and Saelens, 1982; Harrigan, 1988b). According to Sorensen and Reve (1998: 159) 'The selection of partners is one of the most important steps in forming strategic alliances'. Child and Faulkner (1998: 87) observe that 'the choice of a partner is key to the ultimate success of a joint enterprise'. One of the most often cited reasons for alliance failure is the incompatibility of partners (Farr and Fischer, 1992; Dacin et al., 1997; Zahra and Elhagrasey, 1994). The choice of a particular partner is an important variable influencing IJV performance, since it influences the mix of skills and resources which will be available to the venture and thus the IJV's ability to achieve its strategic objectives (Porter and Fuller, 1986).

Chung et al. (2000: 1) note that researchers have focused on two explanations of what drives a firm to form a strategic alliance with a particular partner firm. Scholars of economics and business strategy have emphasized resource complementarity: two (or more) firms enter into an alliance when the pooled resources can create excess value relative to their value before the pooling (Nohria and Garcia-Pont, 1991). Other scholars have emphasized the role of social structural context in alliance formation, where two firms' direct and indirect relational experiences facilitate the formation of future ties (Bourdieu and Wacquant, 1992; Coleman, 1990; Gulati, 1995a).

A large number of selection criteria have been suggested in the literature, for instance, requisite skills and assets (Porter and Fuller, 1986; Sorensen and Reve, 1998), compatibility and chemistry between partners (Kanter, 1994; Sorensen and Reve, 1998), strategic fit and cultural fit (Child and Faulkner, 1998: 92; Kanter, 1989; Lorange and Roos, 1992). While such perspectives are reasonable they do not address the fundamental criteria for partner selection in a parsimonious manner. A significant contribution by Geringer (1988; 1991) has been the suggestion that despite the almost unlimited range of alternative criteria that might exist, it is possible to provide a simple two-fold typology of categories of selection criteria. The typology suggested by Geringer is based on the distinction between 'task-related' criteria and 'partner-related' criteria. A major purpose of this part of the study is to develop further the understanding of the concepts of task-related and partner-related selection criteria by building on prior research.

The rest of the chapter is set out in the following way: the next section presents a review of task-related and partner-related selection criteria and develops the research questions of the study. Section three presents the findings and discussion. Conclusions are in the final section.

LITERATURE REVIEW AND RESEARCH QUESTIONS

Task-Related Selection Criteria

Geringer (1988; 1991) notes that task-related selection criteria are associated with the operational skills and resources that a venture requires for its competitive success, for example, patents or technical know-how, financial resources, experienced managerial personnel and access to marketing and distribution systems. If, for example, a company perceives technology leadership to be crucial for the venture's performance, but that it cannot provide this on its own, it will logically give high priority to finding a partner with which an alliance will be capable of securing that leadership. From Geringer's work and that of others on partner selection, Child and Faulkner (1998: 33) note that the relative importance of a given task-related criterion appears to depend on the partner's perception of how crucial the feature is for the co-operative venture's performance, how strong is the partner's ability to provide or gain access to the feature, and how difficult the partner thinks it will be in the future to compete in terms of the feature. This essentially embodies a 'resource-based' view of IJV formation (Barney, 1991; Grant, 1991; Peteraf, 1993; Wernerfelt, 1984; Tsang, 1998; 2000). It also has antecedents in the resource-dependence argument (Pfeffer and Nowak, 1976), that a strong reason for organizations to collaborate with others lies in their recognition that they lack critical competencies which they cannot develop readily, and/or sufficiently rapidly, on their own.

Clearly, each partner must offer a complementary set of task-related selection criteria. In this sense there is a reciprocal dependency associated with IJV formation. Each partner requires what the other offers for success in the venture. Doz and Hamel (1998: 59) when considering the value creation aspect of alliance formation argue that perhaps the most critical determinant of value creation is the degree to which the partners' contributions are complementary.

Resource complementarity

When resources are idiosyncratic and indivisible, accessing such inputs through market mechanisms is not always feasible (Teece, 1986), and amassing resources inside the firm is not always optimal (Williamson, 1985). In such circumstances, joint venture formation can be the primary vehicle for accessing inputs and the consideration of resource complementarity becomes important (Burgers et al., 1993; Harrigan, 1985; Lorange and Roos, 1992). By pooling resources and capabilities, firms can initiate projects that they could not have successfully undertaken alone (Chung et al., 2000: 3). Mutual gain is possible if partners can complement each other's weakness since each partner in a venture can access the complementary capabilities of their partners (Hamel et al., 1989; Teece, 1986). The complementarity of strengths and assets between firms is often clear even prior to negotiations on the terms of joint ventures because this is what brings the partners together in the first place (Doz, 1988). Support for the logic of complementarity in forming alliances has been found in the biotechnology industry (Shan and Hamilton, 1991). In the global automobile industry, evidence has been reported that firms in certain strategic groups form alliances in a complementary manner with those in other strategic groups to increase the benefits of co-operation (Nohria and Garcia-Pont, 1991). Gulati (1995b) reported that firms occupying complementary niches have higher chances of venture formation. Chung et al.'s (2000) study of US investment banks suggest that resource complementarity plays a significant role in driving joint venture formation. The first research question of the study therefore concerns: *the extent to which task-related selection criteria reflect resource complementarity in IJVs.*

Partner-related Selection Criteria

Partner-related selection criteria refer to those variables that become relevant only if the chosen investment mode involves the presence of multiple partners. Some examples of partner-related selection criteria are national or corporate culture of a partner, compatibility or trust between the partners' management teams, the degree of favourable past association between the partners, and the size or corporate structure of a partner. Spekman et al. (1996) found that past working experience with each other, similarities in corporate cultures, mutual respect and a basic understanding of the other's capabilities helped shape the very early stages of the alliance building process.

Prior collaborative experience

A number of authors have pointed out the importance of prior relationships for the formation of IJVs (Kogut, 1988; Gulati, 1995a). Chung et al. (2000: 5) define a firm's *social capital* as its potentially beneficial relationships with external parties. Firms develop social capital through their participation in collaborations and social capital is, by its nature, dependent upon history. In other words, the current relations of a firm are products of its prior relational activities as well as the basis upon which it establishes future social relations. This social capital can function as a driver of IJV formation. Firms will utilize their social capital in forming IJVs both to decrease the costs of searching for partners and to create new economic opportunities. Under the conditions of information asymmetry and bounded rationality, firms are likely to exchange economic opportunities with the firms that they have collaborated with in the past (Ben-Porath, 1980). Since finding the right partners with complementary resource configurations is a costly and time-consuming process, both direct and indirect prior collaboration experiences come into play in the selection of partners. These experiences provide a firm with valuable information that it can use to seek potentially beneficial partner firms.

In forming IJVs, a natural solution is for a firm to consider first previous partners with which it has had direct prior experiences. Chung et al. (2000) note that the tendency to conduct a limited search will be greater when a firm has more stringent time constraints and is more uncertain about the benefits it derives from the selected option. Co-operative ventures usually involve significant uncertainty about future costs and benefits because of the possibility of opportunistic behaviour and the lack of a clear authority relation. Moreover, each partner has to invest a substantial amount of time and energy to establish a long-term relationship (Burt, 1992). This investment is a fixed or sunk cost and is impossible to recover (Ben-Porath, 1980). Further, changing partners in the short run may involve significant switching costs and the risk that existing relationships will come to an end. Consequently, when trustworthy partners are already available, searching for new partners is difficult to defend. Gulati (1995a) shows that the prior joint venture experience between two firms enhances the possibility of their additional joint venture formation. Chung et al. (2000) found a significantly positive coefficient of direct ties and alliance formation. The second research question therefore concerns: The extent to which a firm's direct prior collaborative experience with a partner is an important element of partner-related selection criteria.

Trust between top management
Buchel et al. (1998: 49) when discussing commitment and trust in IJVs note that a strong conception of an IJV is characterized by the presence of committed individuals amongst the potential partners who support the creation of the IJV. Often this commitment is based on mutual confidence exhibited by key individuals. Also, trust is likely to come more easily where partners have had prior business relationships. A trust-based relationship with repetitive exchanges is beneficial for long-term partners because of the sharing of

opportunities and valuable information (Burt, 1992; Mohr and Spekman, 1994). Information is often difficult and costly to obtain since it is not spread evenly across all firms, but instead becomes available through social contacts with immediate or intimate external parties.

Chung et al. (2000) argue that trust is achieved by the continuity of the relationships between partners through reciprocal exchanges and by the mutual recognition that what one might gain by cheating in a given instance is outweighed by the value of the tradition of trust that make possible a long sequence of future interactions (Schelling, 1960; Zucker, 1986). The trust construct therefore stresses the importance of past experiences in dealing with a particular partner (Elg, 2000).

There are many definitions of trust and an extended discussion of the dimensions of the concept of trust are beyond the scope of this chapter. We adopt the common sense understanding of the concept of trust that pervades many definitions in that 'it refers to the willingness of one party to relate with another in the belief that the other's actions will be beneficial rather than detrimental to the first party, even though this cannot be guaranteed' (Child and Faulkner, 1998: 45). Without imposing a concept of trust on respondents we believe that this common sense understanding of trust would be one recognized by respondents in the discussion of trust.

As noted, for trust to develop, time and repeated interactions are necessary (Buckley and Casson, 1988). However, if prior relationships between partners lead to trust between partners this confounds the partner-related selection criteria as there is likely to be conceptual overlap between the two criteria. This raises doubts as to whether prior relationships and inter-partner trust should be treated as separate independent components of partner-related selection criteria. Although a contentious issue, we adopt the view that trust between the top management teams of the partners and prior relationships can be identified empirically as separate components of partner-related selection criteria. Although the development of trust is closely identified in the literature with prior ties, such ties are not necessary for trust to develop. IJVs are frequently established between partners which have no prior ties, yet it is still possible for trust to develop between top management teams during the negotiation phase of the IJV, a period during which there would be repeated interactions. Moreover, prior ties could exist between partners, firms, for example supply contracts, but these may not have directly engaged the time or attention of the top management teams or led to their interaction. For these reasons we treat trust between top management teams as a separate partner-related selection criterion, which is encapsulated in the third research question: The extent to which trust between top management teams is an important element of partner-related selection criteria.

Status indicators

Firms are likely to consider the status of potential partners when forming IJVs, and will probably establish ventures with firms of similar status (Podolny, 1994). Chung et al. (2000) found that status similarity of two investment banks significantly increases the possibility of their alliance formation, and they provide three possible reasons for this. First, is the signalling role of social interaction. When the quality measure of an output is ambiguous, the status of a focal firm and the quality of its outputs as perceived by others are dependent on the status of other firms with whom the focal firm interacts (Podolny, 1993). The signalling effect of inter-firm alliances encourages firms to collaborate with others of similar status when the results of the transactions are uncertain. Second, is the process of competitive isomorphism. When firms compete with each other on the basis of their status, firms of similar status will be in a similar competitive environment. Therefore, competitive isomorphism will lead firms of similar status to have similar or compatible operating systems and practices. This compatibility in operating systems is a catalyst in helping partner firms co-operate more effectively with each other (Lorange and Roos, 1992). For example, firms with similar administrative systems will find it easier to evaluate, communicate and co-ordinate their co-operative activities in an alliance. Finally, a firm also tends to seek a partner of similar status because doing so makes it more likely that both parties will exhibit increased levels of fairness and commitment in sharing both the costs and benefits of an alliance. Dissimilarity of status is likely to lead to the situation where the commitment of resources by the partner of higher status is the same as the commitment of resources by the partner of lower status. Thus the commitment of resources by the higher status partner will be far less than its capabilities and will be less than what the firm of lower status expects. This is likely to cause the latter firm to reduce the effort it contributes to the alliance. The contrasting expectations of partners can thus lead to conflicts that often make alliances between firms of dissimilar status less effective than those between firms of similar status.

An important status indicator is the reputation of the potential partner firm. By behaving reciprocally, an organization can build a good reputation of being a reliable interaction partner as long as the organization's behaviour is observed by third parties. This reputation makes the organization very attractive to a third party that may be looking for IJV partners, even if this party does not have any direct or indirect ties to the organization (Coleman, 1990; Macaulay, 1963; Raub and Weesie, 1990).

Stuart et al. (1999) argue that an important category of information that influences the perception of the probability that a young company will succeed relates to the attributes of its exchange partners. The prior accomplishments of a new venture are usually insufficient to resolve the uncertainty about its quality;

however, the social structure of business relationships can affect perceptions of the quality and hence value of new ventures. This follows from the notion that firms' reputations are constructed in part from the identities of their associates (Blau, 1964). Organizations that are thought to be reliable, accountable and trustworthy are considered to have higher chances of survival and better performance. The implicit transfer of status across organizational relationships (such as an alliance), builds confidence about the quality of a new venture by key stakeholders such as potential customers, suppliers, employees and investors. In effect, firms often seek a form of endorsement in the market by engaging in alliances with partners of high status. Moreover, through this process companies with prominent partners gain an advantage in the competition for resources. In particular, if prominent organizations have greater or higher quality resources than other firms and if their partners enjoy access to some of these resources then such ties will give a competitive advantage. Stuart et al. (1999: 321) claim that reputation and resource-access effects work in tandem to create advantage for companies with prominent partners. They contend that inter-organizational exchange relations in addition to providing resources also affect reputations, which have a positive effect on performance. In this respect a firm's status may also act as a task-related selection criterion.

This discussion leads to the fourth research question: The extent to which status indicators are an important element of partner-related selection criteria.

Partner differences
It may be more difficult to find compatible partners in cross-border JVs because firms based in different countries may have largely different criteria in selecting partners and thus seek different benefits from the alliances. Dacin et al. (1997: 6) contend that it is unlikely that IJV partners will have complete agreement on alliance objectives and expected benefits because the institutional context in which the IJV is embedded varies by country. A significant amount of economic interaction is embedded in cognitive, cultural, structural and political factors that shape firm behaviour (Zukin and DiMaggio, 1990). Differences and similarities between selection criteria employed by managers is best appreciated, however, in the context of the distinction between task-related selection criteria and partner-related selection criteria. It is to be expected that partners will differ in task-related selection criteria because of the need for synergistic resource complementarities. Task-related selection criteria can be expected to be specific to the particular needs of an IJV, whereas partner-related selection criteria will tend to be a more general set of criteria, and will be far less dependent on the specific requirements for success of the IJV. Firms are therefore unlikely to differ with respect to partner-related selection criteria. This gives our final set of research questions: (i) The extent to which task-related selection criteria does not differ between UK partners

and European partners. (ii) The extent to which partner-related selection criteria does differ between UK partners and European partners.

The set of task-related and partner-related selection criteria used in this study was derived from previous studies (Geringer, 1988; 1991; Glaister and Buckley, 1997). The questions relating to selection variables were *ex post* measures of managers' perceptions of the relative value of the variables at the time of IJV formation. For the interview questionnaire the questions were open-ended. For the self-administered questionnaire, responses were assessed using five point Likert-type scales.

FINDINGS AND DISCUSSION

Task-related Selection Criteria

Resource complementarity
Complementarity of capabilities implies the possibility of synergy when the partners' resources are pooled together and thus enhances the likelihood of IJV formation. Based on the interview data, Table 3.1 shows the task-related selection criteria as identified by the UK partners, the European partners, and the perceptions of the IJV management of the respective partners' task-related selection criteria. Our data analysis revealed that in all but one case there is a high degree of resource complementarity underlying the task-related selection criteria, as indicated in column 6 of Table 3.1. In the single case where there was no obvious task-related selection criteria (IJV 11) the partners indicated the IJV was driven more by collusion (reduction of competition). Apart from this case, the questionnaire data clearly indicates that task-related selection criteria do reflect resource complementarity in IJVs.

While the recognition of resource complementarity between partners is high, we found that there is a more limited recognition between partners and IJV managers, as reflected in the final column of Table 3.1, which shows that the recognition of resource complementarity is high in only six cases. It is not surprising that partners are more acutely aware of resource complementarities and synergistic needs as a rationale for partner choice than are the IJV managers. Nevertheless, as is indicated in Table 3.1, IJV managers broadly recognize the resource complementarities, and are in general agreement with partners regarding the main task-related selection criteria.

A citation count of task-related selection criteria mentioned by partner respondents and reported in Table 3.1, shows that for UK partners the most cited task-related selection criteria are access to technology (9 counts), access to the market (6), links with major buyers (5) and knowledge of the local market (5). For European partners the most cited task-related selection criteria

Table 3.1 Task-related selection criteria: questionnaire data (1)

JV	UK partner wanted access to:		European partner wanted access to:		Recognition of complementarity:	
	UK partner perspective	IJV management perspective	European partner perspective	IJV management perspective	Partners	Partners & IJVM
1	The product Engineering capability	The product Technology	The market Links with major buyers Knowledge of international markets Government bodies	The international market Links to major buyers Knowledge of the market Government bodies Technology	High	High
2	Technology Links to major buyers Foreign Government funding	Access to resources was of low importance. Needed IJV for strategic reasons Markets/links to major buyers Foreign government funding	Skill in financial control Links with major buyers Knowledge of local culture Knowledge of local markets Government bodies	Access to resources was of low importance. Needed IJV for strategic reasons Market/links to major buyers Foreign Government funding	High	Low
3	Technology Technological know-how	Technology	Materials/natural resources Labour Capital/finance Distribution channels Links with major buyers Knowledge of the local market	Market knowledge	High	Medium to high
4	Markets/links with major buyers Government bodies Local culture Capital	Knowledge of systems integration	The product Links with major buyers Knowledge of the local market Government bodies	Process capability	High	Medium
5	Marketing Knowledge of different market Knowledge of culture	Links to buyers Links to distribution channels Knowledge of the market Knowledge of the local culture	Capital/finance	Raw materials	High	Medium

Table 3.1 continued

JV	UK partner perspective	UK partner wanted access to: JV management perspective	European partner perspective	European partner wanted access to: JV management perspective	Recognition of complementarity: Partners	Partners & IJVM
6	Capital/finance Local market Knowledge of the local market	Local market Knowledge of the local market	Business expertise Market knowledge	Business expertise Market knowledge	High	High
7	R&D	R&D	Capital/finance Manufacturing know-how Local Market	Manufacturing know-how Production capacity	High	High
8	Technology Markets Government bodies	Market knowledge Markets	Government R&D funding Government bodies Markets Major buyers	Markets Government R&D funding	High	Medium to high
9	Technology R&D	Technology Plant design Production processes	Inputs Markets Major buyers Distribution channels	Major buyers Distribution channels	High	High
10	Production processes Production planning Brand name	Production knowledge	Technology Design competence	Knowledge of technology development skills	High	High
11	Good dividends from shareholding – good return on investment.	Knowledge of markets Distribution network Geographical market	Not looking for access to resources, involved so the partner would not provide competition	Product range Geographical market	Low	Low
12	Technology The product	Technology The product	Finance Buyers	Finance Buyers	High	High
13	Technology Markets/links with major buyers Knowledge of production process Production capacity Knowledge of the local market	Markets/links with major buyers Knowledge of production processes Knowledge of market Knowledge of local culture	Markets The product	Managerial capability and skills	High	Medium to high

14	Local brand names Technology The product Knowledge of production processes/Production capacity Links with major buyers	Product knowledge Brands	Distribution channels Links with major buyers Knowledge of the local market	Local market Distribution channels	High	Medium to high
15	Knowledge of local market/industry Operating permits Market/Links with major buyers	The market	Technology Finance	Technology Finance	High	Medium to high
16	Growing capacity Natural resources Technology	Technology	Finance Links with buyers	Distribution Access to finance	High	Medium to high
17	Production process Production capacity Market knowledge	Finance Production capacity	Technology Technical knowledge	Technology	High	Medium to high
18	Labour Inputs Regulatory permits Knowledge of local culture Government bodies	Inputs Knowledge of local market Government bodies	Technology Distribution channels Major buyers	Knowledge of the business Cash and funding International market	High	Medium to high
19	Technology The product	Technology	Technology Markets	Product development	High	Low
20	Regulatory permits The market	Regulatory permits The market	Finance Major buyers	Finance	High	Medium to high

41

are access to links with major buyers (11), knowledge of the market (7), access to capital/finance (7) and access to the market (5). At the aggregate level the major difference in task-related selection criteria between the partners is the greater need to access technology by the UK partners and the greater need to access links with major buyers by the European partners.

Questionnaire respondents were asked to assess on a five-point scale 'How important was the formation of the joint venture in allowing access to inputs that *your company* did not have?' In Table 3.2 criteria are ranked by mean order of response. The median value of the five-point scale is 3. For UK partners no task-related selection criterion exceeds this value. However, the high ranked set of criteria for UK partners are access to knowledge of local market, links with major buyers and access to capital and finance. For European partners three task-related selection criteria exceed the median value, in rank order these are access to production capacity, access to distribution channels and access to technology. There is clearly some variation in rank order and level of importance of the task-related selection criteria between the two sets of partners. However, non-parametric tests of difference in means reveals only one significant difference, that relating to access to distribution channels (Mann–Whitney U = 58.0, p = 0.023), where the importance of this criterion is greatest for the European partners. These findings corroborate the questionnaire data in supporting the view that task-related selection criteria reflect resource complementarities in IJVs.

Table 3.2 also shows the ranking of IJV managers' perceptions of task-related selection criteria of the respective partners. Comparing UK partners and IJV management responses, there are some differences in rank order, although the first two ranked task-related selection criteria for UK partners are ranked third and first respectively by the IJV managers. Tests of difference in means indicate there is only one significant difference, that relating to access to distribution channels (Mann–Whitney U = 135.0, p = 0.018), ranked 11 by UK partners but ranked 2 by IJV managers.

Comparing European partners and IJV management responses, again there is some variation in rank order of task-related selection criteria, particularly between the highest ranked criterion for each group. Tests of difference in means indicate only two significant differences, those relating to access to local brand names (Mann–Whitney U = 147.5, p = 0.012) and access to production capacity (Mann–Whitney U =137.9, p = 0.015), both of which are considered more important task-related selection criteria by the European partners than by the IJV management. Overall the findings of the questionnaire data support the findings of the interview data, which are that IJV managers broadly recognize the resource complementarities, and are in general agreement with partners regarding the main task-related selection criteria.

Table 3.2 Task-related selection criteria: questionnaire data (2)

Access to:	UK partners Rank	Mean	SD	European partners Rank	Mean	SD	IJV managers (UK partner perspective) Rank	Mean	SD	IJV managers (European partner perspective) Rank	Mean	SD
Materials/natural resources	13	1.67	1.23	11=	2.13	1.68	14	1.58	1.18	10	1.97	1.28
Technology	5	2.47	1.76	3	3.20	1.74	4	2.74	1.51	6	2.50	1.50
Labour	14	1.53	1.18	9=	2.20	1.42	13	1.61	1.05	12	1.87	1.20
Capital/finance	3	2.64	1.69	13	2.07	1.48	7	2.41	1.18	4	2.62	1.36
Distribution channels	11	1.87	1.25	2	3.27	1.62	2	2.90	1.42	2	2.84	1.48
The product	6	2.33	1.67	4=	3.00	1.65	5	2.67	1.49	5	2.53	1.46
Knowledge of production processes	9=	2.07	1.58	6=	2.67	1.54	8	2.38	1.54	9	2.15	1.32
Production capacity	4	2.53	1.76	1	3.47	1.25	6	2.45	1.46	7	2.44	1.26
Regulatory permits	7	2.27	1.75	14	2.00	1.36	12	1.74	1.34	13	1.53	0.98
Local brand names	12	1.80	1.27	8	2.53	1.55	11	1.87	1.23	14	1.40	0.80
Links with major buyers	2	2.73	1.38	6=	2.67	1.59	1	3.19	1.25	1	2.90	1.42
Knowledge of local market	1	2.93	1.44	4=	3.00	1.46	3	2.87	1.46	3	2.75	1.48
Knowledge of local culture	8	2.20	1.42	9=	2.20	1.47	9	2.32	1.45	8	2.28	1.40
Govt and admin bodies	9=	2.07	1.62	11=	2.13	1.55	10	1.94	1.37	11	1.88	1.26

Note: The mean is the average on a scale of 1 (= 'of no importance') to 5 (= 'very important').

Partner-related Selection Criteria

Prior collaborative experience

A count of the number of prior relationships between the partners reported by the interviewees is shown in Table 3.3. Reported prior relationships included technology transfer agreements, R&D agreements, supply contracts, marketing agreements, relationships as trading partners, licensing/patent agreements, previous joint ventures, and personal relationship between the top management of the partner organizations. It is clear from Table 3.3 that knowledge and recall of prior relationships tended to vary between the partners to an IJV, with one partner usually identifying more prior relationships than another.

Table 3.3 also reports the summary view of the respondents on whether the degree of favourable past association between the partners acted as a partner selection criterion. For the 14 UK partners who identified a prior relationship this was considered to be a relatively important influence on partner selection by nine respondents, but not of importance by four respondents. For the 15 European partners who identified a prior relationship, this was considered to be a relatively important influence on partner selection by nine respondents, but of relatively little importance by two respondents, with a further two respondents not providing an opinion.

The data therefore suggests that the degree of favourable past association often acts as a selection criterion. Further examination suggests, however, that the strength of past association as a selection criterion increases with the number of prior ties. Examination of the partner comments on the degree of favourable past association as a selection criterion summarized in columns 4 and 5 of Table 3.3, by the number of prior relationships, reveals that where there are few prior relationships the degree of favourable past association has a low importance as a partner-related selection criterion. However, where there have been several prior relationships then the degree of favourable past association becomes of greater importance. Although not a monotonic relationship, generally as the number of prior ties increases, the degree of favourable past association becomes of more importance as a partner-related selection criterion. Table 3.3 also shows the degree of similarity of view between the partners with respect to the importance of past association as a selection criterion. In general there is a close similarity of view between the partners, either in terms of the importance or lack of importance of this criterion.

Questionnaire respondents were asked to assess on a five-point scale how much importance they placed on a set of partner-related selection criteria. These criteria are ranked by mean response in Table 3.4. As is shown in Table 3.4, the degree of favourable past association between partners is considered

Table 3.3 Prior relationships and favourable past association as a partner selection criterion: interview data

	Prior ties		Degree of favourable past association between the partners:		
JV	UKP	EP	UK partner	European partner	Similarity of view
1	1	3	Not a key issue	I wouldn't say first on the list but certainly important	Low
2	5	3	Yes, that was strong. That was important, we knew we could work with them	That played a role. Both partners knew each other at the operational level	High
3	0	0	No past association	No past association	High
4	0	2	No past association	Meant very little	High
5	6	7	Of key importance, JV grew out of long-standing relationship	Of key importance, JV grew out of long-standing relationship	High
6	0	0	No past association	No past association	High
7	0	0	No past association	No past association	High
8	1	5	Limited past association, known each other for many years as competitors	Very important	Low
9	1	2	No, this wasn't a factor	No	High
10	4	1	No, that wasn't very important	Yes, that was important	Low
11	3	2	This was very important	–	–
12	0	2	No past association	I believe it was an important criterion	Low
13	2	1	Yes, probably important	–	–
14	1	0	Not important/not relevant	Not particularly relevant	High
15	4	1	There had been associations before and that influenced the decision	There had been associations before and that influenced the decision	High
16	6	3	High importance	Very important	High
17	2	1	I'm sure that had an influence	This was a positive factor	High
18	0	0	Not relevant, no past association	Not relevant, no past association	High
19	1	4	Yes, that was quite good. We've never had negative relationships with them, we've known them for a number of years	Not the most important thing	Medium
20	3	3	That certainly was a factor, there was a very good relationship	The fact that we had a previous relationship was a factor	High

Note: UKP = UK partner; EP = European partner

45

Table 3.4 Importance of partner selection criteria: questionnaire data

Criteria	All partners Rank	All partners Mean	All partners SD	UK partners Rank	UK partners Mean	UK partners SD	European partners Rank	European partners Mean	European partners SD
Trust between the top management teams	1	4.27	0.86	2	4.20	0.94	1	4.33	0.82
Relatedness of the partner's business	2	4.13	1.04	1	4.33	0.82	4	3.93	1.22
Reputation of the partner	3	4.07	0.88	3	4.07	0.96	2	4.07	0.88
Financial stability of the partner	4	3.80	1.13	4	3.60	1.18	3	4.00	1.06
The partner company's size	5	3.33	1.12	5	3.07	1.22	5	3.60	0.99
Degree of favourable past association between partners	6	2.48	1.32	6	2.33	1.29	6	2.64	1.39

Note: The mean is the average on a scale of 1 (= 'of no importance') to 5 (= 'very important').

to be the least important of those listed, with the mean score below the median of the scale. A non-parametric test of differences in means shows no significant difference between the means of UK partners and European partners (Mann–Whitney U = 91.5; n.s.).

Evidence from this sample of IJVs provides limited support for the view that a firm's direct prior collaborative experience with a partner is an important element of partner-related selection criteria. From the interview data it is clear that for any given IJV the degree of favourable past association between partners is neither a necessary nor a sufficient condition for partner selection. However, as the number of prior ties rises, this tends to increase the importance of favourable past association as a partner-related selection criterion. From the questionnaire data the degree of favourable past association between partners is clearly of less importance than other partner selection criteria. This latter finding provides further support for the findings of Geringer (1988) and Glaister and Buckley (1997).

Trust between top management teams

The majority of interview respondents considered trust between top management teams to be an important partner-related selection criterion. Fifteen of the 20 UK partners and 15 of the 20 European partners were of the view that trust between the top management teams was of medium to high importance as a partner-related selection criterion with a clear majority of partners from both groups considering this criterion of high importance. Further examination of the interview data reveals that trust tended to grow over the negotiation phase and/or was associated with the degree of favourable past association between the partners.

Evidence from the questionnaire data on the importance of trust between the top management teams as a partner-selection criterion is shown in Table 3.4. For the partner groups combined and for the individual partner groups, trust between the top management teams is ranked first of all the partner-related selection criteria, with the mean score considerably above the median of the scale. A non-parametric test of differences in means shows no significant difference between the means of UK partners and European partners with respect to the importance of trust between the top management teams (Mann–Whitney U = 105.5; n.s.).

Findings from this sample of IJVs provide strong support for the view that trust between top management teams does comprise an important element of partner-related selection criteria. The findings also provide further support to Glaister and Buckley's (1997) findings that trust between the top management teams is an important partner-related selection criterion.

Status indicators

Based on the prior literature, this study examined three status indicators: reputation of the partner, financial stability of the partner and the partner company's size. A quantitative summary of the relative importance of status indicators drawn from the interview data is shown in Table 3.5. For UK partners financial stability is seen as relatively more important than reputation, with company size being viewed as relatively less important. For European partners reputation and financial stability are viewed as being equally important, with company size only marginally less important. It is not surprising that reputation and financial stability are viewed as being important partner-related selection criteria. Few companies would seek a partner that had a poor reputation or that was financially insecure. Further analysis of the interview data revealed that where the partner was not well known prior to the formation of the IJV then information was obtained to check the reputation of the firm. In addition, reputation appeared to be one of the factors that persuaded one firm to choose a particular partner rather than an alternative. While company size featured as being relatively less important for UK partners there was some evidence from the data that company size was often used as a proxy for financial strength. Where firms were seeking substantial financial inputs for capital investment or to fund R&D, company size was seen as a measure of the ability of the partner to sustain the level of finance required.

The ranking of status indicators from the questionnaire data by mean level of importance is shown in Table 3.4. These rankings are in accord with the findings of the interview data. For both sets of partners, reputation is seen as a more important status indicator than financial stability of the partner, with the partner company's size being marginally less important. For both partner groups, reputation of the partner and financial stability of the partner exceed the median measure of the five-point scale. This indicates the relative importance of these criteria in partner selection. Although the partner company's size is of less importance as a partner selection criterion than other status criteria, the mean values indicate that it is still of some importance. Non-parametric tests of differences in means show that there are no differences between the views of the UK partners and the European partners on the relative importance of status indicators as partner-related selection criteria. The rank order of status indicators support previous findings of Glaister and Buckley (1997) for a sample of UK IJV partners, who reported that reputation and financial stability of the partner were more important than the partner company's size as partner-related selection criteria. In summary, the evidence from this sample of IJVs provides support for the view that status indicators are important elements of partner-related selection criteria.

Table 3.5 Status indicators – quantitative summary: interview data

Status indicators	Important No.	Important Valid %	Not Important No.	Not Important Valid %	Missing No.	Missing %	Total No.	Total %
UK partners								
Reputation	13	72.2	5	27.8	2	10	20	100
Company size	10	52.6	9	47.3	1	5	20	100
Financial stability	16	84.2	3	15.8	1	5	20	100
European partners								
Reputation	17	89.5	2	10.5	1	5	20	100
Company size	14	82.3	3	17.7	3	15	20	100
Financial stability	17	89.5	2	10.5	1	5	20	100
Total partners								
Reputation	30	81.1	7	18.9	3	7.5	40	100
Company size	24	66.7	12	33.3	4	10	40	100
Financial stability	33	86.8	5	13.2	2	5	40	100

Partner Differences

The data provided evidence that there are differences between UK partners and European partners with respect to task-related selection criteria, but there are few differences between UK partners and European partners with respect to partner-related selection criteria. The interview data clearly demonstrate that there are differences between partners with respect to task-related selection criteria based on resource complementarity. While generally supporting this conclusion, only limited statistical support for this finding was provided by the questionnaire data. As expected, there are relatively few differences between UK partners and European partners with respect to partner-related selection criteria, with the interview data and the questionnaire data leading to the same conclusions. Findings from this study indicate that there is greater consensus among the partner groups on the relative importance of partner-related selection criteria than on the importance of task-related selection criteria. Partner-related selection criteria tend to be generic between groups of partners, whereas task-related selection criteria are clearly specific to the needs of the venture. In consequence there will tend to be agreement between partner groups on partner-related selection criteria but more sharply drawn differences on the importance of various task-related selection criteria.

CONCLUSIONS

The ultimate success of an IJV is intimately bound up with the nature of the partner firms. Consequently, the choice of partner is a crucial variable influencing IJV performance. This chapter serves to build on prior research, which has emphasized both resource complementarity and the role of the social structural context in alliance formation, by investigating IJV partner selection through an examination of the nature of task-related and partner-related selection criteria. In doing so it has sought to clarify and elaborate the nature of these types of selection criteria and to identify the relative importance of each from the perspectives of the different elements of an IJV. The contribution of this chapter is to elucidate the interplay of task-related and partner related selection criteria in UK–Western European IJVs. This study is novel in that it has approached partner choice from an examination of interview and questionnaire data obtained from both partners and managers of an IJV.

Findings support the contention of the first research question that task-related selection criteria reflect resource complementarity. Underlying the task-related selection criteria view of partner selection is a contingency view of the merits of a co-operative strategy that emphasizes the matching of partners, rather than looking at co-operation from a single partner's point of view (Faulkner and de Rond, 2000).

On prior relationships (research question two), the findings indicate that the degree of favourable past association between partners appears to become a more important partner-related selection criterion as the number of prior ties between partners increases. The relative importance of this criterion is then itself a function of the number of prior ties. Findings show that trust between top management teams is an important element of partner-related selection criteria (confirming the expectations underlying research question three). Of the partner-related selection criteria examined in the study, trust between top management teams was considered the most important by both UK and European partners. The study confirmed the importance of a number of status indicators as partner-related selection criteria (supporting the expectation underlying research question four). The status indicators of reputation of the partner, financial stability of the partner and to a lesser extent the partner company's size are important elements of partner-related selection criteria. With respect to the fifth research question, the study found that there is greater consensus between the partner groups on the importance of the set of partner-related selection criteria than on the different factors of task-related selection criteria. It is conjectured that this is because the former tend to be general partner requirements, while the latter are specific to the needs of the venture.

It is clear from the findings of this chapter that partner selection is a complex and multifaceted phenomenon. The drivers of partner choice are an inter-linked combination of factors hinging not only on resource complementarity but also on the social structural context of alliance formation in terms of the relational experiences and characteristics of the partner firms. In this context the identification of task-related and partner-related selection criteria provides an appropriate typology of partner choice. While this dichotomy provides an extremely useful perspective on choice of partner, it tends to obscure the fact that in reality partner choice is a synthesis of these two sets of criteria. This presents an ongoing challenge in terms of identifying the dominant force in driving partner choice and in uncovering the hierarchy of choice criteria.

One limitation of the findings to the study is that the sample is drawn from IJVs between partners from the advanced industrial economies of Western Europe. Extrapolating the findings to IJVs between partners from other parts of the Triad or between partners from developed and developing nations may be problematic.

A consideration of the research questions of this study with samples drawn from a broader range of IJV partners represents a further research opportunity. IJV formation is a highly popular strategy employed by many firms, but IJVs continue to have a high mortality rate. It is important for managers embarking on a strategy of IJV formation to know and comprehend the partner company. Clearly, there remains a research imperative to examine and understand the criteria used for partner selection if the success rate of IJVs is to be improved.

4. Management control

INTRODUCTION

A key challenge of corporate governance is the manner in which corporate owners can exercise effective control over the direction of their companies. Control raises questions concerning the rights of smaller versus dominant stockholders and how managers can be held accountable as the agents of corporate owners. These questions have been addressed mainly to unitary enterprises, but comparable issues arise in international joint ventures, where the partners in IJVs are also in the position of co-owners.

IJV governance defines how an IJV is managed, how it is organized and regulated by agreements and processes, and how the partners control and influence its evolution and performance over time (Doz and Hamel, 1998: 120). Management control is the process by which a parent organization influences its subunits (the IJVs) to behave in ways that lead to the attainment of organization objectives and the organization's ability to influence IJV activities and how they are performed (Lin et al., 1997). Control is recognized as a critical issue for the successful management and performance of IJVs (Geringer and Hebert, 1989). Problems may arise both in relations between the partners, who may be concerned with the extent to which each of them can influence the IJV so that it meets their objectives, and between the partners and their agents – the managers of the IJV. Parents must ensure that IJV managers are held accountable for performance to the owners. While this situation is not unique to IJVs, it can be complicated by the presence of multiple partners, who may seek to introduce different performance priorities and different control systems into the IJV.

Despite its importance for partner firms, there is relatively little evidence on control in IJVs, or on the factors which provide for control. Among the prior studies there is also the complication that some have examined control in IJVs between partners from developed countries, while others have investigated control in IJVs between developed and developing country partners (Beamish, 1985; 1988).

The goal of this chapter is to identify and examine the dimensions of control for the sample of UK–Western European IJVs in terms of the mechanisms of control, the extent of control and the focus of control. The chapter is organized as follows: literature on IJV control and research questions relating to the study are discussed in the following section. Findings and discussion are in the fourth section. Conclusions are given in the final section.

LITERATURE REVIEW

IJVs are normally established to exploit complementarities between partners, who supply a range of resources, skills and knowledge (Glaister and Buckley, 1996). IJV partners face the problem of protecting the integrity and use of the resources they supply, and therefore have a motive for seeking a degree of control over the IJV. The need for control is reflected in the threats partners may face to the integrity of the resources they provide (Child and Faulkner, 1998: 185). First, one partner may gain access to the core competencies of the other partner, either deliberately through acts of opportunism or from simple 'leakage' or 'bleedthrough' (Harrigan, 1985; Hamel, 1991), which incurs the risk of undermining the competitive advantage that the supplying partner enjoys and strengthening the competitive position of the receiving partner. Second, a partner will be concerned with how the resources are used in the IJV. A poor use of the resources could damage the reputation of the partner's products in other markets, for example, if their quality suffers and they are provided with inferior after-sales support. Third, a partner may seek to secure IJV control if it believes that a shared system of control may lead to a lack of cohesion and unity that would threaten the operating efficiency and overall performance of the IJV.

The Dimensions of IJV Control

Geringer and Hebert (1989) presented a conceptual framework which suggests three dimensions of parent control of IJVs: the *mechanisms* of control, that is the means by which the control is exercised; the *extent* of control, that is the degree to which the parents exercise control; the *focus* of control – or the scope of control – which is the area of the JV's operation over which control is exercised. Each of these dimensions is now considered more fully.

Control mechanisms
The partners adopt different kinds of control mechanisms depending on levels of strategic interdependence and environmental uncertainty (Kumar and Seth, 1994). These mechanisms range from formal methods of control such as majority equity shareholding, the IJV board, selection of board members, veto rights and appointment of key IJV managers, to more informal methods such as development of personal relations and assigning an executive as 'ambassador'

of the partner. A summary of control mechanisms identified in the literature is shown in Table 4.1.

In order to achieve effective managerial control, the parent companies of IJVs frequently rely upon *majority equity shareholding*. In legal terms formal ownership conveys rights to control an IJV that exist in proportion to the share of equity held. The main mechanism for exercising these rights is the *board of directors* through the powers reserved to the board in the JV contract. The frequency with which the board meets and the scope of its agenda bear upon its effectiveness as a control mechanism for the majority partner. However, control through the board is necessarily qualified. If exercised too frequently and in a domineering manner, it is likely to lead to significant ill will and the eventual breakdown of the IJV.

There are limitations on equity holding as a control mechanism. First, the decisions of an IJV's board of directors cannot be expected to reflect a majority equity position without any qualification. Second, majority equity share can provide for control over IJV policy but may not be an effective means of control at the operational level. This is because considerable reliance often has to be placed upon another partner's managers and staff for the implementation of policy. This is especially true of IJVs whose operations are located in the other partner's country. Concerns over majority equity shareholding as a mechanism of control have led to an interest in mechanisms for control over IJVs other than equity share. This leads to the first research question which concerns *the identification of control mechanisms adopted by partners to ensure IJV control, and the extent to which different partners to a venture may seek to influence IJV management through different mechanisms of control.*

Extent of control

The extent of control is dependent upon the centralization or location of the decision-making process. An important contribution of this perspective is that it regards control as a continuous variable, that is parents can exercise different degrees of control over the IJV rather than it being a question of having either total control or no control. An early study adopting this perspective was that of Killing (1983) who observed that some JVs were easier to manage than others, and this was when one parent was willing to adopt a passive role, leaving the other dominant parent to run the JV. Killing concluded that the more a JV can be run as if it has only one parent, the simpler will be its management task and the better its performance.

Child et al. (1997) identified four significant bases for control in 67 Sino-foreign equity JVs. First, *majority equity share* provided for dominant control over key policy decisions, including a JV's strategic priorities, reinvestment policy and profit distribution. Second, the nomination of the *general manager* and the *heads of certain functions*, particularly finance, increases a foreign

Table 4.1 Control mechanisms

Mechanism	Comment
Formal mechanisms	**Formal methods to improve operational control over an IJV**
Majority equity shareholding	From the legal perspective, formal ownership conveys rights to control an IJV that exist in proportion to the share of equity held.
The board of directors	The main mechanism for exercising rights to control is through the powers reserved to the board. The board normally decides on policy issues such as approval of the IJV's business plans, capital expenditure budgets, senior appointments and overall performance.
Selection of board members	The partners can exercise control not only over the choice of board members, but also over the way they vote on the board.
Right to veto	Parents, including minority parents, may be able to negotiate the inclusion in a JV contract of the *right to veto* board decisions that are important to their interests.
Appointment of key IJV managers	To run the venture or manage critical functions such as marketing or R&D. This can be an important means for a partner to maintain operational control, particularly where the partner is geographically remote or is a minority equity-holder.
Formal contractual agreements	These may set out certain rights to the partner relating to technology (e.g. licensing) or management (e.g. key appointments, management systems and services).
Structuring the IJV–partner relationships	These include the reporting relationships upwards from the IJV to a parent company, formalizing its planning and approval processes for capital budgeting and resource allocation, and laying down procedures and routines for the IJV to follow.

Composition of documents	These set out the obligations of the partner companies. The development of a business plan is the main instrument of control, because it involves shared planning of the IJV's future turnover and making joint decisions on activities and markets.
The provision of HRM programmes and systems	Selection, training and development, career advancement and remuneration, can help to control the quality of the IJV's staff and help to lay down an organizational culture which is consistent with the partner's own.
Incentive systems	Incentive systems for IJV managers increase the likelihood that the management of the IJV will act in the parent's interests.
Informal mechanisms	*Informal methods to improve operational control over an IJV*
Personal relations with the IJV's senior managers	In the course of time, personal contacts develop alongside the official structures. These contacts promote the exchange of information and thus contribute indirectly to the achievement of objectives.
Transfer of loyal members of the partner companies	Loyalty to the partner is strengthened because these managers develop social contacts and become part of an informal network who work in the JV but maintain their relationships with the partner. This loyalty also increases the partners' influence over the JV.
'Ambassador' of the partner	The partner company can assign an executive with sufficient time and resources to monitor the IJV's progress and to support this with the necessary personal contact.
Personal relations between partner and IJV staff	Technical, advisory and managerial inputs offered to an IJV on a continuing basis, and accompanied by the maintenance of close relations between the parent and its IJV, can have a considerable potential for enhancing operational control.

Sources: Tomlinson, 1970; Stopford and Wells, 1972; Lecraw, 1984; Child et al., 1997; Buchel et al., 1998; Harrigan, 1986; Schaan, 1988; Child and Faulkner, 1998; Lyles, 1987; Frayne and Geringer, 1990; Killing, 1983.

parent's control over a wide range of JV decisions. Third, legal *contracts* are intended primarily to provide security for foreign technology, to guard against leakage, to guarantee standards, and to secure an income stream from royalties. They are also used to protect brands. Fourth, provision of *non-contractual support*, including product know-how, production technology, marketing assistance, management systems and training, by Chinese JV parents, added appreciably to the influence they possessed in many areas of JV management.

These findings are broadly comparable with those of Yan and Gray (1996) for US–China JVs, regarding the impact of resource provision by parent companies upon their levels of JV control. Yan and Gray found that the equity share held by a parent is a stronger predictor of what they called strategic control than is non-capital resource provision, while they found that non-capital resourcing is more predictive of operational control.

Glaister (1995) found that those UK partners which owned at least a half share of the IJV not only possessed the control advantages associated with being the majority equity holder, but also in most cases had been able to build upon this advantage by deriving several other mechanisms of control. These included appointing the JV's general manager, sourcing the JV's management team, providing its accounting, planning and control systems, and being the more active partner in its general management and in all the main management functions except R&D and marketing. When the foreign partner held a majority equity share, it was similarly able in many cases to introduce much the same pattern of additional control mechanisms. These findings are in contrast to Schaan's (1988) conclusion that a JV partner can secure control even while owning a minority equity share. Child and Faulkner (1998) point out this may be due to the contrast between IJVs between developed country partners, as in Glaister's study, and those between developed and developing country partners, as in Schaan's sample. In the latter case, IJVs depend quite highly on the developed country partner for technical and managerial skills, thus providing it with a substantial alternative basis for exercising control, even if it has a minority equity holding. By contrast, IJV partners from highly developed countries will tend to be more balanced in their managerial and technological competencies. They are therefore less likely to be able to use these to derive further control advantages unless they enjoy the right to do so which flows from a majority equity share (Child and Faulkner, 1998: 199). In summary, the extent to which partner control will vary with the equity share of the partner appears to be somewhat ambiguous. This leads to the second research question which concerns *how the extent of partner control will vary with the equity share of the partner.*

Focus of control
The realisation that control in IJVs does not have to be an all-or-nothing phenomenon has drawn attention to the possibility that parents may seek to

focus their control on specific activities, decisions or processes which they perceive to be crucial for the IJV's performance or for the achievement of their own strategic objectives (Geringer and Hebert, 1989; Child and Faulkner, 1998: 190). Child et al. (1997) point out that the transactions costs of managing some areas of IJV activity may be less for one partner because of its acquired competence and familiarity than for another partner. These considerations support 'the notion of parent firms' parsimonious and contingent usage of resources for controlling IJVs' (Geringer and Hebert, 1989: 240). They imply that IJV owners may seek to concentrate on providing certain resources and on controlling certain decision areas and activities. Child and Faulkner (1998: 187) argue that a key distinction is that between strategic control and operational control (Yan and Gray, 1994a; 1994b).

Schaan (1983) explored the focus of control in a study of ten IJVs located in Mexico. He explicitly defined control as 'the process through which a parent company ensures that the way a JV is managed conforms to its own interest' (1983: 57), and he demonstrated that parent companies tended to seek control over 'strategically important activities' rather than over the whole JV. Geringer's (1988) study of 90 developed-country JVs supported Schaan's finding that control had a focus dimension, in that parents may choose to exercise control over a relatively wide or narrow range of the JV's activities. Child et al. (1997), using their sample of Sino-foreign equity JVs, also found that foreign- and local-partner control was focused to some extent on those areas of JV activity in which they enjoyed competence advantages. Glaister (1995) also found evidence that supports the view that parents will seek to gain control over particular decisions and activities of the venture, rather than attempting to achieve overall control. The evidence indicated that different parents would be more active in different functional areas of management. The particular focus of control was conjectured to be a function of the relative competencies and pressing interests of the separate partners. This discussion leads to the final research question which seeks to *identify which aspects of IJV control partner firms will choose to focus on and the drivers of this focus of control.*

FINDINGS AND DISCUSSION

Mechanisms of control

The nine most frequently cited mechanisms of control identified by the interview respondents are shown in the columns of Table 4.2, with the partner firms using these mechanisms denoted with an 'X'. The most commonly adopted mechanism of control is through the formal mechanism of board level decisions,

Table 4.2 Mechanisms of control used by partners to influence IJV management: interview data

JV	Board & sub-committees	Appointments to key posts	Geographical proximity	Functional competencies	Executive management team	Personal & professional relationships	Accountancy & reporting practices	Operational control	Financial control	Number of mechanisms used
UKP1	X	X		X	X	X				5
EP1	X	X	X	X	X	X				6
UKP2	X	X					X	X	X	5
EP2	X									1
UKP3	X		X					X		3
EP3										0
UKP4	X		X				X			3
EP4	X						X			2
UKP5	X									1
EP5	X									1
UKP6	X					X			X	3
EP6	X		X			X				3
UKP7	X									1
EP7	X									1
UKP8	X					X				2
EP8	X					X				2
UKP9	X		X			X				3
EP9	X					X				2
UKP10	X	X				X			X	4
EP10	X					X		X		3
UKP11	X									1
EP11	X									1
UKP12	X					X			X	3
EP12	X							X		2
UKP13	X					X		X		3
EP13	X					X		X		3

UKP14	X		X	X	X	5
EP14	X		X	X	X	5
UKP15	X	X		X	X	4
EP15	X		X	X		3
UKP16		X	X			2
EP16		X	X		X	2
UKP17	X	X				2
EP17				X		1
UKP18	X		X	X		4
EP18	X		X	X		3
UKP19	X		X	X		3
EP19	X			X		2
UKP20	X				X	3
EP20	X	X		X		4
Per cent	87.5	27.5	20.0	17.5	15.0	55.0	7.5	25.0	12.5

and/or sub-board level, that is meetings between partners and IJV managers in a structured manner but outside the board meetings (adopted by about 88 per cent of the partners). Other regularly adopted mechanisms are personal and professional relationships (55 per cent), appointments to key posts (about 28 per cent), operational control (25 per cent), and geographical proximity (20 per cent). Other identified mechanisms of control are financial controls, accountancy and reporting practices, and influence through functional competence (for example, where one partner specializes in manufacturing, this partner can influence the IJV management through its close involvement in this activity), and daily dealings with the IJV management through the executive management team.

Although a high proportion of partners seek to influence IJV management through the formal mechanism of the board and sub-committees, closer examination of the data reveals that much of the sub-board control is also informal in nature. Respondents reported that problems were often discussed prior to board meetings and resolved before there was a formal board discussion. In general, there tended to be a fluid system of communication, advice, request and pressure between partners and the IJV management before issues were resolved formally at the board.

While partners acknowledge that they can have an informal influence on the IJV management, in practice they may choose not to exercise this influence but instead operate formally through the board. Some respondents felt that it was legitimate to influence the IJV management *only* through the board and that informal approaches should be avoided. Each partner was then seen to be applying the same rules and this was felt to encourage the development of trust and mutual forbearance, and was likely to promote goodwill and harmony between the partners. In contrast, where one partner was observed to influence the IJV management through informal means, this was likely to lead to tension between the partners and the breakdown of a harmonious and trusting relationship. The relationship between the parents and IJV management is crucial when one partner attempts to influence the IJV management in a surreptitious way. Should this occur there was an expectation that the IJV management would inform the other partner.

It is not particularly surprising that so many partners adopt the mechanisms of direct contact between partners and senior IJV managers through personal and professional relationships, the appointment of key personnel in the IJV, and direct operational control. What is somewhat surprising is the discovery that so many partners use the mechanism of geographical proximity. Where a partner's business operation is located close to the business operation of the IJV (in some instances a partner and IJV shared the same physical site), this physical proximity provides the partner with easy access to the IJV management and an ability to exercise influence in a way that the more distant partner is unable to achieve.

In several IJVs there is a symmetrical pattern of control in that both partners use the same mechanisms of control. This is most clearly the case when control through the board is the only mechanism used by both partners; however, there are three instances (IJVs 8, 13 and 14) where several of the same mechanisms are adopted by both partners. In 14 of the 20 IJVs, however, there is an asymmetrical pattern of control in that the partners to an IJV adopt different mechanisms of control. In IJV 2, for example, the UK partner uses a range of control mechanisms which are not adopted by the European partners; in IJV 15 the UK partner uses four mechanisms of control of which two are not used by the European partner, while the European partner uses three mechanisms of control, of which one is not used by the UK partner; in IJV 20 the UK partner is responsible for financing the IJV so this partner adopts financial control, while the European partner uses functional competencies, and personal and professional relationships, with both partners using the Board and sub-committees, and appointments to key posts.

The final column in Table 4.2 shows the number of mechanisms used by each partner. This ranges from zero in one case (in IJV 3 the mechanisms of control are ceded by the European partner to the UK partner which manages the joint venture) to six with a mean of 2.7. Only nine of the 40 partners do not use at least two mechanisms of control.

The ten most frequently identified mechanisms of control used by UK partners and European partners, as identified by respondents completing the self-administered questionnaire, are shown in Table 4.3 ranked by frequency of adoption. The questionnaire respondents identified a set of mechanisms of control that is similar to that identified by the interview respondents. Together, board and sub-board discussion were reported as being adopted by almost half of the UK partners and the European partners. The differences in rank order of use of mechanisms of control, shown in Table 4.3, indicates that the frequency of use of the mechanisms of control varies somewhat between partners, validating the data reported in Table 4.2.

In summary, the findings of this study show that partner firms seek to use an array of mechanisms to control the IJV. The formal control mechanism of the IJV board is the most often used mechanism of control by both UK partners and European partners, but both sets of partners tend to use a number of other control mechanisms. In the clear majority of cases there is an asymmetrical pattern with one partner tending to use a range of control mechanisms that are not adopted by the other partner. Different mechanisms of control are adopted by partners for a variety of reasons: it may be based on interest, for example, the financial control often adopted by UK partners (shown in Table 4.3); competence, for example, seeking influence through involvement in functional areas of management; and physical proximity, where a close geographical presence allows the development of regular and informal contact with IJV management.

Table 4.3 Mechanisms of control used by partners to influence IJV management: questionnaire data

Method	UK partners Rank	No.	%	European partners Rank	No.	%
Board level discussion	1	19	30.2	1	21	33.3
Stringent financial controls	2	12	19.0	3	8	12.7
Sub-board level discussion	3	11	17.5	2	10	15.9
Appointment of key personnel	4	10	15.9	5	5	7.9
Effective management control system	5	6	9.5	9	2	3.2
JV agreement procedures	6	5	7.9	4	6	9.5
Personal relationship	7=	4	6.3	6	4	6.3
Strategic planning	7=	4	6.3	7=	3	4.8
Majority representation on boards	9=	3	4.8	10	0	0.0
Relevant experience	9=	3	4.8	7=	3	4.8

64

The Extent of Control

The distribution of equity between the partners in the IJVs in the sample is shown in Table 4.4. Of the 20 IJVs in the sample, 11 have a 50–50 equity shareholding, in five cases the UK partner has a majority shareholding and in four cases the European partner has a majority shareholding. Of the nine IJVs with an unequal shareholding, seven may be classed as 'balanced' holdings of equity in that the majority shareholder has at most only two percentage points more equity than the minority partner. In only two cases is there a clear imbalance of shareholding with the UK partner holding a relatively high proportion of the equity in both cases.

Table 4.4 also shows the distribution of IJV board members, and the origin of the IJV general manager/CEO. Partner representation on the board is reflected in the distribution of equity shareholding between partners. In all of the 50–50 IJVs and five of the seven 'balanced' IJVs there is an equal number of partner representatives on the board. In the remaining four IJVs the partner with the majority shareholding has majority representation on the IJV board. Board representation, therefore, follows a predictable pattern with the expected pattern of voting by members of the board in general reflecting the shareholding of the respective partner. Data analysis also shows that in general the nationality of board members also follows a predictable pattern with the majority of board members being nationals of the country of the IJV partner they represent.

The source of the IJV general manager/CEO shows a slight bias in favour of the UK partner. In seven of the 11 50–50 IJVs and three of the seven 'balanced' IJVs the senior manager was appointed from the UK partner firm. Of the seven 'balanced' IJVs the senior manager was appointed in two cases from the UK partner even though they were minority shareholders, and similarly in two cases the senior manager was appointed from the European partner even though they were minority shareholders. With the two unbalanced majority UK shareholding IJVs, in one case the senior manager was appointed from the UK partner, and in the other case the appointment was from the European partner. Further examination of the data shows that in the majority of cases, however, the senior manager of the IJV is a joint or agreed appointment in that the appointment has to be approved by both partners. One partner may have the right to propose the candidate for the post but agreement must be reached with the partner before the appointment may be ratified. There is no real support from the findings of this study that the majority shareholding partner is able to secure the appointment of the senior manager in the IJV.

Table 4.4 also shows for each IJV the source of management below the board level. Of the 11 shared equity IJVs, four (36.4 per cent) have roughly equal proportions of managers from both partners, five (45.5 per cent) have

Table 4.4 Extent of partner control: interview data

JV	Equity share % UKP–EP	Board members Total = UKP + EP	Origin of general manager/ CEO	Main source of management below board	Partner right to veto IJVM	Perception of extent of partners' control UKP	EP	IJVM
1	50–50[1]	6 = 3 + 3	EP	EP	Both	Equal	Equal	EP
2	50–50	8 = 4 + 4	UKP	Equal	Both	UKP	UKP	UKP
3	50–50	6 = 3 + 3	UKP[3]	UKP	Both	UKP	UKP	UKP
4	51–49	8 = 4 + 4	UKP	UKP	Both	UKP	Equal	UKP
5	50–50	8 = 4 + 4	UKP	Equal	Both	UKP	Equal	UKP
6	50.1–49.9	8 = 4 + 4	EP	External	Both	Equal	Equal	Equal
7	50–50	4 = 2 + 2	EP	UKP	Both	Equal	Equal	UKP
8	49.9–50.1	6 = 3 + 3	EP	Equal	Both	EP	Equal	UKP
9	50–50	4 = 2 + 2	UKP	UKP	Both	UKP	Equal	Equal
10	51–49	8 = 4 + 4	EP	Equal	Both	UKP	Equal	UKP
11	50–50	4 = 2 + 2	Third party	EP	Unclear	Equal	Equal	UKP
12	49–51	5 = 2 + 3	EP	External	Both	EP	EP	EP
13	72.5–27.5	7 = 5 + 2	UKP	Equal	Both	UKP	UKP	UKP
14	49–51	5 = 2 + 3	UKP	UKP	Both	Equal	Equal	Equal
15	80–20[2]	5 = 4 + 1	EP	EP	Both	UKP	UKP	UKP
16	50–50	6 = 3 + 3	UKP	EP	Both	EP	EP	EP
17	50–50	4 = 2 + 2	UKP	UKP	Unclear	UKP	UKP	EP
18	50–50	8 = 4 + 4	UKP	External	Both	Equal	Equal	Equal
19	50–50	6 = 3 + 3	EP	Equal	Both	Equal	UKP	Equal
20	49–51	6 = 3 + 3	UKP	EP	Both	UKP	Equal	UKP

Note:
UKP = UK Partner; EP = European Partner; IJVM = IJV Management
1. UKP also holds 35% of EP shares
2. When IJV first started UKP had 51%, subsequently increased to 80%.
3. First from UKP. Second: recruited externally.

sourced more managers from the UK partner and two (18.1 per cent) have more managers from the European partner. Of the seven 'balanced' IJVs, three (42.9 per cent) have sourced managers equally from both partners, with two IJVs (28.5 per cent) recruiting more from the UK partner (in one case the UK partner is the majority owner, and in the other case the European partner is the majority owner) and two recruiting more from the European partner (in both cases the European partner has marginally more equity than the UK partner). For the two IJVs with a relatively high equity share in favour of the UK partner, in one case the management has been sourced equally from both partners and in the other the IJV has drawn on the European partner more than the UK partner for its management. In summary, where the equity share is equal or balanced between the partners, this is not a good indication that the management will be equally sourced from both partners; it is just as likely that only one of the partners will provide most of the IJV management. Similarly, there is no clear indication that the majority shareholder will be the source of most of the management of the IJV; the management is just as likely to be equally sourced from both partners or to come from the minority partner more than from the majority partner.

Whether partner firms have the right to veto decisions made by IJV mangers is also indicated in Table 4.4. Examination of the interview data clearly shows that while most partners have the right to veto, including the minority partner, in practice the veto has not been used. The veto has not been used mainly because of the procedures that the partners and IJV managers go through in their decision making. Sufficient checks and balances on the process of decision making within IJVs make it unnecessary for any one partner to force a showdown through the use of the veto. This was expressed in the following way by the manager of IJV 15: 'The communication is fluent and daily so the IJV management is unlikely to take a decision that the partners then say 'no' to. As an experienced general manager I know how to avoid any conflict.' In summary, while the right to veto by partners may exist, this is rarely used and in most IJVs would not reach such a stage. More significantly, the right to veto is independent of the level of equity shareholding, with most IJV agreements making clear provision for minority shareholders to exercise veto rights in key decision-making areas.

The interview respondents were asked which partner they thought most controlled the IJV. The summary of the responses from managers in each element of the IJV are shown in the final three columns of Table 4.4. Where there is a difference of view on this issue between the three respondents to a particular IJV, the majority view is reported in the following assessment. Of the 11 shared equity IJVs, six (54.5 per cent) are controlled equally by both partners, four (36.3 per cent) are controlled more by the UK partner and the remaining one IJV (9 per cent) is controlled more by the European partner. In the seven balanced IJVs, four (57.1 per cent) are controlled equally by both partners; in two of these IJVs the UK partner is the majority shareholder and in the remaining two the European partner is the majority shareholder. In the other three balanced IJVs, two (28.5 per cent) are more controlled by the UK partner (one where the UK partner is the majority shareholder, and the other where the European partner is the majority shareholder), and the remaining balanced IJV (14.3 per cent) is controlled more by the European partner (which has a majority equity share). In the two IJVs where the UK partner has a high proportion of the equity, both IJVs are controlled more by the UK partner. Of the total of 20 IJVs, half are controlled equally by both partners, eight (40 per cent) are controlled more by UK partners, and two (10 per cent) are controlled more by the European partner.

Questionnaire respondents were also asked who they considered had most control over the IJV; Table 4.5 presents the results. The total percentage responses are close to those obtained from the personal interviews, with about 43 per cent reporting equal control, about 44 per cent reporting that the IJV is controlled more by the UK partner, and about 13 per cent reporting that the IJV is controlled more by the European partner.

This section has considered a range of aspects of IJV management that bear on the extent of control in the context of the equity share of the partners. The study has considered the composition of IJV boards, the source of the senior manager of the IJV, the source of the management below the board level and the right to veto by the partners as indicators of the extent of control. More directly, the study has also considered a perceptual measure of the extent of partner control. For the sample as a whole most IJVs have an equal or 'balanced' shareholding, with only two IJVs having a very unbalanced shareholding. Partner representation on the IJV board is reflected in the distribution of equity shareholding, indicating that voting power at the board level is consistent with equity share. The source of the senior manager of the IJV appears to be independent of equity share and the study does not find that the majority shareholding partner is associated with the source of the senior manager of the IJV. The source of management below board level is not associated with equity shareholding. The right of partners to veto IJV management decisions is not associated with the level of partner shareholding in that it is usual for both partners to hold veto rights. Perceptions on the extent of control indicate that shared and balanced equity IJVs are just as likely to be controlled by one parent as they are to have equal control. Only in the two cases of unbalanced shareholding is there an unambiguous view from the interviewees that the majority shareholder has a greater extent of control over the IJV. The weight of these findings supports the conclusion that for this sample of IJVs the extent of partner control is independent of the equity share of the partner. However, this finding may be largely conditioned by having a sample where

Table 4.5 IJV partners' extent of control: questionnaire data

| Most control over IJV | Respondent ||||||||
| | UK partner || European partner || IJV managers || Total ||
	No.	%	No.	%	No.	%	No.	%
UK partner	5	8.2	6	9.8	16	26.2	27	44.3
European partner	2	3.3	2	3.3	4	6.6	8	13.1
Equal control	9	14.7	7	11.5	10	16.4	26	42.6
Total	16	26.2	15	24.6	30	49.2	61	100.0

in the majority of cases the equity share is equally split or nearly so. The data shows that where the equity share is unbalanced, then the extent of control is more likely to be in accordance with the equity shareholding. For nearly balanced shareholdings, however, the small difference in equity holding does not appear to influence the extent of control.

Focus of Control

The functional areas of management with which each partner was particularly concerned is shown in summary form from the interview data in Table 4.6, where the final column of the table indicates the extent of specialism. In 14 out of the 20 IJVs (70 per cent) there is a medium to high degree of specialization. It is noticeable, for example, that the UK partner firm often takes on functional responsibility for the financial management of the IJV. UK partner firms tend to be more focused on cost control (which may be linked to the short-term perspective of UK firms with respect to financial returns). Other than this, there is no functional area that appears to be dominated by one group of partners.

Questionnaire data indicating the more active partner in the functional management of the IJV is shown in Table 4.7. This data confirms the view that the UK partners are more active than European partners in the financial management of the IJVs. UK partners also appear to be active with regard to planning in IJVs. Apart from the finance and planning areas the questionnaire data supports the interview data in that although there is functional specialization within particular IJVs, there does not appear to be a significant degree of functional specialization between the partner groups as a whole.

Findings from this study support the view that there is a relatively high degree of specialization and division of labour with respect to the functional management and hence the focus of management in IJVs. Further analysis of the personal interview data revealed that functional areas of specialization tend to be based on partner competence, that is functional specialism was basically a reflection of capabilities. UK partners were able to do some things that European partners could not, and European partners were able to do some things better than UK partners. Specialization was based around capabilities, the degree of expertise and perceived importance of the management area by the respective partners. Importantly, the area of specialization is identified at the formation stage of the IJV and is planned to the strengths of the respective partners, as argued by one respondent in IJV 1: 'The nature of functional specialism goes back to the resources and capabilities of the partners ... and the origin of the IJV. I mean, those were the capabilities that we were looking for.'

Table 4.6 Partner involvement in functional areas: interview data

JV	UK partner	European partner	Specialism
1	Marketing and sales. Procurement, estimating.	Product development. Production. System development. Project management and engineering of the product.	High
2	General management. Finance.	Operational functions, including engineering, manufacturing, manufacturing strategy. HRM. Production. Technical expertise.	High
3	All functional areas except production.	Little involvement, some R&D, marketing.	High
4	Little involvement, some marketing.	Little involvement, managed by the IJV managers.	Low
5	Little involvement, managed by the IJV managers. More concerned with obtaining financial information.	Little involvement, managed by the IJV managers. More concerned with personnel policies.	Low
6	Production and marketing.	Legal activities. Financial control. Political assistance, lobbying.	High
7	Little involvement, managed by the IJV managers.	Little involvement, managed by the IJV managers.	Low
8	Limited involvement, managed by the IJV managers. Some concern with financial and accounting control.	Limited involvement managed by the IJV managers. Some concern with overall management control, and marketing.	Medium
9	Production, marketing and finance. HRM.	R&D, product development.	High
10	Limited involvement, managed by the IJV managers. Some concern with product development.	Limited involvement, managed by the IJV managers. Some concern with marketing, sales and distribution.	Medium

Table 4.6 Continued

JV	UK partner	European partner	Specialism
11	Partners equally active in all aspects of IJV management.	Partners equally active in all aspects of IJV management.	Low
12	Quality and volume issues.	More active in all functional areas especially manufacturing, production management and scheduling.	Low
13	Limited involvement, managed by the IJV managers. Some concern with financial systems, accounting, R&D.	Limited involvement, managed by the IJV managers. Some concern with engineering, environmental issues.	Medium
14	Sales and marketing. HRM, finance, logistics.	Manufacturing, marketing, R&D and product development.	High
15	Finance and production.	Technical and legal advice. Marketing and commercial.	High
16	Marketing, R&D, finance.	General management, production.	High
17	Finance and production, general management.	Marketing. Technical expertise.	High
18	Most influence on most of the functional areas, especially technology, marketing, product development.	Political liaison, finance and financial management.	Medium
19	Little involvement, some concern with finance, marketing, R&D.	Little involvement, some concern with R&D, HRM, marketing.	Low
20	More active in managing IJV, especially in general management, finance.	Operations, HRM.	Medium

Table 4.7 More active partner in regard to the functional management of the IJV: questionnaire data

Functional area	UK partner No.	%	Equally active No.	%	European partner No.	%	Not applicable No.	%
Finance	31	49.2	30	47.6	2	3.2	0	0.0
R&D	16	26.7	27	45.0	16	26.7	1	1.7
Production	13	21.0	32	51.6	16	25.8	1	1.6
Distribution	18	30.5	26	44.0	14	23.7	1	1.7
Planning	19	30.6	34	54.8	9	14.5	0	0.0

This general theme was repeated many times. In effect, the functional areas of management in the IJVs were dominated by those partners that had the superior level of competence. For example, the UK partner in IJV 1 was of the view: 'The functional areas of financial responsibility were dominated by [UK partner] because they were better at it. There was no way near the rigour or the accountability required in a French business like [European partner] compared with [UK partner].'

It is apparent that parent companies have particular functional interests. Partners appoint their managers to senior positions in these functional areas, and the partners concentrate on these areas of management in the IJV. While this degree of specialization and division of labour with respect to functional management is likely to lead to operational efficiency of the IJV, one worrying aspect is that this degree of specialization has the potential to have a detrimental effect on learning in IJVs. If each partner concentrates on its own area of specialization and particular interest, then little learning may occur across the range of activities of the IJV, and in consequence little learning may be transferred to the parent organizations. In this sense the natural inclination by partners to focus on those aspects of the IJV in which they have most competence, or are most keenly interested, may ultimately have a negative influence on the rate of generation of new competencies that can be leveraged and effectively used by the respective partners. This may be the case even though in other respects the IJV may be successful.

It should be noted, however, that there is a group of IJVs where functional specialization by the partners is not recognized and where, in effect, the IJV managers take on functional specialization. In these IJVs there is no focus of control as far as functional management is concerned. There may be appointees from the partners to particular functional areas but there is no notion of the partner seeking to be more active in this functional area. The partners cede management to the IJV managers.

It is clear that the concept of control is multifaceted. It also became clear from analysis of the interview data that many managers prefer to view the relationship between partners and IJV as one of 'influence' rather than 'control'. The manager from IJV 9, for example, stated:

> I'm not sure that control is the right word. Influence might be a better word. Because the IJV is on the UK partner site, because the UK partner deals with it day in day out and knows the running of the plant and everything else and all the people, and the IJV joint general manager is co-opted from the UK partner. . . . I think the influence of the UK partner is by virtue of those issues greater than the European partner.

Another perspective on influence was provided by the UK partner in IJV 8 who argued:

In what the French regard as the key positions, they appoint themselves to them. . . . They have sufficient control . . . in their eyes. . . . The other side of that is that we have sufficient influence in our eyes to make the thing worthwhile. There's a difference between influence and control isn't there? . . . They find it very hard to do anything of real substance that was against our interest.

In the first example the partner is seen to influence the direction of the IJV rather than controlling it. In the second example, while the partner does not have control it is still able to achieve a degree of influence over the IJV. So although one parent may have control, the other parent is content to allow this, providing that they have what they regard as influence. Providing the degree of influence is sufficient for each partner, that is one partner might cede control but believes that they have sufficient influence to affect the process and the outcome, they are therefore content to cede control. The concept of the focus of control then becomes relative. Complete dominance of control, even of a particular area of the IJV, is unlikely. There will be shades of control associated with shades of influence from the other partner. One partner may be seeking sufficient control in its own terms, which is conditioned by influence exerted by the other partner. The partner with influence as distinct from control provides itself with a degree of involvement, so it at least feels it is not totally excluded from the particular management area of concern. An exception to this is where the partner is willing to cede control entirely to the other partner.

CONCLUSIONS

This chapter has concentrated on three control dimensions as they apply to IJVs. These are the mechanisms by which control is exercised, the extent of control exercised by partners over the IJV, and the activities which they control (focus). The study found that IJV partner firms seek to use an array of mechanisms other than equity shareholding to ensure control. The formal control mechanism of the IJV board is the most often used mechanism of control by both UK partners and European partners. Both sets of partners tend to use a considerable number of other control mechanisms, however, including sub-board level discussions, appointment of key personnel, personal relationships, and for UK partners especially, financial controls. The study also found that different partners to an IJV will seek to influence IJV management through different mechanisms of control. Although a similar set of control mechanisms tend to be used by both partner groups, within a particular IJV one partner often uses a range of control mechanisms which is not adopted by the other partner.

The findings show that for this sample of IJVs the extent of partner control is independent of the equity share of the partner. However, this finding may be largely conditioned by having a sample where in the majority of cases the equity share is equally split or nearly so. Finally, it was found that partner firms seek to concentrate on particular aspects of IJV control associated with their key skills and competencies. The findings from the study clearly indicate that partner firms do seek to concentrate on particular aspects of control. The areas that partners specialize in tend to be associated with their key skills and competencies, which is reflected in functional specialization.

There is clearly scope for further work on management control in IJVs. Future studies should attempt to gather data from a larger number of IJVs in order to undertake hypotheses testing on the findings reported in this study. The relationship between the nature of management control and IJV performance warrants investigation. It would also be fruitful to pursue the distinction and clarify the meaning of 'influence' and 'control' in IJV management.

5. Decision-making autonomy

INTRODUCTION

International joint ventures stand between the traditional economic co-ordination mechanisms of market and hierarchy. They provide a way of combining the strengths of different firms which is not available in market-oriented exchange relationships but without incurring the disadvantages of a merger or acquisition (Buckley and Casson, 1988; Buchel et al., 1998: 4). In practice, however, IJVs pose extremely difficult challenges to management. Co-operating with another company is a demanding and often unfamiliar task, which may be hindered by the divergence between parent firms with respect to goals, strategies, culture, autonomy and control.

A wide variety of motives have been suggested for the establishment of joint ventures (as examined in Chapter 2). The transaction cost approach identifies three inter-linked motives (Buckley and Casson, 1988, following Coase (1937) and Williamson (1975)). These are (i) the existence of net benefits in one or more intermediate markets between the joint venture and the parties' other operations, (ii) an element of economic indivisibility which results in benefits from avoiding the splitting of the JV into one or more separately owned facilities and (iii) the existence of obstacles to merger. The resource-based view (Wernerfelt, 1984; Barney, 1991; Grant, 1991) sees links between the internal capabilities of the parent firms where each gains access to others' internal capabilities without the risk of outright ownership (Hamel et al., 1989; Hamel, 1991; Glaister, 1996, Eisenhardt and Schoonhoven, 1996). Thus capabilities can be leveraged outside the firm in combination with complementary capabilities or competencies (Contractor and Lorange, 1988). IJVs and a network of IJVs give firms the advantages of flexibility in the face of a hostile and turbulent global economy (Buckley and Casson, 1998b).

The achievement of these aims depends on linking the IJV closely with the parents to achieve the requisite internal market and resource links whilst allowing a certain degree of decision-making freedom to the IJV managers who are closest to its environment and internal capabilities. This is the dilemma of 'autonomy' which we seek to explore. After investigating the issue in the round, we seek to identify the areas in which the IJV is allowed autonomy in decision making by separating strategic from operational decisions and by examining those areas of decision making which are formalized within the IJV's business plan from those which are excluded. Our expectation is that the key areas identified by the theory above will be (a) defined as strategic rather than operational and (b) included in the IJV's business plan. Thus our empirical investigation can be seen to uncover the key theoretical drivers of transaction cost theory and the resource-based view of the firm.

The issue of how much decision-making autonomy, if any, to grant an IJV has been identified as a major issue faced by both researchers and practitioners (Newburry and Zeira, 1999: 263). Research on the nature and meaning of IJV autonomy is a relatively neglected area in the examination of IJV activity. The purpose of this chapter is to provide new evidence on the nature of autonomy. The rest of the chapter is set out in the following way: literature relating to IJV autonomy and the research questions are discussed in the following section. The third section presents a discussion of the findings. Conclusions are in the final section.

LITERATURE REVIEW

For an IJV, autonomy is defined as the freedom to make and implement decisions independently of the parents. It is clear that autonomy is a concept that is capable of a number of interpretations based on managers' differing conceptual understanding partially influenced by cultural differences. This 'native category' problem (Buckley and Chapman, 1998) was confronted by a careful contextualization during the interview phase of the study, by leading managers through an understanding of autonomy as defined above. A perceptual measure of autonomy across the IJV system provides information regarding the extent to which the IJV is viewed as autonomous by the respective parents and the IJV management. This represents a novel departure in the study of IJV autonomy.

IJV Governance and Autonomy

The primary meaning of governance is that the decision takers in the firm must be responsible to the ultimate owners for their actions (Buckley, 1997). Where equity IJVs are structured by the ownership of their parent companies, governance by owners is twice removed and concerns that they act in accordance with the goals of these owners is increased. This agency problem (Jensen and Meckling, 1976; Arrow, 1985) is exacerbated by national and cultural distance in IJVs, so a balance needs to be struck between excessive control and laxity in supervision. This is the context in which we investigate the elusive notion of IJV autonomy.

Several contributions to Bleeke and Ernst (1993a) warn that over-control by parent companies may inhibit the flexibility that their IJV needs in order to develop within it its own competitive environment. Buchel et al. (1998: 98–99) conclude that the optimal level of autonomy is that at which objectives can be met while total costs are kept to a minimum. There is, however, no consensus in the literature either for or against the granting of autonomy to IJV managers. As Lyles and Reger (1993: 398) conclude, 'The desirability of less control for parents and more autonomy for joint ventures has not been explored'. (A survey of the arguments for and against autonomy in IJVs has been provided by Newburry and Zeira, 1999: 266–7.)

Buchel et al. (1998: 100) note that the pattern of control and autonomy depends on two variables: strategic interdependence and environmental uncertainty. Usually, the greater the strategic interdependence, that is the dependence of two organizations on each other's inputs and outputs, the more control the partners exert over the IJV. The greater the environmental uncertainty, the higher the level of autonomy needed by the IJV to make independent adjustments to environmental changes. Low autonomy needs exist when resources are shared and when the IJV makes an important contribution to the value-added chains of the partners. However, too much control by the partners reduces the IJV's decision-making efficiency and can damage its market competitiveness. In contrast, in highly competitive, dynamic industries, the JV needs considerable autonomy: it must be adaptable and flexible enough to hold its own in the market; and it must gain legitimacy as an independent organization (Buchel et al., 1998: 102).

Empirical Evidence

There is limited empirical evidence on autonomy in UK IJVs with partners from developed countries. In a study of UK IJVs Glaister (1995) found little evidence of IJV autonomy; however, many IJV managements had independent decision-making responsibility in a number of key areas. Glaister concluded that there is nothing particularly contradictory in this finding, rather it is an example of the way in which IJV control tends to be a complex and subtle phenomenon. Newburry and Zeira (1999) using data from 49 IJVs located in Britain found that permitting an IJV to develop local HRM policies and to implement business plans independently contributes to IJV effectiveness. They also found that IJVs which have the freedom to implement their strategic business plans independently are more effective than IJVs which lack the freedom to do so. They also demonstrated that autonomy is a multidimensional construct and suggested a model of relative recommended autonomy levels for different IJV activities.

The perspective from which an IJV should be viewed raises a number of concerns, largely because there are a number of different viewpoints on the venture, including the parent firms and the IJV management (assuming that the venture has a separate workforce, which is not necessarily the case). This means that there might be different views on aspects of autonomy, which may vary between partners and between partners and IJV management. In principle, therefore, estimates of autonomy should incorporate multiple viewpoints. Because of the difficulties of finding an objective, culture-free and context-free measure of autonomy, our approach is to tackle the concept by exploring the managers' (native category of) understanding in context and in stages. First, we explore the differences in perception between the parent managers (UK versus non-UK), then we explore the 'vertical' differences of understanding (parent managers versus IJV managers). We then unpack the overall concept of autonomy by discussing differences in the management and control of decision making as categorized by operational versus strategic decisions and between decision structure formalized within the business plan versus those outside it. Furthermore, we consider the influence on autonomy of IJV performance and IJV duration.

While there has been some attempt in the literature to develop a measure of IJV autonomy (for example Newburry and Zeira, 1999), in general studies have not relied on perceptual measures of autonomy. This is in contrast with the literature relating to IJV performance where concerns over the ability of financial and objective measures to effectively capture alliance performance have led several researchers to turn to perceptual measures of a parent's satisfaction with alliance performance (Killing, 1983; Schaan, 1983; Beamish, 1985; Inkpen and Birkenshaw, 1994; Lyles and Baird, 1994; Dussauge and Garrette, 1995). In order to explore the degree to which parent firms grant the IJV management autonomy we first *consider differences in perception of the extent of autonomy between the various elements of the IJV system according to context.* We address both the horizontal difference in parent perceptions of autonomy, that is, differences between UK parent managers and non-UK parent managers, and the vertical difference in perception between parents and IJV managers.

There is a clear distinction between strategic and operational control in organizations, which applies *a fortiori* to IJVs. Child and Faulkner (1998: 190) point out that it is effective for IJV parents to exercise control selectively over those activities and decisions the parent regards as critical. Furthermore, Child et al. (1997) point out that the transactions costs of managing some areas of IJV activity may be less for one partner because of its acquired competence and familiarity in so doing than for another partner. These considerations support 'the notion of parent firms' parsimonious and contingent usage of resources for controlling IJVs' (Geringer and Hebert, 1989: 240). They imply that IJV owners may seek to concentrate on providing certain resources and on controlling key decision areas and activities. Child and Faulkner (1998: 187) argue that a distinction that may inform this selection is that between strategic control and operational control (Yan and Gray, 1994a; 1996). Extending this line of argument to the notion of autonomy, it is likely that parents will seek to exercise more control over issues relating to the strategic management of the IJV and grant autonomy to the IJV with respect to operational management. In order to establish this distinction, the partners are likely to rely on the procedures established in the original documents drawing up the IJV and in the business plan and other planning documents. In this respect, Buchel et al. (1998: 83) emphasize that the joint production of a business plan is an important instrument of strategy development for the IJV. The business plan specifies the common strategic guidelines and the planned development objectives for the IJV and it documents the outcome of the partners' negotiations on strategy. They further contend that the joint development of a business plan offers significant opportunities for the cohesion of the IJV system. The second set of research questions therefore relate to *differences in IJV autonomy between operational decision making and strategic decision making, and the extent to which autonomy for IJV managers is formalized within the IJV's business plan.*

The performance of the IJV is likely to be a moderating variable on IJV autonomy. Killing (1983) noted that JV parents loosen or increase control over their ventures as a response to their performance. Yan and Gray (1994a) reported data that suggests that performance also shapes the relative levels of bargaining power and the pattern of the sharing of management control between parents. In general it may be argued that where the parents perceive the performance objectives of the IJV to be at least satisfactory and to be improving beyond some minimum requirement, then they are more likely to grant greater decision-making autonomy to the IJV management. In contrast, where IJV performance is unsatisfactory in terms of objectives or generally declining, then the parent firms are more likely to withhold or withdraw autonomy and take a greater role in the decision making of the IJV. The third research question therefore concerns *the extent to which satisfaction with IJV performance is related to the perceived extent of IJV autonomy.*

Another moderating variable on autonomy is likely to be the duration or age of the IJV. The 'parent–child relationship' (Harrigan, 1986) emphasizes the extent to which the IJV is dependent upon the partner firms. However, over time, the nature of the relationship between the partners and the IJV may change fundamentally. In particular, as IJVs age they may gain more autonomy from the parent firms (Lorange and Roos, 1992). In new and immature IJVs the parent firms are likely to scrutinize carefully the decisions of the IJV management and to control tightly the decision-making process. As the IJV matures and as the parents' confidence in the IJV management grows it is likely that the partners will grant increased autonomy to the IJV management.

The final research question thus concerns *the extent to which the age of the IJV is related to the perceived extent of autonomy of the IJV.*

In the design and conduct of the interviews, account was taken of the 'native category' issue. By 'native' in this context we mean self-generated, and valid in the local context (Buckley and Chapman, 1998). There can be no guarantee that words and categories are congruent from one context to the next, so we did not assume that managers shared our 'objective' understanding of categories or words such as 'autonomy'. Qualitative results for answers to questions were obtained only after a full exploration of the issue under discussion. For instance, in the interview schedule, the word 'autonomy' is used only once in a prompt to the final question, after a full exploration of the issues surrounding decision making (Briggs, 1984). This represents an innovative attempt to introduce qualitative and perceptual data into a study of the transactions cost and resource based views of IJV management.

FINDINGS AND DISCUSSION

Perceptions of IJV Autonomy

Perceptions of IJV autonomy were explored in order to clarify the concept. Following this conceptual clarification respondents were asked to assess the overall level of IJV autonomy on a five-point scale (from 1 'no autonomy', to 5 'completely autonomous'). This was a broad, preliminary assessment of the perception of autonomy in the IJV, as precursor to a more fine-grained examination of the concept in detail. The mean responses are shown in Table 5.1 panel (i). For each category of respondent the mean score is above the median measure, indicating the perception of a fair (but certainly not a complete) degree of autonomy of decision making on the part of IJV managers.

Tests of pairwise differences in means shows that there are no significant differences between the mean scores for each category of respondent. On this basis it may be argued that perceptions of IJV autonomy do not vary significantly between partners or between each parent and the IJV management. However, this would be misleading. Correlation coefficients between the three elements of the IJV are shown in Table 5.1 panel (ii). This shows only one moderately high and significant correlation ($p < 0.01$); that between the European partners and the IJV management. There are low and non-significant correlations between the partners and between the UK partner and the IJV management.

To explore further perceptions of autonomy between the three elements of the IJV we measured the extent of agreement between the ratings by computing the kappa coefficient.[1] Although only one of the kappa coefficients shown in Table 5.1 panel (iii) is significant (p < 0.10), it is clear that the values shown represent poor levels of agreement beyond chance.

Based on a perceptual measure of IJV autonomy, while there appears to be a recognition by each of the elements of the IJV of a similar level of autonomy, there is a lack of correlation of perception 'horizontally' between the partners and a lack of correlation of perception 'vertically' between the UK partners and the IJV management. Moreover, there is evidence of a low level of similarity of rating of perception of autonomy between the three elements of the IJV. The interview data for this study appears to provide little evidence to reject the view that there will be differences in the perceptions of the extent

Table 5.1 Perceptions of IJV autonomy

(i) Perceptions of IJV autonomy: interview data

	Mean	SD
UK partners	3.35	1.18
European partners	3.85	0.98
IJV managers	3.55	0.88

Notes:
The mean is the average on a scale of 1 (= no autonomy) to 5 (= complete autonomy).
SD = Standard deviation.

(ii) Correlations between perceptions of autonomy: interview data (Spearman's rho)

	1. UK partners	2. European partners
1. UK partners		
2. European partners	0.23	
3. IJV management	0.01	0.58***

Note: *** $p < 0.01$

(iii) Comparison between perceptions of autonomy: interview data

Perception of autonomy	Kappa
UK partner – European partner	0.08
European partner – IJV management	0.17
UK partner – IJV management	0.23*

Note: * $p < 0.10$

and scope of IJV autonomy horizontally and vertically between the elements of the IJV. Clearly, these findings raise the issue of what is understood by 'autonomy'. This question is addressed later in the discussion where the attempt is made to disaggregate the managers' overall understanding of autonomy by contextualizing its various elements.

Autonomy in Operational Decisions and in Strategic Decisions

The questionnaire survey obtained autonomy data on a broad spectrum of decision-making autonomy. Respondents were asked to indicate on a five point scale (from 1 'no autonomy', to 5 'completely autonomous') the extent to which the IJV was autonomous in its decision making across a range of decisions. The mean responses for all categories of respondent are shown in Table 5.2. It is clear from Table 5.2 that the greatest level of IJV autonomy is in the day-to-day management of the IJV, with a mean score well above 4, indicating a relatively high level of IJV autonomy.

Table 5.2 also shows that five other decision-making areas achieved a mean score above 4, indicating a relatively high level of autonomy in hiring and firing of non-technical personnel and technical personnel, process technology, manufacturing and marketing. In contrast, relatively little local control was

Table 5.2   IJV decision-making autonomy: questionnaire data

	Rank	Mean	SD
Day-to-day management	1	4.47	0.76
Hiring and firing non-technical personnel	2	4.23	1.05
Hiring and firing technical personnel	3	4.10	1.17
Process technology	4	4.07	1.20
Manufacturing	5	4.03	1.15
Marketing	6	4.01	1.26
Cost control	7	3.98	1.08
Distribution	8	3.90	1.38
Pricing	9	3.84	1.21
Technology & engineering of products	10	3.83	1.28
R&D	11	3.78	1.31
Patents & trademarks	12	3.65	1.29
Hiring and firing senior JV managers	13=	2.57	1.17
Deciding capital expenditures	13=	2.57	1.19
Financing of JV	15	2.23	1.25
Location of JV	16	2.21	1.20

Note: Mean is average on a scale of 1 (= no autonomy) to 5 (= complete autonomy).

reported in the decisions to locate the IJV, its financing, deciding capital expenditures, and hiring and firing senior IJV managers.

It is apparent from Table 5.2 that while there is a perception across respondents of a reasonable amount of autonomy, there is a spectrum of local control across decision-making areas. IJV managers have most decision-making freedom in regard to daily management and ongoing operational issues and least autonomy in regard to longer-term financial issues and senior management appointees. This indicates that IJV managers have a relatively high degree of operational autonomy but relatively low levels of strategic autonomy in decision making.

This situation becomes clearer when we consider the extent of joint decision making in the IJVs across a number of areas. Questionnaire respondents were asked to indicate on a five point scale the extent to which a set of decisions were taken jointly (from 1 'no extent', to 5 'great extent'). The decisions ranked by mean score are shown in Table 5.3. Three decision areas have a mean score greater than the median measure, indicating a relatively high extent of joint decision making, that is these decisions involve the parent companies as well as the IJV management. These decision areas relate to the budgetary process of the IJV, they are non-operational decision-making areas and are concerned with medium-term decisions of the IJV. In contrast the lowest ranked decision areas, each below the median measure, indicate a relatively low extent of joint decision making, that is these decisions tend to be taken by IJV management without the involvement of the parent companies. These decisions relate to operational matters. The findings reported in Table 5.3 clearly indicate that while the IJV management is concerned with operational decisions, the partners tend not to be so, but rather are involved with strategic decisions relating to the IJV. These findings add further support to the view that the IJV managers will have decision-making rights in operational management but not in the strategic management of the IJV.

Table 5.3 Extent of joint decision-making: questionnaire data

	Rank	Mean	SD
Budget capital expenditures	1	3.92	0.94
Budget sales targets	2	3.79	1.01
Budget cost targets	3	3.66	1.04
Replacing a functional manager	4	2.73	1.22
Product pricing	5	2.60	1.47
Quality standards	6	2.46	1.32
Product design	7	2.36	1.39
Production process	8	2.28	1.21

Note: Mean is average on a scale of 1 (= no extent) to 5 (= great extent).

Aspects of decision-making autonomy were also directly explored in the personal interviews by asking respondents whether IJV partners, the IJV management, or combinations of partners and IJV management were responsible for decision-making and in particular those decisions relating to pricing and quality. Triangulation across the different respondents for each IJV revealed a high level of consistency. Table 5.4 provides a summary of the interview responses.

Investigation of the interview data reveals that there is a large measure of agreement between managers in the three elements of each IJV system on the locus of decision making with regard to pricing and quality issues. Although there is not complete agreement across the three categories of respondent as to the nature of decision making within each of the IJVs, it is the case that in about three-quarters of the IJVs there is such agreement. Moreover, even where there is disagreement over the locus of decision making with regard to pricing and quality there is general agreement that daily operating decisions lie with the IJV management within the constraints set by the partners and that strategic decisions lie with the partners. The responses clearly indicate the separation of strategic control and operational control between partners and IJV managers (Child and Faulkner, 1998).

The summary of interview responses shown in Table 5.4 reveals that some firms had only limited autonomy even in operational decisions, indicating extensive control by the partners. An examination of the relationship between the partners and the IJV showed that for most of this category of ventures the output of the IJV was being sold as an input to one of the partners, or being supplied to one of the partners for onward distribution. In these circumstances the parents tended to exercise greater control and grant less autonomy of operational decisions than when the output of the IJV did not go directly to one of the partners. This supports the view of Buchel et al. (1998: 100) that the pattern of control and autonomy in part depends on strategic interdependence. The findings indicate that the greater the strategic interdependence, that is the dependence of one organization on the outputs of another, the more control the partners exert over the IJV and the less autonomy is granted. This is striking confirmation of the transactions cost view that there are net benefits of internalizing key markets across the IJV system and that indivisibilities are important.

The findings of this study support the view that there is a risk of IJV autonomy becoming a rather fuzzy concept unless the distinction is drawn between strategic autonomy and operational autonomy. In the former case there is practically no autonomy for this sample of IJVs, in the latter case there is a high level of autonomy. The areas where IJV managers have no autonomy are in the location of the IJV which is largely predetermined, and the hiring and firing of senior managers. Partners also generally control the raising of finance and capital expenditure by being closely involved in the approval process for

Table 5.4 Nature of IJV decision-making: interview data

JV	Summary of responses	Strategic	Operational
1	Most strategic decisions the partners take together; price proposal requires the backing of both partners. Product decisions (e.g. a new feature) would be a decision for the IJVM; other decisions IJVM have autonomy.	No	Yes
2	Strategic decisions taken by the partners. Prices determined by IJVM; IJVM have operational autonomy	No	Yes
3	Strategic decisions taken by the partners. Pricing and quality decisions left with IJVM; IJVM have operational autonomy	No	Yes
4	Price and quality set by the board; IJVM decisions approved by the board	No	Limited
5	Pricing and quality decisions are left to the IJVM	Unclear	Yes
6	Parents only influence strategic decisions. Pricing, quality and operational decisions are left to the IJVM.	No	Yes
7	Most decisions are made by IJVM. Some decisions vetted by the board before they are implemented	Limited	Yes
8	Quality decisions taken by IJVM. Price decisions taken by IJVM subject to financial return expectations of partners.	Unclear	Yes
9	Price and quality decisions taken by IJVM, providing they satisfy the broad guidelines of the partners. Other decisions, e.g. changes in capacity are taken by the board.	No	Yes
10	Price and quality decisions taken by partners. Production flow and internal efficiency. decided by IJVM	No	Limited
11	Pricing and quality decisions made by IJVM.	Unclear	Yes

87

Table 5.4 Continued

JV	Summary of responses	Strategic	Operational
12	Pricing is agreed between the two partners and IJVM; quality and production level determined by the partners. Within planned production limits IJVM takes decisions.	No	Limited
13	Pricing and quality decisions made by IJVM, within the agreed budget.	No	Yes
14	Pricing and quality decisions made by IJVM, within the agreed budget.	No	Yes
15	Parents set strategic direction and the budget. Pricing, quality and day-to-day running decisions taken by IJVM.	No	Yes
16	For all major decisions the parents make the decisions jointly. Pricing and quality decisions taken by partners and IJVM. Day-to-day management decided by European partner and IJVM.	No	Limited
17	Partners take capital expenditure decisions. Price and quality decisions influenced by partners. Daily operating decisions taken by IJVM	No	Yes
18	Acquisitions and major investment spending agreed by the board. Price, quality and other decisions taken by IJVM, provided they are within the business plan.	No	Yes
19	General strategy, acquisitions, major investment decisions made by parents. Pricing and operational decisions made by IJVM.	No	Yes
20	General strategy influenced by partners. Pricing determined by partners and IJVM. Quality and operational decisions taken by IJVM.	No	Yes

significant levels of investment. In most other areas IJV management run the venture as if it were their own operation. This position was neatly encapsulated by an IJV manager from IJV 18, a telecommunications JV between a UK partner and a Dutch partner, who reported that although the partners may query the 'how' of what the IJV management are doing, the IJV management are still expected to come up with the 'how', and not to be told 'how'.

In summary, we observed a consistent pattern across respondents clearly indicating that there is a recognition that IJV managers have operational autonomy, which in large part extends to issues of pricing and quality. However, if the IJV management wanted to develop strategic initiatives, such as developing new markets or investing above a certain level, they have to go to the IJV board to seek approval from the parents. These findings add further support to the view that autonomy for IJV managers will be greater in operational decisions than in strategic decisions.

Autonomy and the Parameters of the IJV's Business Plan

Further investigation of the personal interview data showed that operational decision making by IJV managers takes place within the context of a set of constraints established by the partners and decided through the board of the IJV. These constraints are set out particularly in terms of budget limits and ceilings on capital expenditure. The limits within which the IJV managers have autonomy are established within the context of the IJV's business plan. Provided that IJV managers' decisions are within the acceptable boundaries of the business plan then partners allow IJV managers decision-making autonomy.

The interview data reveals that the overall strategy for the IJV is determined by the partners. Further, in order to ensure that IJV managers work to the goals set for the IJV, the parameters of the venture are defined by the business plan and agreed by the partners. Once the plan has been agreed on an annual basis with a budget, then the IJV management are expected to deliver and the IJV management's performance is monitored through the board. As long as IJV managers work within the parameters established in the business plan they have a fair degree of autonomy. Autonomy allows IJV managers to choose what they want to do within these parameters. Clearly, it is not in their interests to ignore all of the wishes of the partners, but autonomy allows the IJV managers to choose whether or not they want to follow the wishes of the partners fully, and in general terms the IJV management are free to work within the business plan assumptions. To a large extent then, the parameters have little impact on the IJV management, the biggest impact probably being on capital expenditure decisions. In this regard, however, IJV management tends to be no more circumscribed than are the management of subsidiary firms, who would have to go to their respective company boards for permission to spend beyond agreed levels of investment. There is thus a hands-off approach by the partners to the operational management of the IJV. The IJV managers are knowledgeable of what they are required to do to run the business and to satisfy the partners. As long as they provide the necessary information through the board and they act in the way they are expected, they are allowed a relatively high degree of operational autonomy. The operational control very much belongs to the joint venture. Problems arise, however, when the managers of the IJV brush up against the boundary of what is established in the business plan.

Our data analysis revealed that the IJV managers have the freedom to run the business knowing the performance outcomes expected by the partners. It is necessary, of course, for partners to communicate their expectations clearly to IJV managers, and for IJV managers to be aware of the partners' goals for the IJV. This points up the relevance of the planning and budgeting process and in particular the importance of the business plan agreed through the board. At the same time IJV management have to conform to reasonably rigorous reporting to the partners. This process is likely to lead to a clear understanding between the elements of the IJV system and to an amicable and appropriate working environment.

Evidence supporting the importance of the business plan as a mechanism of IJV control was present in the data. The business plan establishes the ground rules, however, typical evidence from the interview data also indicates that in general it is not dictated by the partners to the IJV management, rather it is an agreed process. In other words, the business plan is not necessarily 'handed down' to the IJV management from the partners, but may be developed by the IJV management and 'sold' to the partners. Giving an IJV management enough autonomy to genuinely run an independent business, but at the same time making sure that major strategic decisions are taken by equity partners is a delicate task. On the one hand it is necessary for the IJV management not to feel emasculated, but at the same time the partners should feel sufficiently confident that they have control over major issues. This is recognized by interview respondents as a difficult balance in practice.

Performance and IJV Autonomy

Evidence relating to performance and autonomy derived from the questionnaire data is shown in Table 5.5, where correlations between the perception of satisfaction of performance and the perception of the extent of autonomy across a number of dimensions of decision making are reported for different groups of respondents.[2] Significant positive correlation was expected between performance and the various areas relating to decision-making autonomy. For

Table 5.5 Correlation between satisfaction and autonomy: questionnaire data (Spearman's rho)

Extent of IJV autonomy	All	Both partners	UK partner	European partner	IJV management
Hiring and firing non-technical personnel	0.233**	0.092	0.154	-0.031	0.379**
Patents & trademarks	-0.016	-0.289*	-0.581**	0.113	0.249
Technology & engineering of products	-0.205*	-0.315*	-0.405*	-0.275	-0.097
Process technology	-0.163	-0.236	-0.124	-0.381*	-0.123
R&D	-0.150	-0.249*	-0.074	-0.391*	-0.081
Financing of JV	0.256**	0.346**	0.368*	0.359*	0.234
Deciding capital expenditures	0.192*	0.285*	0.212	0.427*	0.122
Location of JV	0.061	0.083	0.258	-0.083	0.048
Hiring and firing technical personnel	0.298***	0.170	0.344*	-0.174	0.433***
Pricing	0.054	-0.029	-0.024	0.031	0.117
Distribution	0.068	0.091	-0.119	0.342	0.044
Marketing	0.139	0.037	0.257	-0.186	0.272*
Day-to-day management	0.247**	0.334**	0.405*	0.291	0.173
Hiring and firing senior JV managers	0.334***	0.255*	0.093	0.525**	0.417***
Cost control	0.211*	0.305*	0.257	0.398*	0.082
Manufacturing	0.046	0.057	-0.105	0.238	0.024

Notes:
* $p < 0.1$
** $p < 0.05$
*** $p < 0.01$
(1-tailed tests)

the partners and IJV management together (the 'All' column in Table 5.5), significant positive correlation is found for hiring and firing non-technical personnel, technical personnel and senior JV managers. Clearly, for the respondents as a whole as IJV performance improves there is an expectation of the granting of autonomy to the IJV managers in terms of hiring or dismissing the key personnel of the IJV. Considering the other respondent groupings, however, it is apparent that these correlations only remain consistently significant for the IJV managers. This would appear to indicate that the partner firms are less prone to grant such autonomy than the expectation of the IJV management to receive such decision-making autonomy when performance is perceived to be good. For the 'All' group other significant positive correlations are found for the financing of the JV, deciding capital expenditures, cost control and day-to-day management. These correlations are significant for both partners together but not for the IJV management alone. This indicates willingness for the partners to cede financial and investment decisions to the partners as performance improves but a lack of awareness of such increasing decision-making autonomy on the part of the IJV managers. It is also interesting that the day-to-day management coefficient is low and non-significant for the IJV managers, perhaps indicating that they expect the greatest level of decision-making autonomy over the day to day running of the IJV irrespective of the IJV's performance.

Contrary to expectations there are a number of significant negative correlations reported in Table 5.5. This is the case for: patents and trademarks (for Both partners and the UK partner); technology and engineering of products (for the 'All' group, Both partners and the UK partner); R&D (for Both partners and the European partner). These findings indicate that partners appear to be reluctant to grant autonomy to IJV managers in these areas even when performance is good or improving. These decision-making areas are characterized by technological know-how and are probably core to the competitive position of the partner firms. Partners may be unwilling to cede decision-making autonomy in these areas in order to preserve their key competencies and to prevent acts of opportunism on the part of the partners who would be more able to appropriate this know-how if it was passed into the IJV. This supports the contention of the resource-based theory that while the extension of capabilities is a major reason for the establishment of IJVs, it is still necessary to protect core capabilities from being appropriated by partner firms.

Correlations between perceptions of performance and perceptions of autonomy for the interview respondents are shown in Table 5.6. For this broad measure of autonomy there is only one significant positive correlation. In general, correlations from the interview data provide at best weak support for the view that as performance improves the partners will grant increased autonomy to the IJV managers.

Table 5.6 Correlations between (i) Satisfaction with performance and perception of IJV autonomy
(ii) Age of JV and perception of IJV autonomy: interview data (Spearman's rho)

	(i) Performance	(ii) Age
All	0.15	–0.14
Both partners	0.21*	–0.26*
UK partner	0.10	–0.56***
European partner	0.22	0.06
IJV management	–0.08	0.11

Notes:
* p < 0.10
*** p < 0.01
(1-tailed tests)

Further examination of the interview data, however, clearly revealed a recognition by respondents that IJV management autonomy is not guaranteed, but is contingent on performance. We found that if the IJV is performing well then the IJV management will be afforded a high level of autonomy; however, if the IJV is performing poorly then the autonomy of the IJV management is curtailed through the frequent and direct intervention of the partner firms. Deviation from the budget, for example, tends to cause debate and possible further direction to be provided to the IJV management. If the business is not achieving its budgetary targets it is likely to come under a far greater degree of control from the board of directors. So for many IJVs the budget setting and the target setting are key to the level of autonomy that the IJV management are allowed. The IJV management will achieve more autonomy the closer they are to budget, and the closer they are to delivering the targets that the board of directors set. The UK partner in IJV 15, for example, reported that the business was not performing too well, so there was a high degree of intervention from the board of directors and consequent loss of autonomy on the part of the IJV management.

A key finding from this study is that in general greater IJV autonomy is positively associated with perceived performance of the IJV, but that the nature of this autonomy needs to be carefully specified. It appears that partners allow IJV management autonomy as long as performance is acceptable to them, but only in certain areas of decision making. If performance deteriorates, or is below what is expected, then there tends to be greater parent involvement and intervention in the operational running of the IJV and in the IJV decision-making processes. Overall, evidence from this study supports the view that the level of autonomy granted to IJV managers and IJV performance are correlated, but not always positively so. Moreover, the interview data in particular would tend to support the view that the level of autonomy is a function of performance, rather than IJV performance being a function of the level of autonomy.

IJV Age and Autonomy

It is necessary to recognize the dynamic evolutionary nature of IJV governance systems. Autonomy is not a static concept so the nature of the autonomy extended to the IJV management is likely to change over the evolution of the IJV. Evidence relating to age of the IJV and autonomy derived from the questionnaire data is shown in Table 5.7. It is apparent that relatively few of the correlations are significant, providing little evidence of a relationship between age and autonomy. The significant positive correlations are: financing of the JV (for the 'All' group, Both partners, the UK partner, and the IJV management); deciding capital expenditures (for the 'All' group, Both partners and the UK partner); the location of the JV and the hiring and firing of technical personnel (for the IJV management); and hiring and firing senior managers (for the 'All' group, Both partners, the European partner and the IJV management). As the IJV matures it can be expected that partners will increasingly grant autonomy to IJV management in these areas.

A number of significant negative correlations are also shown in Table 5.7. The significant negative correlations are: technology and engineering of products (for the 'All' group, the European partner, and the IJV management); process technology (for the 'All' group, Both partners, the European partner and the IJV management); R&D (for the 'All' group, Both partners and the European partners); marketing (for Both partners). As the IJV matures it can be expected that partners will be unwilling to grant autonomy to IJV management in these areas. These findings broadly support the correlation findings related to perceived satisfaction of performance and autonomy. Partners appear to be unwilling to cede decision-making autonomy over the duration of the IJV, particularly in areas associated with proprietary technology, for reasons outlined above.

Evidence relating to age of the IJV and autonomy derived from the interview data is shown in Table 5.6. Only two of the correlation coefficients are significant and both are negative (for both partners and the UK partner). This indicates that for the broad conception of autonomy there is no underlying relationship of increased autonomy as the IJV matures.

Overall, the findings of the study are mixed with regard to IJV duration and autonomy. Some aspects of decision making are likely to be granted to the IJV management as the venture matures while other areas, particularly

Table 5.7 *Correlation between age and autonomy: questionnaire data (Spearman's rho)*

Extent of IJV autonomy	All	Both partners	UK partner	European partner	IJV management
Hiring and firing non-technical personnel	0.077	−0.034	−0.081	0.059	0.190
Patents & trademarks	0.008	−0.019	−0.116	0.030	0.073
Technology & engineering of products	−0.229**	−0.181	0.003	−0.385*	−0.260*
Process technology	−0.252**	−0.321*	−0.225	−0.519**	−0.188
R&D	−0.243**	−0.337**	−0.214	−0.435**	−0.118
Financing of JV	0.290**	0.323**	0.416*	0.158	0.239*
Deciding capital expenditures	0.175*	0.371**	0.533**	0.202	−0.099
Location of JV	0.109	−0.097	0.026	−0.291	0.250*
Hiring and firing technical personnel	0.046	−0.145	−0.138	−0.164	0.236*
Pricing	−0.032	−0.099	−0.063	−0.067	0.051
Distribution	−0.126	−0.046	−0.224	0.192	−0.197
Marketing	−0.162	−0.267*	−0.224	−0.303	0.004
Day-to-day management	−0.010	−0.038	−0.034	−0.039	0.043
Hiring and firing senior JV managers	0.291***	0.296*	0.136	0.441**	0.241*
Cost control	−0.017	0.098	−0.049	0.212	−0.270*
Manufacturing	−0.129	−0.132	−0.393*	0.035	−0.136

Notes
* p < 0.1
** p < 0.05
*** p < 0.01
(1-tailed tests)

those associated with proprietary technology, are not. Broadly, the evidence from this study indicates that autonomy cannot be expected to increase simply as the IJV matures.

Dynamics of autonomy in IJVs

Figure 5.1 illustrates the nature of decision-making autonomy in IJVs as reflected in the findings of the study.[3] The horizontal line in Figure 5.1 shows a continuum of decision making from strategic decisions to operational decisions. To the left of the continuum are strategic decisions relating to the IJV. In the main, strategic decisions will be made by the partner firms. Moving to the right along the continuum there will be a range of decisions (which may be termed tactical decisions) that will be taken jointly by the partners and the IJV management. To the right of the continuum are operational decisions relating to the IJV. In the main, operational decisions will be taken by the IJV management. Autonomy of decisions making occurs when the IJV management are solely responsible for decision making. The findings of the study as reflected in Figure 5.1 show that IJV autonomy largely encompasses operational decisions.

The trajectories along the ellipses in Figure 5.1 recognize that changes in decision-making autonomy will take place and movements backwards and forwards along the continuum will occur as the performance of the IJV varies. Improvements in performance will tend to encourage the granting of autonomy. A decline in performance will encourage the withdrawal of autonomy. There is thus a cycling of joint decision making and IJV autonomy as performance changes. The findings from the study indicate that when IJV performance is at least satisfactory to the parents and appears to be improving, there will be a greater willingness of the partners to grant autonomy of decision making to IJV managers, indicated by the rightward facing arrows on the ellipses in Figure 5.1. Decisions that were formerly taken jointly will tend to be taken by the IJV management alone, thus extending the extent of IJV autonomy. As noted, however, not all decision-making areas will be subjected to greater autonomy. Conversely, when IJV performance is less

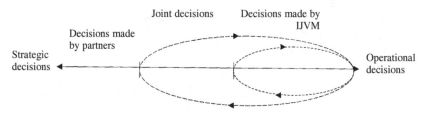

Figure 5.1 Dimensions of IJV decision making

than satisfactory and appears to be deteriorating, there is likely to be a withdrawal of autonomy of decision making by the parent firms. As indicated by the leftward facing arrows along the ellipses in Figure 5.1, parent firms will increasingly become involved in operational decision making, and IJV management will become less involved in joint decision making over tactical decisions.

The cyclical nature of decision-making autonomy as a function of IJV performance has important implications. First, the extent of autonomy in an IJV is dynamic. The dynamic nature of autonomy indicates different levels of autonomy over time for a particular IJV, and different IJVs will each tend to be at different stages in the cycle of decision making. One-period cross-section studies of autonomy are thus unlikely to capture the nature of the changing dimensions of autonomy. Second, different IJVs will have different limits over which the cycles occur. In other words the extent of the cycle over the continuum will be more constrained for some IJVs than for others, depending on the particular circumstances of the IJV, including the proclivities of the partners to engage in decision making. Hence the extent and scope of autonomy will vary between IJVs. The cyclical nature of autonomy also makes it unlikely that researchers will find a simple positive linear relationship between autonomy and the performance of IJVs and autonomy and the age of IJVs.

CONCLUSIONS

This is one of the first studies to report a perceptual measure of autonomy considering the managerial context in all three elements of an IJV, and to relate this to the theoretical underpinnings of IJV governance. The perceptual measure shows that partner firms and IJV managers consider that there is a relatively high degree of autonomy afforded the IJVs in this study, with no significant difference in the mean scores for perception of autonomy between the partners or between each of the partners and the IJV management. However, a more detailed examination of the perceptual measures shows weak correlation and low similarity of rating, both (a) horizontally between the partners and (b) vertically between each of the partners and the IJV management. The findings of the study show that there is a spectrum of autonomy across decision-making areas. IJV managers have a relatively high degree of operational autonomy but relatively low levels of strategic autonomy in decision making. The findings show further that operational decision making by IJV managers takes place within the context of a set of constraints established by the partners and decided through the board of the IJV. The limits within which the IJV managers have autonomy are established within the context of the IJV's business plan.

The relationship between IJV performance and autonomy is not clear cut. As performance improves, an extension of autonomy is likely to be granted in some decision-making areas, in part those associated with the financing and capital investment of the IJV. Performance improvement is not likely, however, to be associated with an extension of decision-making autonomy over the proprietary technology of the IJV. Similar conclusions apply to the relationship between the duration of the IJV and autonomy. In broad terms IJV management cannot presume that there will be a simple extension of autonomy of decision making as the venture matures.

IJV autonomy is a rather fuzzy concept unless the distinction is drawn between strategic autonomy and operational autonomy. Giving an IJV management enough autonomy to genuinely run an independent business, but at the same time making sure that major strategic decisions are taken by equity partners, is a delicate task. The difficulty of this task is compounded by the dynamic evolutionary nature of the partner–management relationship over the life-cycle of the IJV. Further, IJV management autonomy is not guaranteed but is conditional on IJV performance satisfying partner goals.

The interpretation of these findings in terms of the theory of IJVs is instructive. Transaction cost theory posits that key markets will be internalized, particularly where strong indivisibilities are present. Our findings that internal markets in management skills, technology and capital are largely under system-wide control exactly confirm this. There is also confirmation of the resource-based view of the firm that key capabilities are protected (by devices such as the business plan established by parent firms) and extended (by mutual activities across the parents and the IJV) by the exercise of variable levels of autonomy.

There are several possible future research opportunities to extend our findings. First, the identification of the stage of the life-cycle of the IJV at which increasing levels of autonomy are granted by the parents. Second, clearer identification of the variables that condition the granting or withdrawal of IJV autonomy by parents. Third, the nature of the relationship between autonomy and the dimensions of management control in IJVs. Fourth, the relationship between autonomy and effectiveness of the IJV, an issue which has begun to be addressed by Newburry and Zeira (1999). Fifth, comparisons of subjective (perceptual) measures and objective measures of autonomy would be instructive. Patterns of behaviour in the IJV, for example, morale and motivation, may be more a function of the perceptions of the autonomy condition rather than the objective condition; this seems worthy of future research. Sixth, comparison studies of autonomy in subsidiary companies and IJVs would be a welcome addition to the literature.

NOTES

1. Cohen's kappa measures the agreement between the evaluations of two raters when both are rating the same object. The difference between the observed cases in which the raters agree and the proportion expected by chance is divided by the maximum difference possible between the observed and expected proportions, given the marginal totals. A value of 1 indicates perfect agreement. A value of 0 indicates that agreement is no better than chance.
2. Care must be taken when comparing means for the self-administered questionnaire data, which is not as uniform as the personal interview data. With the latter there are data from matching interviews across each element of the IJV, that is 20 UK parents, matched with 20 European parents, matched with 20 IJV managers. With the self-administered questionnaires, although the data is drawn from the same 20 IJVs as the interview data, there are not 20 matching sets of responses. This is because for several IJVs one or more elements of the IJV have not responded. Hence when comparing categories of respondent for the questionnaire data the discussion should be couched in terms of UK firms, European firms and IJV management, because of the inexact matching of the data set.
3. A similar diagrammatic representation of centralization and autonomy in the context of multinational control of subsidiaries is found in Brooke (1984).

6. Learning to manage international joint ventures

INTRODUCTION

Increasingly knowledge is considered a vital ingredient in competitive success. As the integration of global markets intensifies competition, companies must devote more attention to ways of acquiring the knowledge resources that they need. With constantly shifting technologies, products and processes, competitive advantage may rest on the ability of a company to learn and diffuse accumulated knowledge throughout the organization (Garratt, 1987; Choi and Lee, 1997; Nonaka, 1991, 1994; Lynn and Rao, 1995; Spender, 1994). In this context the possibility of using co-operative strategies, especially international joint ventures, as instruments for gaining knowledge is being more readily acknowledged (Lyles, 1987; Inkpen, 1995).

The importance of learning within organizations has long been considered an important determinant of technological progress and the raising of efficiency and productivity. Child and Faulkner (1998: 287) maintain that the ability to learn is probably the most important intangible asset that a company can possess. In the mainstream economics literature the phenomenon of 'learning by doing' (that is, increases in output without additional investment) was formally elucidated in the 1960s by Arrow (1962), Levhari (1966), and Sheshinski (1967). More recently, the learning process in organizations has been examined within the realms of organizational theory and strategic management (Huber, 1991). This literature focuses not only on the outcomes of learning but also on the processes of learning, that is, on the methods used by firms to utilize knowledge and develop organizational efficiency. Principally, this is done through more effective use of skills in order to achieve the outcome of raising productivity or retaining or enhancing competitiveness (Dodgson, 1993).

A number of types of learning have been postulated, including higher and lower level of learning (Fiol and Lyles, 1985), generative and adaptive learning (Senge, 1990), strategic and tactical learning (Dodgson, 1991) and single-loop, double-loop learning (Argyris and Schon, 1978) that involves detection and correction of errors (for an elaboration of these concepts, see Dodgson, 1993).

Although IJVs provide a vehicle for learning, and while alliances create value (Chan et al. 1997; McConnell and Nantel, 1985), Anand and Khanna (2000) note that there is widespread recognition of the difficulty inherent in this process of value creation. This is evidenced by the relatively high failure rate for IJVs and cross sectional studies which 'point to a consistently low level of satisfaction with IJV performance, especially in developed countries' (Beamish and Delios, 1997b: 108). The failure rate is likely to differ, however, between the type of firm generally thought to be able to manage alliances well, and the type thought to be poor at managing alliances (*Alliance Analyst*, 15 August, 1997). Clearly, the lessons of managing IJVs are important to practising managers, as successful management is likely to improve the performance of IJVs. It is therefore important to identify what IJV experienced partners and managers suggest are the key lessons of managing IJVs, which is the basic goal of this chapter.

Recent research on IJVs shows that the learning process, broadly defined, is an important determinant for the formation of strategic alliances (Hamel, 1991; Kogut and Zander, 1992; Inkpen and Beamish, 1997). There is a basic distinction to be made between learning from the partners, and learning about how to form and manage IJVs. Inkpen (2000: 1020) elaborates on this distinction and notes two forms of learning from partners: first, firms may seek access to partners' knowledge and skills but not with the aim of integrating the knowledge in their own operations. This type of partner learning is necessary when firms seek to combine their skills successfully in an alliance. Second, a firm may acquire knowledge from its partner that can be used to enhance strategy and operations in areas unrelated to the alliance activities. Learning from partners occurs largely through the transfer of tacit knowledge, in order to enhance competencies, and the competitive position of the parent firm – a view given prominence by the resource-based theory (Hamel, 1991; Glaister, 1996). Learning about how to form and manage IJVs involves the acquisition of knowledge useful in the design and management of other alliances which may be applied to the management of future alliances (Inkpen, 2000). The focus of this chapter is on this type of learning. There is paucity of data and analysis with respect to the *types* of lessons learned after a period of an IJV's existence – or after its termination. This chapter attempts to fill this lacuna by reporting empirical data from the survey of UK–European IJVs in order to elucidate the management lessons that are deemed important. This framework is broader in scope than research such as that by Lyles and Salk (1997) and Child and Markoczy (1993) which focused mainly on the scope of IJV companies learning from parents.

The chapter is organized as follows: a literature review is set out in the next section. Section three elaborates upon the major management lessons discerned from the interview and questionnaire data; section four provides a discussion and development of future research propositions. Conclusions are in the final section.

LITERATURE REVIEW

Learning to Manage IJVs

Two different objects of learning are identified in the prior literature (see for example Tsang, 1999; Buchel et al., 1998: 25), they are 'learning the other partner's skills', that is, co-operating to learn, and 'learning from strategic alliance experience', that is, learning to co-operate. Co-operating to learn means using JVs as a medium for organizational and inter-organizational learning. This concept of learning dominates the literature on learning in the context of alliances and defines learning narrowly. The object of learning from a partner is usually a certain technology, or other types of know-how, of the other partner. This learning motive is strong in alliances where the firms desire to discover new opportunities or to acquire new capabilities (Koza and Lewin, 1998; Khanna et al., 1998; Nti and Kumar, 2000; Dussauge et al., 2000; Lane et al., 2001). Hence increasing numbers of IJVs are being created because both partner companies hope to acquire new competencies by combining their resources in a process of inter-organizational learning (Buchel et al., 1998: 245). Doz and Hamel (1998: 52), for instance, emphasize that alliances are often the best way for companies to acquire and deploy new skills quickly. Knowledge can be used jointly and combined across different functions. This can only succeed, however, when both partners see the co-operation as offering a win–win situation. If one partner hopes to learn at the expense of the other, the co-operative venture cannot be learning-oriented in the full sense of the term.

Learning to co-operate means striving towards a growing understanding of the processes and specific problems involved in IJVs, and continuing to develop one's own practices and competencies in IJV management. Buchel et al. (1998: 25) argue that the important thing is to learn how a JV works, the problems that arise and the possibilities that exist for organising, guiding and developing in different areas. This concept of learning emphasizes that managing an alliance with a partner is itself a great learning experience, especially if the partner is a foreign company. As noted in the introduction, this type of learning is the focus of this study.

Child and Faulkner (1998: 289) note that collaboration can enhance organizational learning through the accumulation of experience and knowledge about how to manage alliances. Moreover, this benefit is becoming increasingly significant at a time when more business activity is being organized through strategic alliances. Clearly, collaborative know-how might be used later in the design and management of other collaborations.

Buchel et al. (1998: 244) point out that managing a JV is a demanding leadership task in which the main day-to-day challenge is to resolve the difficult conflicts which repeatedly threaten the existence of the co-operation. The scope of management thus extends far beyond organizing the operational side of the company and assigning tasks to different people. It is a complex process which takes place at different levels in the JV system and which cannot be reduced to a matter of formal rules, contracts, business procedures or sequential planning. Tsang (1999) notes that Parkhe (1991) identifies five dimensions of inter-firm diversity in global strategic alliances, namely societal culture, national context, corporate culture and strategic direction, as well as management practices and organization. Parkhe argues that the diversity has negative effects on the longevity and effective functioning of an alliance, but organizational learning and adaptation can mitigate the impact of diversity, that is the partnership can be strengthened when the partners learn to analyse their diversity and to devise solutions to accommodate the differences. This implies that in modern business, the know-how of managing international strategic alliances has become an essential resource of most firms, and learning is the means to acquire and accumulate the resource.

'Learning from strategic alliance experience', requires an experiential learning process, as distinct from 'learning the other partner's skills', that entails a vicarious learning process (Tsang, 1999). Vicarious learning is more focused and requires the staff concerned to have the necessary background knowledge. As Tsang (1999) notes, this does not imply that the partners must have an intent to learn. Individual and organizational learning may be an unconscious activity. However, an intent to learn may spur an organization on to higher levels of learning. Hamel (1991) argues that a partner's intent to internalize the other's skills is a key determinant of learning; the stronger the intent, the higher the chance that the partner will win the learning race. Tsang (1999) argues that although learning intent is not a necessary condition for learning, especially experiential learning, to take place, the presence of learning intent in a company is the first step towards effective learning.

In asking how exactly firms might learn to manage alliances, or acquire an alliance capability, Anand and Khanna (2000: 298) break the question down into two parts: first, how individuals within the firm learn and, second, how firms harness the learning experiences of such individuals. They note that repeated exposure to different partners exposes individuals within the firm to a broad repertoire of experiences. This facilitates the interpretation of new unforeseen contingencies in their subsequent alliance interactions. The ability to learn from a particular alliance is thus likely to be enhanced by the set of problems encountered in prior learning experiences. The knowledge built up in this way will in part be about learning skills themselves (Ellis, 1965), or more broadly about 'learning to learn' (Estes, 1970).

Anand and Khanna (2000) point out that 'learning to learn' at the firm level is a complex function of the individual level phenomenon. Cohen and Levinthal (1990) relate each firm's learning ability to its 'absorptive capacity'. Absorptive capacity refers to the ability of a firm to understand and exploit knowledge in various knowledge domains, and may be used as a measure of a firm's ability to appropriate knowledge from an alliance relationship. The greater the absorptive capacity of a firm, the more knowledge it can appropriate from a given volume of alliance-generated knowledge. Differential learning may also occur because the division of work may expose the firms to different amounts of alliance-generated knowledge. Nti and Kumar (2000) note that absorptive capacity is a characteristic of a firm that is required and shaped over many years and is not likely to change during the course of a particular alliance relationship. Absorptive capacity is a product of the firm's organizational culture, which shapes its motivational orientation, technological competence, and the quality of the human assets it attracts and develops. The process of accumulating absorptive capacity depends on a firm's prior preparation and requires continuous and sustained investment (Cohen and Levinthal, 1990; 1994).

Cohen and Levinthal (1990) also point to the possibility of path dependence in learning to learn. Firms that have learnt to learn will continue to do so at an increasing rate, while those that have never invested in learning from different experiences will not find it optimal to do so. In the context of alliances, this would imply that heterogeneity in alliance capabilities will persist over time (Anand and Khanna, 2000). It seems that what is learned in a focal IJV is likely to vary with JV prior experience. This JV prior experience may be a function of the number of JVs the partner has had and the number of JVs the respondent has been involved in – these might be two different things. It is unlikely to be the case that learning in either respect is a monotonic increasing function. It might be better to think of 'learning to learn about managing IJVs' as an inverted U-shaped function, that is learning increases in the early phases of IJV partnering, peaks, and then declines with further experience as learning opportunities diminish with further experience. In asking respondents to indicate what they have learned from a focal JV, the responses are likely to vary with prior experience.

Despite support for the idea that learning to manage alliances might be important, there has been little empirical analyses on this issue. Lyles (1988) found unanimous agreement among managers and staff of two US and two European firms, with a successful history of operating IJVs, that there was a valuable transference of experience from previous ventures. This transference took place largely through the sharing of experiences, the continuity of top-management oversight, and the development of management systems. The companies were also able to use their experience as a credential that made it easier for them to form new IJVs. In related empirical work Gulati (1995a) shows that pairs of firms appear to learn over time to manage their collaborative activities more efficiently. Anand and Khanna (2000)'s empirical analysis identifies two important factors that drive value creation in alliances: a firm's experience in managing alliances, and the existence of persistent firm-specific differences in the ability (or inability) to create value through alliances. They find strong evidence that firms learn to create more value as they accumulate experience in joint venturing. They also find strong and persistent differences across firms in their ability to create value and interpret these differences as reflecting differences in 'alliance capabilities'.

While the prior literature demonstrates the importance of learning to cooperate, there has been little elaboration of the key areas in which such learning improves the management of IJVs. Consequently, the basic research question to be explored in this study is the nature of the lessons learned in *the management of IJVs*.

LESSONS LEARNED

Coding analysis of the interview data revealed a large number of categories of lessons learned that were highlighted as being important – these are listed in Table 6.1. A large number of categories elicited responses from only one or two of the interviewees. However, several categories elicited eight or more responses; these involved lessons associated with culture, the strategic vision of the IJV, issues of operational decision making, the anticipation of implementation issues, the management of a 50–50 equity relationship, and matters of trust. It is apparent from the crude listing of the categories of response that the UK managers were able to identify more lessons learned in the management of IJVs (47 citations) than were European partners or IJV managers (37 citations each).

Of the 63 completed self-administered questionnaires received, 41 answered the question on lessons learned. The total number of citations was 68 spread over 27 broadly distinct categories, as shown in Table 6.2. Again most categories elicited responses from only one or two of the respondents with five categories cited five or more times. The most frequently cited categories from the questionnaire data largely conformed to those of the interview data in that they were concerned with lessons associated with shared strategic vision, matters of culture – either national or corporate culture, communications and operational decisions. The identification of lessons of managing IJVs were more readily expressed in the questionnaire responses by the IJV

Table 6.1 Categories of lessons learned from interview data

Lesson	Total	UK partner	European partner	IJV management
Culture	17	8	3	6
Shared strategic vision	15	7	3	5
Issues of operational decision making	9	2	3	4
Anticipating implementation issues	8	5	2	1
50–50 relationship	8	3	3	2
Trust	8	3	3	2
Personal relationship	5	3	1	1
Exit strategy	4	3	1	0
Clearly identifying complementarities	4	2	1	1
Commitment	3	1	2	0
Past relationships	3	0	1	2
Calculating financial return	2	1	1	0
Autonomy for JV	2	0	1	1
Avoid JVs	2	1	1	0
Issue of JV autonomy	2	0	1	1
New competencies	2	0	1	1
Surface disagreements	2	0	1	1
Learning from partner's practices	2	0	1	1
Inculcating JV perspective	2	1	0	1
JV agreement	2	1	1	0
Due diligence analysis	1	1	0	0
Process of ongoing learning	1	0	1	0
How to structure the JV	1	0	0	1
Avoiding faults	1	0	1	0
Understanding consequences of negotiation	1	0	0	1
Nothing	1	0	1	0
Financial strength	1	0	1	0
Balanced partnership	1	1	0	0
Frustration of seconded managers	1	0	0	1
Integrity	1	0	0	1
Anticipate change	1	1	0	0
Clear definition of what is to be shared	1	0	1	0
Appropriate incentives	1	0	0	1
Resource availability	1	1	0	0
Advice from consultants	1	0	1	0
Neutral IJV management	1	0	0	1
Even-handed decision making	1	1	0	0
Partner selection procedure	1	1	0	0
Understanding the partner	1	0	0	1
Total	**121**	**47**	**37**	**37**

managers (39 citations) followed by the UK partners (20 citations) and then the European partners (nine citations).

While the data coding revealed a large number of distinct responses to the question of lessons learned, further examination of the interview transcripts and written questionnaire responses revealed that these categories broadly grouped into three distinct areas of learning with respect to the management of IJVs: the management of the IJV formation process, management of the boundary relationship between partners, and the management of the operations of the IJV. These three areas include not only findings which confirm the

Table 6.2 Categories of lessons learned from questionnaire data

Lesson	Total	UK partner	European partner	IJV management
Shared strategic vision	9	4	0	5
Effort to manage different corporate culture	7	1	1	5
Importance of good communication	6	0	1	5
Agreeing key operational decisions at formation	5	2	0	3
Don't underestimate national cultural differences	5	1	1	3
Define clear lines of responsibility between partners and JV managers	4	1	1	2
Need more effort to win people over	3	0	0	3
Careful selection of senior managers of JV	3	1	2	0
Let JV managers manage within agreed plans	3	1	0	2
50–50 causes severe problems	2	0	0	2
Regular review of performance needed	2	1	0	1
Nothing specifically new	2	1	0	1
Importance of openness and speed	2	1	0	1
Early financial commitment necessary	2	0	0	2
Takes long time to establish coherent management	1	1	0	0
Much easier when JV profitable	1	1	0	0
Assumption of successful outcome before contract finalized brings operating benefits	1	1	0	0
Using strengths of parent company	1	0	1	0
Need for structured plan to keep control	1	0	1	0
Partner selection by competencies/requirements	1	0	0	1
No previous experience – all new knowledge	1	0	0	1
Learn to compromise and respect each other	1	0	0	1
Initial contingency planning facilitates later agreements	1	0	0	1
Equal power sharing	1	0	1	0
Have controlling influence in day-to-day management	1	1	0	0
Simplicity in JV agreement	1	1	0	0
Preparedness to change personnel quickly	1	1	0	0
Total	**68**	**20**	**9**	**39**

expectations confronted in the prior literature (IJV formation process and IJV operational management) but also one unexpected group of findings – the importance of boundary relationships between the elements of the IJV. These three areas of management and the key lesson categories are illustrated in Figure 6.1. As shown in Figure 6.1 several of the categories of lessons impacted on more than one of the broad groupings. The following subsections elucidate the lessons regarding these three areas of IJV management.

IJV Formation Process

By far the clearest lesson regarding management of the IJV management process is the need for the partners to establish a clear *shared strategic vision* for the IJV. At the formation stage both parents must broadly agree their respective objectives in regard to the IJV over its long-term duration. This means recognizing that parents initially may have different goals with respect to the venture, but these must be reconciled and in so doing, agreement reached in regard to common goals and strategy for the IJV. There was a general view from respondents that this leads to a smoother and more efficient running of the IJV. It follows, therefore, that where there is significant divergence in goals and strategy, there is a fear that this will have a detrimental effect on a JV's performance. The UK manager of JV 1 provided a typical view in regard to common goals/strategy:

> I think the first thing is to make sure that both parties understand very clearly why they are getting together so they have a common aim, and in that sense sharing the strategic vision, i.e. not what's right today, but what is going to be right in the long term, what both companies strive to achieve.

It is clear that one partner should be very careful when selecting the other partner company. Respondents identified a number of lessons in connection with *partner selection*, but of particular importance is the identification of skill and resource complementarities between the partners, ensuring that resources are available and establishing clearly what is to be shared between the partners. During the IJV formation stage partners should undertake a formal analysis of the financial viability of the proposed venture, and even undertake a due diligence analysis to ensure that what the partner promises is actually delivered. During the negotiation stage one respondent recommended that advice be obtained from third parties, particularly consultants, who can provide an objective view on the proposed venture and help to avoid problems from the beginning.

The atmosphere in which the negotiations are conducted is also relevant, particularly the need for partners to have a high degree of integrity. An IJV is a partnership, and the partners must be open and seek to avoid hiding anything

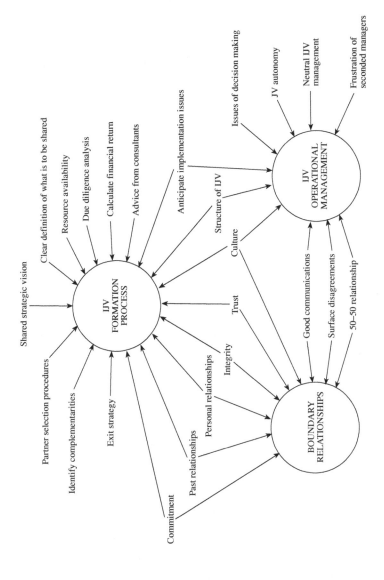

Figure 6.1 Lessons in the management of IJVs

that is to their advantage and not to the benefit of the IJV. The atmosphere of negotiations is also affected by the degree of trust and commitment between the partners as well as the nature of prior and current business and personal relationships between the partner companies. These issues will be examined when considering boundary relationships.

During the formation process it is necessary to determine the structure of the IJV and to anticipate implementation issues. These factors have an obvious bearing on the operational management of the IJV and will be discussed in more detail when examining the lessons of IJV operational management.

A minority of respondents emphasized the need to anticipate an *exit strategy* from the IJV. This should be undertaken not in the sense of planning for failure but ensuring that there is a contingency arrangement should the partner seek an exit position. The options of acquiring the partner's share, selling to the partner, selling to a third party or liquidating the business should be carefully considered. It was suggested by one respondent with a great deal of IJV experience that there must be an exit strategy included in the contractual arrangement, because inevitably there will come a point in time when the strategies of the partners change and consequently their attitude to the IJV. This may come about, for example, from the change of ownership of the partner, through merger or acquisition. At this point the partner should ensure they are not locked into a relationship they would rather dissolve. In the euphoria of establishing the IJV when each partner is displaying a strong commitment, often a 'divorce settlement' is not negotiated or not well considered because of the negative overtones. For some respondents, however, negotiating an exit strategy is a very important part of the formation process. The basic lesson is to have a clear way out of the relationship before it formally begins.

Boundary Relationships

All of the boundary relationship issues are also associated with either the IJV formation process or IJV operational management. This is hardly surprising as the boundary relationship is key to both activities. Those lessons that bear on both the IJV formation process and boundary relationships will be discussed first. One lesson is that the partners should fully commit themselves to the IJV. Evidence from respondents indicates that it is probably better not to enter into an IJV than to do so in a half-hearted manner or with second thoughts. Commitment requires the full involvement and confidence in the IJV of the top management of each partner. Concomitant with this should be the participation of senior managers in the formation stage of the IJV. Supporting prior research which identifies a greater propensity of firms that have allied in the past to do so again (Gulati, 1995a), management of the IJV formation process and boundary relationships can be improved if senior managers from the partners have had a previous business relationship. Respondents argued that this past relationship is beneficial in part because it provides an informal mechanism for keeping control of contentious issues, in that the relevant parties should be able to communicate with each other outside formal meetings. The past relationship also provides cohesion between the partners and lays the foundation for trust. Partly engendered by past relationships, but also growing out of the focal IJV, several respondents stressed the importance of managers forging personal relationships beyond the business relationship. The development of personal relationships in turn nourishes trust and understanding. Good personal relationships at the senior level of the partners are seen as important in fostering beneficial IJV performance. The view was expressed that when the partners' senior managers most directly responsible for the JV have a good personal relationship there is a greater probability that the venture will work well. A good relationship between senior management of parents is considered beneficial; whereas if this relationship is poor, problems invariably arise. This was explained by the European manager of JV 20:

> And with the two partners, if there is a knowledge at the management level of the two partners, due to past experiences or working relationships, and trust between [them], it is clearly a help. Because ... the top management has clearly a positive and strong effect on the workforce, the managers of the joint venture, they feel supported, they feel confident.

A concern for JV partners that stems from difficulties of joint ownership is to minimize conflict and disputes. The importance of a good personal relationship appears to be key in addressing dispute resolution. Though formal mechanisms are almost always established to resolve potential disputes and disagreements – usually through board level discussion – there is a reluctance to go down this path. A desired alternative is for senior managers to have good working relationships with their counterparts so that tension is reduced from the outset.

In situations where personal relationships are not maintained, then problems are likely to arise which will ultimately affect the performance of the IJV. Enduring personal relationships may be most difficult to maintain when the IJV involves two partners that are considerably different in size. This was noted by one of the interview respondents from a relatively small partner company. The larger partner rotated its personnel so that the smaller partner rarely saw the same set of managers. This may be particularly problematic when the managers involved in drawing up the original IJV agreement are not the same people the partner has to deal with subsequently, and who do not have the same tacit understanding of the meaning of the agreement. This leads to the recommendation that those who negotiated the IJV agreement should at least spend some time 'bedding in' the working arrangements of the IJV in order to develop a better interface between the partners. Ultimately, past and current relationships should lead to a better understanding of the partner. In any event each partner must make the effort to understand the other. This entails an understanding of the partner's business, objectives, culture, and so on. There may be a reluctance to surface some sensitive issues so partner understanding requires patience to tease the crucial issue to the surface.

The importance of *trust* was emphasized by several respondents. There are many definitions of trust and we did not impose a particular meaning of the concept on respondents. As noted in the Research methods section in Appendix 1, in the conduct of the interviews account was taken of the 'native category' issue. The concept of trust discussed by the respondents was therefore valid in the context of their own experience. It was clear, however, that there was a common sense of understanding of the concept of trust by respondents that pervades many definitions in that 'it refers to the willingness of one party to relate with another in the belief that the other's actions will be beneficial rather than detrimental to the first party, even though this cannot be guaranteed' (Child and Faulkner, 1998: 45).

The key lesson learned with respect to trust stems from the familiar worry that the partner is acting, or will act, opportunistically. If this happens it is a sure sign that the JV's future is in jeopardy, hence, trust between parents helps the IJV. Issues of trust and partner integrity are acknowledged to be important determinants in the IJV decision-making process so concerns in regard to these ought to be widely expected. Although trust may naturally evolve through regular interaction between the partners, respondents recommended that attempts should also be made deliberately to inculcate trust, because it cannot be assumed that it will occur spontaneously. Deliberate efforts to build up a degree of trust may come, for example, through team building in the joint management of the IJV.

Many of the facets of the boundary relationship are clearly mutually reinforcing. There is likely to be a positive cycle of relationship reinforcement beginning with a history of prior co-operation that builds into strong supportive personal relationships between senior managers. This in turn will lead to partner understanding and commitment for the IJV. In turn the partner interactions are likely to be characterized by integrity and trust, which serves to reinforce the positive nature of the personal relationship, commitment and understanding. The generation of this positive process of interaction will in general improve the boundary relationship and enhance the success of the IJV. Conversely, where there is obstructed development of personal relationships, this will negatively impact on partner understanding and commitment, which is likely to foster low levels of integrity and trust, to the ultimate detriment of IJV performance.

As shown in Figure 6.1, culture is relevant to the IJV formation process, boundary relationships and IJV operational management. The aspect of culture that particularly affects the IJV formation process and boundary relationship is that of national culture. The importance of national culture is recognition that cultural issues such as language and national work practices (as distinct from firm-specific operating culture discussed below) in general are nominally extraneous factors keenly impinging upon inter-firm collaborative activity. It is a factor that cannot be controlled – hence it should be carefully evaluated before proceeding with the IJV. Each partner should identify what kinds of differences they can and cannot tolerate. This suggests that a 'soft issue' such as national cultural differences can act as a decisive influence in the formation of a JV so that on occasion, even where there is potentially a 'good fit' between two partners, the country of a parent company or the intended country for a JV's operations can prevent the partnership from proceeding for reasons of cultural mismatch. The key lesson here is the belief that forming IJVs with firms from countries with sharp national differences in culture presents additional difficulties in the smooth running of a JV and hence should be entered into warily. To proceed with the venture entails ensuring that the cultural differences are both understood and managed. Respondents stressed the importance of showing respect for and sensitivity to the national culture of the partner. Moreover, managers have to learn to deal with these differences. This requirement has implications for the kind of people that are placed in a boundary relationship or an IJV management role, and in turn for staff training and preparation for undertaking such roles. Such people should be tolerant of the nationality of the foreign partner, or at least should be willing to understand the culture of the partner. Education and training practices of the partners should involve thinking beyond the national culture and embrace multicultural perspectives. Unless partners can develop an understanding and tolerance of different cultures the venture is likely to head for trouble.

Several of the categories of lessons were pertinent to both boundary relationships and IJV operational management. The importance of *good communication* stems from consistently and clearly informing the partner about relevant information pertaining to the JV. It therefore follows that lack of effective communication may cause misunderstandings between the partners or between partner and JV management which may, in some circumstances, lead to a loss of trust and ultimately to weakening in JV performance. Related to this is the imperative to air disagreements. Problems should not be hidden or avoided but should be brought to the surface very early. This is in order to prevent ill feelings or disagreements from lingering. It is necessary for partners to be frank with each other and to state the unpalatable in order to clear the issues out of the way.

We found that a contentious issue is the division of equity shares between the partners and in particular the problems that may arise from a 50–50 split. Such IJVs have often been characterized as particularly sensitive to cultural differences and parental tensions (Killing, 1983; Salk, 1992). With respect to lessons learned concerning 'difficulties of 50:50 JVs', respondents noted the potential for constant arguments between the parents leading to the slowing down of the decision-making process with, ultimately, a damaging impact on the JV. Generally, those who cited this lesson thought that one partner needs to have majority shareholding.

Partners need to assess carefully the pros and cons of an equal equity partnership. Negative views from respondents on a 50–50 split were that it imposes a burden on the IJV and a disincentive to the teams of people working in the venture. Decision-making took much longer and bickering between the shareholders adversely affected the performance of the IJV management. Compromises thus have to be arrived at in order to make the relationship work, which may lead to sub-optimal decisions. Alternatively, compromises cannot be arrived at, which frustrates the IJV management. A partner can stop the operation of the JV if one of them does not agree with the proposed solution.

Many respondents favoured an unequal equity split in order that the dominant partner could, in effect, take control of the IJV. An unequal equity share avoids conflicts that cannot be solved easily. In general the view was that the IJV would perform better if there were a dominant partner. These sentiments echo the conclusions reached by Killing (1983). We also found, however, that some respondents had a favourable view of 50–50 relationships, reporting positive experiences. Dividing the equity 50–50 and putting control procedures on an equal footing was considered by some respondents to be a better arrangement than an unequal equity distribution where difficulties may be experienced by minority partners in influencing the majority partner. A 50–50 division of equity in creating a situation of equality between the partners may also tend to foster the development of trust. Further, it may be conjectured that the equity share will play a role in the IJV formation process. The division of the equity shareholding is clearly a contentious issue, of which potential partners to an IJV must be aware.

IJV Operational Management

A lesson cited frequently by respondents was the need to *anticipate implementation issues* and relatedly, to identify responsibilities in the management of the IJV. From the outset, partners must clarify issues of management control, management structures, and management roles and how they will rotate. This is in order to ensure there is no ambiguity, and that managers know what their future roles are to be.

Data indicated that through the formation process and into the ongoing operation of the venture it is necessary to identify which party will be responsible for delivering which end result and to know how the implementation plan will evolve as the IJV matures. It is necessary to define clearly who is responsible for each activity and to avoid having more than one person responsible for the same thing, with associated lines of demarcation in terms of reporting. This prevents one party playing off the other. It also prevents a more senior manager playing politics between the two.

It should be made clear exactly who is responsible for which set of decisions. This means identifying the levels of decision making – which decisions go to the parents, the IJV board, and which are handled by IJV managers. This requires effective communication between all the parties. It also requires effort to be put into team training in order to encourage practical working together from both sides. Partners should recognize that it will take some time to bring together different systems, ways of thinking and approaches to problem solving, and to resolve the personality clashes that are inevitably going to occur. A further lesson is to develop a succession plan for the senior management who will operate at a strategic level.

Allied to anticipating implementation issues are the lessons from the actual *issues of operational decision making*. A fundamental point is that a partner cannot take the decisions that it could with its own business, because it simply does not have the freedom to act. Consequently, operational issues may be a problem because the decision-maker has to take into account the opinions of a number of other parties, and these may differ. This is why an effective decision-making process is required. One respondent argued that this is facilitated best through a flat management structure. At some point disagreement will inevitably occur and as all parties have to overcome these disagreements, the flatter the hierarchical structure, the better.

The fact that there will be occasions when it is not possible for the IJV management team to move quickly on decisions that require approval of both of the shareholders, is likely to lead to frustration within the management team. As a consequence there is a requirement for mature and experienced managers in an IJV, probably more so than if the venture were a wholly owned subsidiary. This is because the IJV managers have to learn to deal with these frustrations, to manage round them and to achieve the consensus that is required. Related to this, respondents noted that because of the greater difficulty of running an IJV, more people are probably required to staff it than would be the case with a wholly owned subsidiary.

The management of the IJV leads to a number of related issues noted by respondents. A somewhat controversial area is the extent of autonomy that should be granted to the IJV managers. There are arguments for and against autonomy in IJVs (for a survey see Newburry and Zeira, 1999: 266–7). One respondent acknowledged that for him this was an unresolved issue. From other respondents there was a view that parent companies must give guidelines but not be involved in the day-to-day business and tactics of the IJV. While there is no clear prescription from the respondents in our sample with regard to the extent of IJV autonomy, it is clear that this is an issue parents must confront. One point stressed was the need for neutrality on the part of IJV managers in that they must not favour one partner, even if they are seconded to the IJV from one of the parent companies. It is necessary for the IJV management to consider themselves as working for the JV and not to operate as part of the parent company. In this respect it is necessary that IJV managers do not bring the baggage of the previous relationship with them and do not make assumptions that things will be done in a particular way. Respondents emphasized that it is important that decisions are made in the best interests of the IJV, and that the decision-making approach has to be even-handed so that one partner is not favoured over another. It is recommended that if necessary the managers must be trained to that view.

Seconded managers may also have personal concerns. Such managers could feel frustrated if they believe they are being kept in the IJV management team because they are performing well, but at the same time this constrains them from being considered for career advancement elsewhere in the parent company. Ultimately, this could cause deterioration in morale and effort on the part of the affected managers. In this regard career progression should be identified for IJV managers with ease of re-assimilation into the parent company provided as an option.

Lessons concerning the *operating culture* were emphasized by many respondents. A well identified lesson involves the problems of bringing together two culturally different organizations in a JV and trying to develop to a common culture. This can be a frustrating process but it may also impose real costs on the IJV if the resulting problems and conflicts cause personnel to leave the business. This element of IJV management should not be underestimated. Partners should be aware that that there is a need to ensure that the culture of the IJV is developed and evolves. Moreover, the culture of the partners should be well understood by the operating managers within the JV.

Lessons learned concerning operating culture relate to the full gamut of the *modus operandi* of a JV. This subsumes how a JV is managed. One lesson is to identify carefully the allocation of parental responsibility for the various functional areas of the JV, that is, production, quality, finance, marketing, R & D, pricing, investment, reporting mechanism and so on, as well as agreeing to the limits of the JV's autonomy as noted above. The interviewee responses show that there is great concern to ensure that the operational aspects of a JV are ones that parents are comfortable with. If this is not so, then there is a real danger of tensions arising between the partners and problems within the JV itself, with the risk of the IJV failing. In the sample this was most apparent between those IJVs involving private parent companies (all British) and some state-owned European companies. This is where the clash of operating culture was greatest – with very different histories, traditions, working practices and goals.

Another aspect of culture is the lingua franca to be used. In all of the IJVs in the sample, the English language was used between the partners. However, some European respondents noted that even though English was the agreed medium, they were at times irritated by the UK partner's failure to appreciate that they were communicating with those for whom English was not the mother tongue. This, in turn, led to operational tensions.

DISCUSSION AND RESEARCH PROPOSITIONS

The formation of an IJV assumes superiority of organizational mode over alternatives such as market contracting or the creation of a wholly owned subsidiary (Buckley and Casson, 1988). However, exit from the JV relationship is likely to be more difficult than vis-à-vis market exchange whilst control of the JV is likely to be more problematic than in comparison with a subsidiary. The formation of a JV implies, indeed requires, mutual forbearance on the part of parent companies that needs to be balanced with moral hazard implicit in a JV contract of which there are two main types: actions taken by one parent to the detriment of the other, and actions taken by the JV management that are detrimental to one or both parents. Both stem from insufficient information and consequently, the JV contract is inherently incomplete. The prevention, therefore, of such opportunistic behaviour (Williamson, 1975) necessitates effective monitoring and control procedures over the JV (Buckley and Casson, 1988; Beamish and Banks, 1987). Nonetheless, the co-operative nature of a JV contract necessitates a degree of trust in the partner (Faulkner, 1995; Madhok, 1995) so that trust becomes a crucial variable in the JV phenomenon. Parents must trust or learn to trust both their partner as well as those managing the JV. This requires refraining from opportunistic behaviour and trusting that both the partner and JV management shall do likewise (Nooteboom, 1999). There is, however, always the risk of a breach of trust and parent companies are cognizant of this. To ensure that potential losses emanating from this possibility are minimized may ultimately require the termination of the JV contract so that an exit strategy needs to be planned either at the initial agreement stage or during the course of the JV's existence. Thus, the intermediary, hence potentially more unstable, nature of the JV is likely to give rise to distinct problems and considerations so that the learning experience will be novel and lessons learned will reflect this.

To the extent that learning allows the partner companies to better manage the IJV it is expected that performance outcomes will be a function of this learning. IJV failure rates among firms generally able to manage IJVs will be expected to be lower than failure rates among those firms thought to be poor at managing IJVs. More generally the performance objectives are more likely to be met in those IJVs where the partners have absorbed the lessons of managing IJVs.

These observations give rise to a number of research propositions: These propositions are better regarded as identifying some important research topics than portraying a comprehensive research agenda.

- P1: The necessity for mutual forbearance will give rise to concern for issues of trust.
- P2: The potential threat of opportunistic behaviour will focus attention on an exit strategy.
- P3: Performance outcomes will be superior in those IJVs that have learned better how to manage IJVs.

Differences in lessons across characteristics of the sample are difficult to test with this sample because of the large number of interrelated lessons and the relatively small sample size. However, future research should consider how lessons learned may vary with the following characteristics: motive for IJV formation, previous IJV experience by parents, cultural distance of the partners and the number of parents. Young et al. (1989: 19) have noted that it is necessary to distinguish between the role of alliances in establishing corporate linkages, such as sharing investment risks, attainment of economies of scale, exchange of complementary technology, and so on, as opposed to their role in corporate entry strategies, principally entry to new geographical markets. This suggests greater difficulties and possibly greater risks involved in market entry IJVs and highlights the importance attributed to a close knowledge of national cultural factors when a new market is being envisaged. In this respect examination of how lessons differ within IJVs designed for market entry as compared to other motives for formation would be instructive.

The more inexperienced the parent firms are in the formation and operation of IJVs, the greater the rate of new learning is likely to be. Parent companies starting with their first few IJVs are likely to be more naïve and prone to making errors than are more sophisticated partners that have been involved in the process several times. The nature of the learning is therefore likely to be an inverted U-shape with respect to the number of previous IJV relationships.

The data from this sample emphasizes the importance of cultural issues in relation to the lessons learned in managing IJVs. The nature of these lessons is likely to vary with the cultural distance between the partners. *Ceteris paribus*, where cultural distance is great this is likely to promote a greater learning experience than where cultural distance is small.

These observations give rise to the following propositions:

- P4: The lessons of managing IJVs will vary with the motives for IJV formation.
- P5: The lessons of managing IJVs will vary with the extent of prior IJV experience of the partners.
- P6: The lessons of managing IJVs will vary with the cultural distance of the partners.

CONCLUSIONS

This chapter has reported on an area of IJV research that has hitherto been relatively neglected, namely, the major types of lessons learned from the IJV experience. When discussing their findings, Anand and Khanna (2000) note that they cannot distinguish whether learning occurs as a result of firms getting better at screening their alliance partners, or because they get better at interfacing with these partners (perhaps through designing better contracts or through getting more adept at managing relationships). The findings from this study indicate that each of these processes are likely to occur. Learning to manage IJVs occurs across the areas of formation, partner relationships and operational management of the IJV. Learning to managing IJVs is a multifaceted and interrelated process. Not only are many of the individual categorisations of learning interrelated, but they also mutually reinforce each other into either positive, or negative, cycles of experience and effect on IJV performance. A direct consequence of this interrelated and interdependent learning activity is that better performance from learning to manage IJVs may be causally ambiguous, in that direct relationships between facets of learning and performance may be extremely difficult to identify. Unravelling the relationship between learning to manage IJVs and performance outcomes is a challenge for future research. Some directions that future research effort may take are identified in the suggested research propositions.

7. Partnering skills and cross-cultural issues

THE CONCEPT OF SKILLS

The skills required to undertake co-operative ventures are different from those in a normal competitive environment, and those of co-operating with a partner from a different cultural background are more complex again. This chapter utilizes personal interviews of managers from all three elements of the sample of IJVs (two parent partners and the IJV itself) to identify the key collaborative or 'partnering' skills deemed to be important by managers. These skills are cross-classified by the context in which they need to be utilized to provide an 'analytical matrix' of partnering skills.

The concept of skill is not easy to define. Cockburn (1991) suggests that skill consists of at least three things: 'the skill that resides in the person himself, accumulated over time, each new experience adding to a total ability', 'skill demanded by the job – which may or may not match the skill in the worker' and 'the political definition of skill'. Payne (1999) goes further, arguing that skill 'has expanded almost exponentially to include a veritable galaxy of "soft", "generic", "transferable", "social" and "interactional" skills, frequently indistinguishable from personal characteristics, behaviours and attitudes'. As Attewell (1990) says 'like so many common-sense concepts, skill proves on reflection to be a complex and ambiguous idea'. In view of this complexity, we did not specify in advance the definition of skill, nor did we delimit in any way the manager's responses. This is in accord with the 'native category' approach derived from social anthropology and ethnomethodology, which allows the respondent managers to choose their own 'native' categories of skill (Buckley and Chapman, 1998).

SKILLS IN IJVs

The view that there may be certain skills necessary for undertaking successful alliance activity is a relatively novel one as is evidenced by a dearth of studies that investigate this proposition. In studies where the importance of collaborative skills is acknowledged, it is suggestive, given in the form of advice rather than being supported by empirical data (as in Lewis, 1990). Arino's (1997) work on co-operative behaviour and by implication co-operative skills, examined only two – veracity and commitment: there are, of course, other 'skills' that need to be discerned. We may conjecture that the reason for this neglect is obvious and understandable: the dominance of the competitive paradigm, reflected in management perception of focusing predominantly on those skills necessary for their personal as well their firms' success in a hostile competitive environment; notwithstanding the fact of a rapid increase in co-operative activity. However, beyond the realms of the mainstream competitive paradigm and Western business practices evidence exists, for example in China, of a high degree of co-operation via business networks through *guanxi* (that is, good inter-personal relationships) that involve the promotion of 'mutual awareness and understanding which can be readily communicated through informal and social channels' (Yeung, 1997). Elements of *guanxi* involve what can be considered good partnering skills (for example obligation and reciprocity, trust and respect) which are embedded in the culture and thus also permeate business practices. A similar phenomenon of business networks has long existed in other East Asian countries, notably in Japan and Korea. Nonetheless, within the global economy, such practices are exceptional, and where firms collaborate they have to do so without recourse to an array of informal traditional networks – a logical outcome of the modern globalization process. In terms of the nature of partnering skills, however, the *guanxi* categories do provide a core set of skills which can be considered universally desirable for collaborative activity, arguably even more so for firms from different countries and cultures. Moreover, the co-operative alliance literature has highlighted the importance of two such categories – trust and reciprocity – in the IJV process, so skills that accentuate these must be considered critical. Indeed, collaboration entails not just trust and reciprocity but also the elimination of opportunism (where one or more of the elements of a JV act in their own self-interest to the detriment of the others) and mutual forbearance (a level of tolerance of partner's shortcomings) (Buckley and Casson, 1988): consequently, core partnering skills can be expected to bear upon these strongly.

A further omission from the established literature on co-operative alliances is the potentially vital issue of IJV managers learning how to manage their parents. This reflects the 'top-down' attitude of much of the management literature – but 'upward' management skills might be of great importance in IJVs.

Equity joint ventures imply that the parents possess joint ownership, hence joint interests, in the JV company. At the same time, however, there is invariably a divergence of interests between parent companies in regard to the JV, which may therefore exhibit a 'mixed motive scenario' involving both interdependence and conflict (Schelling, 1960). So effective partnering skills need to emphasize the joint interests whilst minimizing real or potential conflict, and JV managers will seek to lessen conflict between the parents given the possible damage such conflicts can inflict upon the JV. It should be stressed, however, that the nature of a JV's operation, the external environment, and its performance might limit the extent to which partnering skills can contain conflict and expand joint interests. Nevertheless, under normal conditions, it is reasonable to assume that certain partnering skills do have a positive impact on JV conduct and performance and so need to be nurtured and developed.

This brief discussion illustrates clearly that 'skills' in the context of IJVs are difficult to separate from behaviours and beliefs. 'Veracity' and 'commitment' have moral dimensions as well as skill dimensions. '*Guanxi*' has skill elements such as good communications as well as elements of social context. Partnering skills are very much embodied in culture – both national and company culture – and these need to be expressed in the plural to capture the context of IJVs. It is when they encompass differences of both national and company culture that the concept of partnering skills in the IJV context gains its complexity, intellectual excitement and analytical intractability.

AN ANALYTIC MATRIX OF IJV MANAGEMENT

Figure 7.1 illustrates the operation of skills involved in managing an IJV with two parents. Four categories of skill are shown.

1. Inter-partner skills, that is establishing the IJV and fostering the relationships between the partners;
2. the skills required by the partner managers to manage the interface between the two partner firms and the IJV;
3. the skills required by IJV managers to effectively cross the interface between the IJV and the partners;
4. the skills required by the IJV managers to ensure successful operation and performance of the IJV itself.

Table 7.1 lists broad categories of partnering skill that emerged from our interview study. These skills can be related to our four categories above and to 'levels of influence' – the areas where the operation of these skills are particularly crucial. We identify these areas as:

1. national/macro elements;
2. industry or sector-level factors;
3. organizational and firm levels; and
4. perceptions of individual managers.

Partnering skills and cross-cultural issues 123

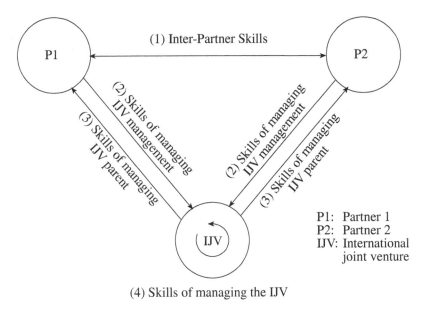

Figure 7.1 IJV skills set

This chapter classifies the skills listed in Table 7.1 into their most appropriate use in the complex process of managing a two partner IJV, and by combining the four levels of influence with the four categories of skill, we have been able to summarize our results as the analytical matrix in Table 7.2.

(1) INTER-PARTNER SKILLS

Flexibility and Diplomacy

Co-operation necessarily implies regular consultation with the partner, and a number of respondents referred to 'diplomatic' skills in this context. In essence, this involves the ability to listen and compromise, attributes that underpin reciprocity and forbearance. Hence, it is not surprising that such skills were among the most cited. A typical example is that given by the European partner of JV3:

> But the people must be flexible – he does not have to agree every time, but he has to be flexible, he has to be open to discussion, he has to take into account the point of view of the other. He's not a politician but he has to be a diplomat and he has to think that maybe he is not right, even if he is French or English.

Table 7.1 Categories of partnering skills from interview data

Partnering skill	Citations
Diplomatic approach	16
Take broad view and accept other cultures	10
Shared objectives and vision	10
Understand goals of both parents	8
International experience	6
Ability to trust and show honesty	6
Commitment to JV	6
No hidden agendas	5
Long-term view	4
Knowledge of JV's business	4
Communication skills	4
Open exchange of information	4
Team player	4
Language skills	3
Management experience and skills	3
Work with partner to achieve consensus	3
Knowledge of and respect for partner	3
Leadership skills	2
Good negotiating skills	2
Adopt best practices	2
Commercial experience	1
Clear responsibilities	1
No partnering skills needed	1
Independent JV management	1
Parents involved in JV's development	1
Total	110

Similarly, the UK partner of this JV states:

> So I think you have to think a little bit more before you say something and put yourself in their place and recognize that you are two separate companies. I mean it's very easy to you as the managing business, as we were, to sort of sideline these guys and just use technical advice, you need to remember that their money was in there as well and their reputation and their name indeed was in there as well. So I do think it requires probably more diplomacy, certainly than normal business situations.

In JVs where one partner has a large majority equity share and hence implied strong control over the JV, it might be possible to temper diplomacy. Evidence, however, from the data suggests that this is a rare occurrence. Doz

Table 7.2 IJV skills set matrix

Level of influences → ↓ IJV skills	(A) Macro	(B) Industry/sector	(C) Firm	(D) Individual manager
1. Inter-partner skills	Cultural sensitivity Language skills Cultural brokers 'Diplomacy' Communication	Industrial cultural brokerage	Ability to forbear Importance of clear vision Trust	Flexibility in outlook Credibility Empathy
2. Skills of managing IJV	'Diplomacy' Cultural sensitivity Language skills Communication Commitment Setting clear goals	Understanding industry sector of IJV operation	Ability to be flexible	Ability to influence across the boundaries of the firm
3. Skills of managing parents	**Managing cultural differences including language skills**	**Ability of IJV managers to harness industrial culture**	**Ability of IJV managers to mesh into two company cultures**	**'Upward' management skills. Communication skills Good negotiating skills Handling ambiguity**
4. Skills of managing IJV	Shared objective and vision	Industry experience and knowledge	Leadership skills	Experience Commitment

and Hamel (1998) note that while marriage is a commonly used analogy in the literature of strategic alliances, a better analogy is found in statecraft. IJVs maintain the separate identities and integrity of individual partners and, in so doing, protect their self-interests. Doz and Hamel conclude that the 'parallels between geopolitical and business alliances are many, and that managers should turn to history as a worthy source of inspiration and guidance'. This perspective clearly has resonance with the key partnering skill of 'diplomatic approach' identified in this study.

The Importance of Clear Vision

The importance of the partner managers setting a clear vision for the IJV was a consistent theme among the responses. The manager of JV7 expressed this clearly:

> They have to have a shared belief which is fairly obvious but a shared belief in so much as that what they're trying to achieve is actually, for both of them, the same objectives. The problem with that is that when it's across geographical boundaries and cultures, it's very difficult to know whether . . . they are actually expressed in the same priority as each of you would expect.

It was important that partner managers had to have the skill of enthusiastically communicating this vision within their own organization, across to the partner firm and into the IJV. This ability to communicate, that some respondents referred to as 'skills of selling' is important in order that those involved in the JV buy into its meaning and purpose. The vision of the JV should not remain the property of the top management of the partner firms, but should be accepted broadly by all those involved in its establishment and implementation.

The setting of clear objectives and measurable outcomes for the IJV is closely associated with the development and communication of the vision. The parent managers must be able to develop a clear understanding of each other's main objectives: objectives that are hidden from a partner may create major disappointments or misunderstandings when attempts are made to achieve them. It is crucial that the espoused objectives should recognize the synergy between the partners so that there is a clearly identified common purpose. The partner managers must identify a positive gain by both parties and a gain they would be unable to achieve on their own. As one respondent noted, the key is in the word 'partner' with both parties recognizing that they should be giving something to the other and not just taking. Translating that purpose into a commercial entity needs thorough research and a JV agreement and business plan that is rigorous and comprehensive and that is fully owned by both parties. In this sense those establishing the IJV must have the skills to develop a common view of a *valid* enterprise – a common view of a fundamentally weak business enterprise is futile. A balance needs to be struck between the possible detrimental effects to a partner by a certain course of action, and the gains such action may bring about to the JV, and the skill of fully understanding the other partner's objectives helps to strike the right balance. The UK partner of JV4 put it as follows:

> Someone who understands what both ... partners, both shareholders whatever, what their aspirations are and can bring them together but at the same time, realizes that you may have to tread on certain toes in both to get the end result. My view is that both partners won't mind as long as the end result is there.

Partner managers must be tenacious and consistent, and convinced that the IJV is the right thing to do: if they are not, this will be communicated to the partner and the IJV managers, with detrimental effect. The partnering skills are thus fundamentally about leveraging the resources and capabilities in a synergistic mix that will produce benefits for both sides. To produce this synergistic mix between the partners, the partnering skills themselves must be complementary. The ability to develop a clear management structure and a clear implementation process is also important. The structure of managing the JV, with clear responsibilities assigned between the partners, must be known before the JV starts.

Although the importance of a clearly articulated vision of the venture, with stated objectives and an identified implementation process, might appear obvious, the reason these are demanding criteria is that partner managers need the skills to do these things well while working in the context of resolving conflicts of culture and understanding a range of different practices, in addition to the normal demands of managing this process. Partner managers need appropriately developed skills to handle this situation.

Credibility

To liaise effectively with the partner company the partner managers must have credibility. Good knowledge of the business and the ability to deliver will tend to make the foreign partner managers more inclined to listen and to do business. We found that it was necessary for managers to display a knowledge and respect for the partner, to understand how the partner runs their business, and to have a genuine desire to recognize the partner's strengths.

JV14 UK partner:

> I think the people in the joint venture have to be credible, and what do I mean by that? They have to be people whose functional skills can be respected by individual partners, and can therefore command respect and know what they are talking about.

Negotiating skills

Relationship-type skills – that is, the capability to 'give and take' and the ability to negotiate – were clearly important. One respondent observed that every time there is a meeting between partners they are effectively negotiating and, therefore, partner managers need to have polished skills in this area. Partners need the capability to manage relationships and to influence relationships, and for some respondents this was again reminiscent of elements of sales skills. The need was also identified for thinking at the parent level to be in broad envelope, strategy-plan terms, and to avoid being too much involved in detailed control, which was perceived as a separate line of management. In that sense, it is necessary for the parent managers to learn to 'let go'.

Skills of Fostering the Partner Relationship: Trust, Empathy and Cultural Awareness

In order to foster the relationship between the partners, several skills were identified. Fundamentally the partner managers must be able to inculcate trust, noted earlier as an extremely important facet of JV relationships (Faulkner, 1995; Madhok, 1995). Trust as a partnering skill involves convincing the partner of your own honesty, that you trust them in their dealings with you and also that you trust the JV management to act in accordance with the interests of both parents. The UK partner of JV18 highlighted this as:

> So you've got to be honest, you've got to be honest in your relationships and dealings with people. You can adopt a sophisticated, assured, negotiated stance and that might get you some way, but you would not get all the way with that and people would see through it – they would detect a lack of honesty there. They would detect that that was not a reflection of your true honesty.

We found that trust developed from openness and honesty between the partners: frank, even-handed and transparent dealings without hidden agendas created the climate for success. The personal integrity of the partner managers is thus important along with an ability to act with mutual forbearance and reciprocity.

The willingness and ability to provide information was seen as important in confirming an honest attitude and developing trust. At the same time as providing information, partner managers should be open to the receipt of information. Expertise in listening, being able to fully comprehend and relate to what the others are saying, was identified as being an important skill by several respondents. Good listening was seen as underpinning the ability to develop understanding of the real issues through discussion, and as offering a sign of respect for the other partner's position and opinion.

Our data also suggests that empathy is an important attribute, associated with an ability to give and take, and the eschewing of the position that the manager or the parent always have to win. It was not seen as helpful for the IJV relationship to be dominated by people with competitively driven psyches: rather, the requirement was for managers who genuinely do care about the other partner and spend time thinking about how the partner can be put into a situation where he can go back a 'winner'. Of course, a firm should not give away its key resources and capabilities, but it should always consider what really matters to the partner.

JV8 UK partner:

> I can think of some individuals... who are quite unsuited to deliver win-win situations. I know one very senior manager.. whose idea of a win-win is to win and then tell you he has won. I think that is completely counter productive. So you want managers who really do care about the other partner, genuinely.

JV18 partner:

> You need to be able to listen and not to impose, it's important to be able to comprehend and relate to what the others are saying.

Not seeking to dominate all stages of the relationship, not trying always to do better than the partner, were associated with the recognition that ultimately the IJV is about a long-term win–win position for both partner companies. This is reflected in the skill of reaching a compromise associated with the desire for consensus and the aim of seeing the partnership work. This does not mean that the competitive instinct in the managers is diluted, rather that it needs to be controlled and to be shared. It is necessary for a manager to compromise, to understand the partner's point of view and to try to work within that and to come to a common agreement. Reaching a compromise is thus recognized as a strength rather than a weakness. Conflict resolution and the ability to find joint solutions become recognized as important traits. This requires managers who are prepared to adopt best practice, even if these do not come from their own firm. Our data also suggested that frustrations and problems had to be expressed immediately but objectively, and conflicts resolved or the partnership dissolved. Simply continuing in such situations was not thought a feasible option, ultimately leading to a bad and unsuccessful relationship.

Underpinning empathy and the need to compromise is an ability to be flexible. In an IJV relationship, managers have to be more adaptable, to be perceived as someone who will resolve things in a way that the partners are comfortable with, rather than imposing a dogmatic solution. Each side will have views, and the flexible attitude will take the best from both of them.

Clearly distinct from the notion of 'wishy-washy' compromise, such flexibility was seen as a strong ability, going hand-in-hand with the strength to insist on things where necessary.

Our data analysis further revealed that a key aspect of flexibility is cultural awareness. The notion of diplomacy brings with it overtones of relationships and negotiations between countries, and an effective international relationship was seen as requiring knowledge and empathy for another country's culture and traditions. Similarly, dealings between partners from different countries are made easier and more productive where there is an acceptance of cultural issues, and a recognition that cultural issues such as language and national work routines affect inter-firm collaborative activity. Respondents noted that showing respect for, and being sensitive to, the national culture of the partner constituted important partnering skills. A typical example is from the manager of JV13: 'Partnering skills [are] absolutely essential because you are constantly having to resolve conflicts of culture, of practice, of everything else on top of the normal conflicts. And so being able to handle that is very important.'

There was clear evidence in the data that partner managers need to have an understanding of the different cultures or they need to be able to pick up these differences relatively quickly. Managers who were not alert to cultural differences risked making the presumption that both sides had the same understanding of a particular issue, when that might not be the case.

(2) SKILLS OF MANAGING THE IJV MANAGERS

Partner Skills of Managing the IJV Interface

Managers in partner firms need parenting skills. In part, during the early phase of the operation of the IJV, the parent managers may need to coach the IJV management through the running of the enterprise. Our data suggests, however, that eventually parent managers need to develop a 'hands-off approach', trusting the IJV management with the freedom to do what is in the best interest of the venture. A balance of skills is required here. Some degree of parent control is required with guidelines on appropriate ways of managing but, at the same time, this should not be perceived by the IJV management as interference. We found that the parents should establish the parameters within which the IJV management may operate, and have an agreed understanding of how they are going to monitor the IJV practice and performance, but should then keep a distance, avoid interfering with the IJV, and grant a high degree of operational autonomy.

JV4 UK partner:

It is an understanding, an awareness of what the rules are and making sure that you can live within the rules but achieve the end result. And if the rules of the structure do not allow you to do that, you have to be a big enough individual to come back and say 'I can't work within these parameters, it doesn't work' and you can modify the parameters.

Our data analysis also revealed that some of the characteristics appropriate to the partner managers should also be inculcated in the IJV managers. We found, for example, that partners from one firm need to signal that JV management should be open and straightforward in its dealings with the other partner. Appropriate behaviour on the part of IJV management is thus encouraged by partner expectations.

Skill Set of IJV Managers

In many respects the skills of managing an IJV are the same as the skills required in any business, for example, respondents identified the need to be a leader, to set goals, to be able to discuss problems and to motivate people. However, because IJV managers have to deal with people from another country this imposes extra burdens on them and so, in some respects, they need a more highly developed set of skills. Our data analysis revealed that IJV managers require many qualities. As seen in Figure 7.1, we first distinguish between the skills of managing the interface between the partners and skills of managing the IJV.

(3) SKILLS OF MANAGING THE PARENTS

IJV Manager Skills of Managing the Parent Interface

The ability of IJV managers to manage their project's relations with its parent companies successfully was often emphasized by interviewees, and the importance of this interface appears to be a significant omission from previous literature on joint venture management. We are able to identify the skills of managing parents, which we identify in Table 7.2, as:

i. the ability of the IJV managers to mesh two company cultures, including cultural and language skills; and
ii. 'upward management skills', including communication skills, good negotiating skills and handling ambiguity.

(i) Meshing Different Cultures
By definition, an IJV is a cross-cultural entity. Managers in all elements of the IJV need to be able to mesh the different cultural contexts in which the firm is operating.

JV8 UK partner: 'The ability to communicate and work effectively inter-culturally is essential.. the successful people are those who are able to work inter-culturally.'

JV13 JV manager:

> ... you are constantly having to resolve conflicts of culture, of practice, of everything else on top of the normal conflicts. And so being able to handle that is very important... And within that you need to have an understanding of the cultures or you need to be able to pick it up pretty quickly, otherwise you're going to be in real trouble.

Cultural awareness

JV2 foreign partner: 'These people have to be very open minded, they have to like different cultures, different languages, different people, it is essential.'

JV3 UK manager: 'You need more highly developed skills because you're dealing with people from another country where, if you scratch deep enough, the prejudices will surface.. ... So you have to think a little bit more before you say something and put yourself in their place and recognize you are two separate companies.'

Success in coping with cultural awareness comes in part from taking into account the parent's views. The IJV manager has to identify with the needs of the parent and to consider whether any action by the IJV can put the parent in a difficult position. The IJV manager should be open about what needs to be done and why, and be receptive to the views of the parents and prepared to look to them for solutions. This involves developing an appropriate relationship with managers from the parent firms.

(ii) Upward management skills

One key element of managing the parents is a flexibility of approach that can be referred to as 'diplomacy', 'give and take' or political skills. Negotiating skills are a manifestation of these generic skills which obviously include an element of cultural sensitivity.

JV15 UK partner: 'There needs to be a degree of flexibility. They will have views, we have views and there needs to be flexibility in taking the best from both of them.'

JV18 JV manager: 'The capability to "give and take". I think an element of negotiation, along with that give and take type approach.'

JV4 JV manager: 'An ability to try and compromise, which comes out of being a good negotiator.'

JV14 foreign partner: '...running a joint venture takes some political skills undoubtedly... the partners have to be very careful *vis-à-vis* each other, and the man in between has to be even more careful... It does take some diplomatic talent.'

Where more than one partner is involved, tolerance of ambiguity is a major skill which is complementary to the meshing of different country and company cultures.

JV14 UK partner: 'I think you have to put in people who, firstly, can handle a degree of ambiguity or frustration, because it takes longer and you have to take more factors into account.'

Our data suggests that ultimately the IJV management and not the parents must take responsibility to ensure that the governance structure and the direction being received from the two parents are being followed. At the same time, the individual needs to accept responsibility for the management of the IJV, and challenge the parents to provide a united approach. When necessary, the IJV manager must have the confidence and strength of mind to go to the parents and express concern about the parameters the parents intend to establish, seeking to modify them if necessary. Rather than being torn apart by contrasting demands from each parent, the IJV management needs to express such concern openly and press on the parents the need to come together to facilitate a convergence of views. This takes managers with confidence and, to be effective, this must be done early in the life of the IJV. The position of the IJV managers requires them to be tough-minded with an ability to stand up for themselves. At the same time social skills are required in order to interface successfully between the two parents.

Clearly, the individual must accept the role of the manager of the JV, and not be allied to either parent, even though previously they might have been (and might be again) an employee of one of the parent firms. The perspective of the IJV manager should be one that does not favour one parent over another, and our data strongly suggests that what makes a good IJV manager is somebody who works for the joint venture and nobody else. An IJV manager appointed from one of the parent companies may inevitably feel a certain affinity towards their former employer, but we found evidence to support the view that the ability to develop a neutrality *vis-à-vis* the parents was recognized as a necessary skill. The IJV manager must be someone who understands the aspirations of both parents, and can bring them together, but at the same time realizes that it may be necessary to tread on certain toes in both camps to get the end result.

(4) SKILLS OF MANAGING THE IJV

Competencies

As with the parent managers the IJV manager should also be a diplomat – a role that indubitably requires more diplomacy than in normal business situations. Managers generally have a natural sense of authority, issuing orders and instructions, and setting directions. The parents have to deal sensitively with each other in these matters, and the IJV manager, as the person in between, has to show even greater care. To manage this position appropriately, therefore, requires diplomatic talent: in fact running an IJV requires a degree of political skill.

We found that the ability to integrate within the IJV was an important skill. The management of the IJV was regarded as a difficult position. The parent shareholders are effectively two bosses and the IJV manager may be under competing pressures to satisfy both. Consequently, successful IJV managers were those who were seen as having successfully managed the potential conflict of interest between the parents. They had an ability to negotiate and compromise, were considered to be patient and to have had a focus on the long-term and a degree of tenacity. Such managers are able to act in a consultative manner and introduce a greater degree of joint consideration in decision making. They are able to tackle problems or issues in a broader way, and to avoid being very narrow-minded. In turn, this requires the IJV manager to be able to handle a degree of ambiguity or frustration, because, with more factors having to be taken into consideration, the decision-making process often takes longer.

IJV managers need the skills and abilities to work within different cultures and to produce a new joint culture. Although the IJV is the employer, the origin and the background culture of the employees cannot be erased immediately. IJV employees from the parents will arrive with a dominant and often contrasting paradigm (Johnson, 1992), and their behaviour will be affected by which partner they have come from, and their own views and experience. It is essential therefore that the IJV manager can accept, and be sensitive to, different cultures. In the early life of the IJV, the managers should resist dogmatic approaches to the way things are done, seeking to accommodate differences. The ability to communicate and work effectively inter-culturally is therefore essential as the IJV manager seeks to weld a new culture positively. In part this may require emphasizing the success stories of working with the parents and expunging the stories of failure or mistakes.

The Importance of Experience

We found that an important influence on the competencies of the IJV managers was their previous experience. It is important that the managers of the IJV appear credible, in the eyes of the parents, the employees of the IJV, and its major customers. IJV managers should know the business of the venture, have had appropriate commercial and management experience, and should be people whose functional and management skills are recognized by individual partners, and can therefore command respect from all parties.

Although the interviewees expressed some divergence of views, there was a broad consensus that an important element of competence and previous experience was having international exposure from previously working overseas. Exposure to different international cultures was considered particularly relevant in developing a degree of empathy towards different cultural backgrounds and working practices. This is closely related to cultural issues, where managers simply recognize that previous international experience (not necessarily of IJVs) assists in the better understanding of how business is conducted across national boundaries. The UK partner of JV13 put it as follows: 'I think that one thing I would tend to look for is did the person have international experience, because I think what makes them unable to see other people's points of view is the fact that they've been rather closeted in their own culture and background.'

In general it was argued that people with international experience would tend to make better IJV managers because they would understand the cultural differences better and would be more able to understand the partner cultures, especially if the personnel concerned have worked in the home country of the partner. Such experience enables partner firms to 'pick horses for courses' in the sense of matching the country experience of the individual with the country of the partner. For instance one respondent noted that the Dutch are delightfully pleased by their bluntness, that is, they have a style which is direct and open. Quite a number of British people would find this difficult to cope with, but prior experience of the culture would make working with the Dutch much easier.

Commitment

An important consideration for some firms was the selection of the JV 'start up' team. One argument strongly put was that a proportion of those involved in establishing the IJV should also become involved in its management, not necessarily in roles that would keep them in the IJV for the long term but in the role of helping bed in the venture. If there is a complete separation of the team that establishes the IJV from the team that subsequently manages it, the latter may not fully comprehend the rationale of the IJV and may be less emotionally committed to making it work. So some of the people who negotiate the deal and set up the IJV, should follow through to IJV management roles to carry through the concept of understanding and ownership of and commitment to the IJV. This also avoids the danger that a fresh IJV management might redefine the venture through lack of understanding of it which comes from being involved in its formation. This view was summarized by the UK partner of JV19: '... and making sure that they perform those tasks that are necessary in order for the joint venture to be a success so that they are committed to it and committed not only just to the joint venture but making sure that they support it within their own activities.'

JV10 UK partner: 'Commitment on both sides, common vision, common objectives, common goals. Commitment must be sustained over a period of time, and longevity of commitment emerges as consistency of strategy.'

JV20 foreign partner: 'You have got to be consistent. You have to be fully convinced that it is the right thing to do, because it will show if you are not. You've got to live with the whole thing ... and be able to carry it among all the difficulties.'

THE ANALYTICAL MATRIX COMPLETED

Figure 7.2 encompasses and synthesizes our findings. Its rows examine the IJV skills that emerged from our interviews, while the columns focus these skills by the level of utilization. One row (3) is highlighted to show the importance of the skills of managing the parents by the IJV. Our study shows that the 'upward management skills' are unjustifiably neglected as they contribute to our understanding of partnering skills in IJVs. The matrix is a useful analytical engine and managerial device enabling outside analysts to focus on key areas in formulating and managing successful IJVs, as well as enabling managers to pinpoint real and potential difficulties in establishing and running an IJV. It is a diagnostic tool that should help managers to isolate and remove problems. It also has a dynamic element: as the IJV's lifecycle extends, so the crucial management issues move from columns (A) and (B), which are most important in the pre-operational phase, to columns (C) and (D) which dominate the set-up and ongoing operation phases.

MANAGERIAL IMPLICATIONS

Selection and Training for Partner Interface and JV Management

Our data analysis revealed the growing importance of selection and training for partner interface and IJV management. Firms are increasingly realizing that the way forward for them strategically is to partner with other, often competing, firms. With the proliferation of alliances and IJVs there has been a growing awareness of the need proactively to develop the skills required for partner interface and IJV management. We found that some of the partner firms invest quite heavily in training – including the need to appreciate the differences of managing to compete, and managing to co-operate. Selection procedures are important because some types of individuals are considered inappropriate for such roles even though they may be intrinsically good managers. This is particularly the case for those lacking the fundamental partnering skills identified above and those with no international experience.

Several firms were conscious of the need to help individuals to develop, and to use them in relation to their strengths. In that context we found that staff rotation through different parts of the business, including overseas postings and cultural exposure, was important. This was to ensure that they see every aspect of the company, including using the opportunity of an overseas post to perceive the company more from the perspective of a partner or a customer and to learn something as a result. The more a company is able to do this, the more it is able to build a group of people who will be adept at managing the elements of the IJV. Training programmes are also recommended to develop clear thinking and a constructive approach to the firm's IJV strategy.

Finally, consideration should be given to succession planning in IJV management. The IJV may have been formed and successfully managed by a group of people who then move on. This incurs the risk of having new people come in to manage the IJV who might have a different agenda and might not have the same rapport or communication with their opposite numbers or the partners. It should be acknowledged that personnel changes can have a significant impact on the IJV, and parent firms and incumbent IJV managers should carefully plan for management succession in order to minimize disruption to IJV performance.

CONCLUSIONS

There is nothing inevitable about the success or failure of IJVs. Management makes the difference. This chapter provides new perspectives on partnering skills in IJVs that are crucial to successful IJV performance. From the analysis of interview data, four categories of skills were identified: inter-partner skills, 'downward' skills of managing the IJV managers, 'upward' skills of managing the partners, and skills of managing the IJV. The chapter presented an analytical matrix formed from the delineation of these skills across the context in which these skills need to be used. This matrix functions as an analytical device and as a diagnostic tool, facilitating the analysis of real and potential problems in the management of IJVs.

8. Performance assessment in IJVs: The relationship between subjective and objective methods and the influence of culture

INTRODUCTION

The motives for international joint venture (IJV) formation include access to markets, cost and risk sharing, economies of scale, and access to new technologies (Contractor and Lorange, 1988; Glaister and Buckley, 1996). These motives indicate that the competitive advantage of the firm is increasingly dependent on the scope of the firm's co-operative relationships with other firms (Parkhe, 1991). Despite the benefits of co-operation, IJVs have relatively high failure rates (Beamish and Delios, 1997b). This has given rise to a substantial literature on the determinants of IJV performance. One major issue is the appropriate measure of IJV performance. In his comprehensive review of measuring strategic alliance performance, Olk (2001: 5) notes that there is no single view of how to measure organizational effectiveness and that there are challenges in measuring effectiveness that are unique to strategic alliances. Most obviously, alliances are hybrid structures, with somewhat fuzzy boundaries which makes performance evaluation more difficult. Furthermore, there are multiple members – an IJV system has at least two partners and (usually) an IJV management – with no clear basis for evaluating the range of interests. These features add to the already complex issue of how to evaluate performance. Consequently, there is no consensus on the appropriate definition and measure of IJV performance.

Early studies of IJV performance used a variety of financial indicators such as profitability, growth and cost position, or objective measures of performance including survival of the IJV, its duration, instability of (significant changes in) its ownership, and renegotiation of the IJV contract. Later studies used subjective measures such as managers' satisfaction with performance. A particularly contentious issue is the extent to which the objective measures and subjective measures of IJV performance are correlated (Glaister and Buckley, 1998a, 1998b; Geringer, 1998).

This chapter addresses some key research issues of IJV performance measurement using data from IJVs between UK firms and partner firms from Western Europe. Its fundamental purpose is to replicate and extend previous studies relating to IJV performance assessment. The replication undertaken in this study has been classified by Tsang and Kwan (1999: 768) as 'generalization and extension', where different research procedures are employed and a sample is drawn from a different population of subjects. Hubbard and Vetter (1996) in undertaking an examination of replication studies in economics, finance, management and marketing, contend that the majority of the business literature consists of fragments and isolated findings. It may be argued that this is particularly so in the field of research which concerns IJV activity (Parkhe, 1993). Uncorroborated studies, even those accompanied by statistically significant results, provide a weak foundation for the development of theory and practice. In order to contribute to the accumulating body of work relating to the measurement of performance in IJVs, the specific aims of the study are as follows: (i) to consider the relationship between objective and subjective performance measures, (ii) to examine the extent to which different measures of IJV performance measure different phenomena, (iii) to clarify the reliability of single respondents reporting IJV performance compared to multiple respondents reporting IJV performance, (iv) to examine the influence of the national culture of the partner on performance evaluation as the literature identifies this as an important determinant of performance measurement. The next section discusses the issues involved with IJV performance measurement and develops the hypotheses of the study. The following section sets out the research methods for the study. The fourth section presents the findings and discussion. Conclusions are in the final section.

ISSUES AND HYPOTHESES DEVELOPMENT

The Relationship between Objective and Subjective Performance Measures

Objective performance measures of IJVs include financial indicators, such as profitability (Lecraw, 1983), IJV survival (Harrigan, 1988a; Geringer, 1990; Geringer and Woodcock, 1995), IJV duration (Harrigan, 1986; Kogut, 1988), instability of IJV ownership, reflected in significant changes in the equity holdings of the parents (Gomes-Casseres, 1987; Beamish and Inkpen, 1995), and re-negotiation of the IJV contract (Blodgett, 1992). Frequently there is difficulty in obtaining financial data relating to the IJV, because financial results are usually subsumed into the partners' accounts. IJVs are often used to engage in a high level of complex tasks that have uncertain outcomes and so their financial performance is only relevant in the long term (Anderson, 1990). Moreover, objective indicators like IJV duration or survival may measure both success and failure of the relationship – termination may reflect IJV success when its objectives have been achieved. An alliance that ends is not necessarily an alliance that fails. As Olk (2001: 6) notes, the indicator of longevity does not apply in all contexts and it does not capture the learning and other goal-related activities that occur. Geringer and Hebert (1991) stress the failure of financial and objective measures to reflect the extent to which an alliance has achieved its aims. They argue that despite poor financial results, liquidation or instability, an IJV may have met or exceeded the parents' objectives and so be considered successful by one or all of the parents. Conversely, an IJV may be viewed as unsuccessful despite good financial results or continued stability. Concerns over the ability of financial and objective measures to capture IJV performance led researchers to adopt perceptual measures of a parent's satisfaction with IJV performance (Killing, 1983; Schaan, 1983; Beamish, 1985; Inkpen and Birkinshaw, 1994; Lyles and Baird, 1994; Dussauge and Garrette, 1995; Osland and Cavusgil, 1996). An advantage of subjective measures is that they are able to provide information on the extent to which the IJV has achieved its overall objectives.

The extent to which there is a positive and statistically significant relationship between objective and subjective performance measures has been the subject of debate (Glaister and Buckley, 1998a, 1998b; Geringer, 1998). Geringer and Hebert (1991), for a sample of US IJVs, reported significant and positive correlation between the objective measures of survival, stability and duration and subjective measures of IJV performance. In their sample of UK IJVs, Glaister and Buckley (1998a) found that the objective measure of survival had the strongest and most significant set of correlations with subjective performance measures, while the correlations for duration and stability were weak and non-significant. Hatfield et al. (1998), using a sample of US domestic JVs, reported correlations that were consistent with those obtained by Geringer and Hebert (1991), but contradicting Glaister and Buckley's (1998a) findings. Ali and Sim (1999) from a sample of private sector IJVs in Bangladesh, found that the subjective measurement of overall performance was strongly and positively correlated with goal achievement and JV survival. Correlations between overall performance and JV stability were positive but barely significant, a result that is marginally different from Geringer and Hebert's (1991) finding but closer to Glaister and Buckley's (1998a) finding. Ali and Sim further report that overall performance is not correlated with JV duration (close to zero), contradicting the findings of Geringer and Hebert (1991) and of Hatfield et al. (1998), but lending support to Glaister and Buckley's (1998a) finding. It is apparent that prior work has led to conflicting findings, which makes it difficult to generalize. To help resolve the current lack of empirical consensus, this study's first hypothesis is:

H1: *There will be a significant and positive correlation between objective and subjective measures of IJV performance.*

Do Different Measures of IJV Performance Measure Different Phenomena?

Hatfield et al. (1998) take the debate further by suggesting that objective and subjective performance measures are not assessing the same phenomenon. If partners perceive JVs as successful, then the partners are more likely to continue the relationship, extending the duration of the JV, which in turn affects JV survival. But they note that this does not prevent the possibility that environmental and strategic factors affect duration and survival more than partner goal achievement. For instance, termination may result from changes in a partner's strategy or environment, as well as from the successful accomplishment of a partner's goals or organizational learning. For Hatfield et al. (1998) this indicates that although partner goal achievement, duration and survival may be positive and causally related, these variables do not measure the same phenomena. Using regression analysis they found support for the hypothesis that partner assessment of JV goal achievement, JV duration and JV survival measure different phenomena. Ali and Sim's (1999) findings using regression analysis provide support for the view that goal achievement, JV duration, survival and stability measure different phenomena. Our second hypothesis is:

H2: *Satisfaction of performance, performance achievement, IJV survival and IJV duration measure different phenomena.*

The Reliability of Single Respondents Compared to Multiple Respondents

The entity responsible for IJV performance assessment is another controversial question, that is which perspective should be used to assess performance – the partners or the IJV management (Anderson, 1990)? The existence of different members of the IJV may produce diverse points of view and may generate contradictory opinions about overall IJV assessment. A comprehensive perspective of performance seems to be required, by incorporating assessments from the different participants involved. As Geringer and Hebert (1991) pointed out, however, collecting responses from all participants is complex and costly. The key issue is thus the extent to which the assessment by one element of the IJV is related to and representative of the other elements' overall assessment of IJV performance. A finding that a consistent relationship exists between the assessment of performance among the elements of an IJV would provide the confidence to reduce the number of responses required and lead to important reductions in research costs. Geringer and Hebert (1991) found strong similarity in evaluation between IJV managers and partner managers, and between the two partners. Their conclusion is that measures from one partner reflect the performance of both partners.

If the partners have a similar perception of IJV performance, and IJV management has a similar perception of performance as the parent firms, we would expect a positive and significant correlation between the performance assessments. This is reflected in the following hypotheses.

H3a: *There will be a significant and positive correlation among the parents' assessment of IJV performance.*

H3b: *There will be a significant and positive correlation among the parents' and the IJV management's assessments of IJV performance.*

Geringer and Hebert (1991: 252) also focus on the extent to which data collected from one element of the IJV represents a reliable estimate of the other element's perception of this performance. They argue that shared ownership and decision making in IJVs indicates that one element of the venture will demonstrate some awareness of the other element's assessment of performance. So it will be expected that the first partner's evaluation of the second partner's satisfaction regarding performance will be correlated with the second partner's actual reported satisfaction, and similarly, with respect to the partners' evaluation of the IJV manager's satisfaction regarding performance, and the IJV managers' assessment of the partners' evaluation of performance.

H3c: *There will be a significant and positive correlation between a parent's satisfaction with IJV performance and perceptions by the other partner and the IJV management of this parent's satisfaction.*

H3d: *There will be a significant and positive correlation between the IJV management's satisfaction with IJV performance and perceptions by the partners of the IJV management's satisfaction.*

The Influence of the National Culture of the Partner on Performance Evaluation

Geringer and Hebert (1991) also considered the influence of national culture on performance evaluation. They contend that agreement on an IJV's performance between its parents may be influenced by the national cultural similarity among them. Where there are national cultural similarities, this will tend to produce a greater agreement among the parents regarding the IJV's performance. In contrast, dissimilarities in national culture may lead to differences in the partners' perceptions of each other and the IJV and result in a lower degree of agreement regarding IJV performance. For their Canadian sample, Geringer and Hebert reported correlations between partners' assessments of specific aspects of IJV performance that were significantly positive as well as being stronger for partners where there was a cultural similarity. Glaister and Buckley (1998a) supported Geringer and Hebert's conclusion on national cultural differences, making the distinction between respondents for whom national culture was, or was not, apparent rather than from the location of the partner firms. In an attempt to replicate and extend these findings, this study's final hypotheses (based on Geringer and Hebert, 1991) are:

H4a: *Correlations between partners' assessments of IJV performance will be stronger in IJVs involving parents with similar national cultures.*
H4b: *Correlations between UK partners' assessment of IJV performance and the IJV management's assessment of performance will be stronger in IJVs involving parents with similar national cultures.*

RESEARCH METHODS

Measurement of Variables

Objective performance measures
IJV survival was measured using a dichotomous variable based on the survival or non-survival (that is, termination) of the IJV from the time of its formation until the data collection point. *IJV duration* was measured by the number of years between the IJV's formation and either its termination or the collection of performance data, whichever came first.

Subjective performance measures
The respondents' subjective level of satisfaction with the IJV's *overall performance* was assessed using a five-point Likert-type scale (from 1 = 'very dissatisfied' to 5 = 'very satisfied'). On the same scale, partner respondents were also asked to provide a measure of satisfaction that they believed applied to their foreign partner and the managers of the IJV. Similarly, IJV manager respondents were asked to provide a measure of satisfaction that they believed applied to each of the IJV parents.

As well as providing subjective measures of overall IJV performance, using the same five-point Likert-type scale respondents were asked to rate satisfaction with the IJV's performance in the following five areas: profitability, growth of sales, market share, efficiency and quality. These five items were also averaged into a *performance index*. The reliability coefficient of the items (Cronbach's alpha = 0.80) was found to be high and acceptable (Nunnally, 1978).

The operationalization of the performance variable does not capture all the nuance of the potential multiple objectives of IJVs, such as learning, and this is a limitation of the analysis.

Cultural difference
Difference in national culture was measured in two ways: by culture clusters and the Kogut–Singh index of cultural distance.

Culture clusters: Ronen and Shenkar (1985) synthesize the results of eight studies to provide a set of country clusters. The principal dimensions underlying the country clusters are geography, language and religion. The UK falls into the Anglo cluster, which does not contain any IJV partner countries from the sample in this study. The nationality of the European partner firms falls into three of Ronen and Shenkar's clusters: Germanic (partners from Germany), Nordic (partners from Norway and Sweden), and Latin European (partners from France, Italy and Spain). The partner country missing from Ronen and Shenkar's synthesis is Holland. Of the eight studies examined by Ronen and Shenkar only one includes Holland (Hofstede, 1980), where it is included in the Nordic cluster. Ronen and Shenkar (1985) point out that two studies they examined did not differentiate between the Nordic and Germanic clusters and the two clusters were combined into a Northern European cluster. For the purposes of this study two country clusters are delineated – Northern European and Latin European. On the basis of the underlying dimensions of the country clusters it is assumed that the national culture difference will be smallest between the UK and the Northern European cluster and greatest between the UK and the Latin European cluster.

Kogut–Singh index of cultural distance: From information provided by 88 000 respondents from 66 countries, Hofstede (1980) developed indices to measure four dimensions of national culture: power distance, uncertainty avoidance, masculinity/femininity, and individualism. Kogut and Singh (1988) employed these indices to compare cultural distances between the United States and other countries. Using their computational formula, we measure cultural distance as follows:

$$\text{Cultural distance } j = \sum \{(I_{ij} - I_{iu})^2 / V_i\}/4,$$

where Iij stands for the index of the ith cultural dimension and jth country, Vi is the variance of the index of the ith dimension, u indicates the UK, and Cultural distance j is cultural distance of the jth country from the UK. Countries with small values of cultural distance are culturally similar to the UK, with larger values signifying increasing dissimilarity. The values of cultural distance were France 2.27, Germany 2.34, Holland 1.87, Italy 0.91, Norway 2.39, Spain 2.37 and Sweden 2.50.

Data analysis techniques

In the questionnaire data, where there were multiple responses from one element of the IJV, these were averaged to produce a single questionnaire response from this element. To enhance the findings and to maximize the sample size in the statistical analysis, the interview data and the questionnaire data were pooled. Regression analysis was used to test H2 (Hatfield et al., 1998). Spearman rank order correlation coefficients were computed to test all of the other hypotheses (Geringer and Hebert, 1991).

RESULTS AND DISCUSSION

Hypothesis 1

Means and standard deviations of the objective and subjective performance measures are shown in Table 8.1.

Table 8.1 Means and standard deviations for hypothesized variables

Performance variables	All partners (n=53–80) Mean	SD
Overall satisfaction	3.33	1.29
Profitability	3.13	1.37
Growth of sales	3.05	1.03
Market share	3.29	0.95
Efficiency	3.56	0.83
Quality	3.72	0.83
Performance index	3.38	0.77
IJV survival	1.20	0.40
IJV duration	3.95	1.95

Results relating to H1 are shown in Table 8.2. The correlations between the objective measure of IJV survival and the subjective performance measures are for the most part weak and non-significant, with several displaying relationships in a direction contrary to that proposed in H1. The only significant correlation is that between IJV survival and the single item measure of performance assessment, *overall satisfaction*, which evidences moderate significant positive correlation ($p < 0.05$). This finding supports the findings of previous studies (Geringer and Hebert, 1991; Glaister and Buckley, 1998a; Hatfield et al., 1998; Ali and Sim, 1999), albeit with a correlation which is much weaker than those reported in prior studies. In contrast, the multi-item measure of performance assessment, *performance index*, evidences a low, negative and non-significant correlation.

There is a radically contrasting set of findings relating to correlations between the objective performance measure of IJV Duration and the subjective performance measures. All of the correlations are significant ($p < 0.05$ or better), moderately strong and in the direction hypothesized. The correlation between *overall satisfaction* and IJV duration is 0.38, while marginally weaker than the correlation reported by Geringer and Hebert (1991) and Hatfield et al. (1998), it conforms to their findings, but is in contrast to Glaister and Buckley (1998a) and Ali and Sim (1999) who both reported correlations close to zero.

Table 8.2 *Spearman rank order correlations for hypothesized variables: all partners*

Subjective performance measures Pooled data	n	Objective performance measures IJV Survival	IJV Duration
Overall satisfaction	62	0.307**	0.386***
Profitability	56	0.162	0.466***
Growth of sales	55	0.003	0.356***
Market share	53	0.074	0.396***
Efficiency	55	−0.087	0.458***
Quality	55	−0.017	0.296**
Performance index	50	−0.032	0.484***
IJV survival	80	–	0.055
IJV duration	80	0.055	–

Notes
Four of the IJVs had been terminated at the time of data collection.
* $p < 0.1$; ** $p < 0.05$; *** $p < 0.01$

The correlation between *performance index* and IJV duration is moderately strong, positive and significant, with a correlation coefficient of 0.48. This finding provides further support for Geringer and Hebert (1991) and Hatfield et al. (1998).

Clearly, most support for H1 comes from the set of correlations between IJV duration and the subjective performance measures. Little support is provided for H1 from the set of correlations between IJV survival and the subjective performance measures. This set of findings is in broad contrast to the findings reported by Glaister and Buckley (1998a), who found support for H1 from correlations between IJV survival and subjective performance measures, and little support from correlations between IJV duration and subjective performance measures (a finding also reported by Ali and Sim, 1999). The contrasting findings perhaps indicate that although, in general, there will be significant and positive correlation between objective and subjective measures of IJV performance, this relationship is unstable between data sets and measures of subjective performance. Nevertheless, and while not unambiguous, the findings of this study do add weight to the view that objective and subjective measures of IJV performance are positively correlated.

Following Hatfield et al. (1998) regression analysis was also used to test H1. Hatfield et al. (1998: 363) note that existing theory does not predict cause and effect relationships among the variables under study, so all possible paired combinations of objective and global subjective performance measures were examined. If standardized betas are positive and the F-values of the regression models are significant, then the performance measures are positively related. The results are shown in Table 8.3. *Overall satisfaction* and IJV survival are positively and significantly ($p < 0.01$) related. The *performance index* and IJV survival are negatively and non-significantly related. *Overall satisfaction* and IJV duration, and *performance index* and IJV duration are positively and significantly related ($p < 0.10$). Surprisingly, the regression pair of IJV survival and IJV duration are found to be positively but not significantly related, which is in contrast to the positively and significantly related finding of Hatfield et al. (1998) and the negatively and significantly related finding of Ali and Sim (1999). Also included as a regression pair in Table 8.3 are *overall satisfaction* and the *performance index*, which are positively and significantly related. As far as H1 is concerned, the regression results are similar to those shown by correlation analysis, and largely support the hypothesis.

Hypothesis 2

H2 may also be assessed by the findings presented in Table 8.3, which indicate a degree of support for the hypothesis. Excluding the regression model containing the two subjective performance measures, the regressions indicate

Table 8.3 Regression analysis for variable sets

Variables	All Partners			
	Standardized beta	R^2	F	df
Overall satisfaction IJV survival	0.350***	0.123	8.386***	61
Overall satisfaction IJV duration	0.392***	0.154	10.901***	61
Performance index IJV survival	−0.010	0.000	0.005	49
Performance index IJV duration	0.503***	0.253	16.228***	49
IJV survival IJV duration	0.052	0.003	0.209	79
Overall satisfaction Performance index	0.837***	0.701	112.605***	49

Note: *** $p < 0.01$

either no significant relationship, or a significant relationship, but with no measure explaining the majority (that is over 50 per cent) of the variance in another measure. All the R^2s for the significant regressions were 0.253 or lower, which in line with Hatfield et al.'s (1998) findings indicates that the variables measure different phenomena. For instance, while the *performance index* and IJV Duration are positively related, the R^2 of less than 0.30 indicates that duration is affected by other factors. The exception is the regression of the two subjective performance measures, which explains well over 50 per cent of the variance. Not surprisingly this finding indicates that it cannot be concluded that *overall satisfaction* and the *performance index* measure different phenomena.

Hypothesis 3

Findings relating to H3a are shown in Table 8.4. The *overall satisfaction* measure and the *performance index* measure evidence strong, positive and significant ($p < 0.01$) correlation among the partner firms. For the individual performance measures there are three significant positive correlations ($p < 0.10$ or better). Although weaker in strength, these findings are in line with similar correlations reported by Geringer and Hebert (1991). On balance these findings provide support for the view that there will be significant positive correlation among the parents' assessment of IJV performance.

Table 8.4 Spearman rank order correlations between assessments of performance

	n	UK partners and European partners	n	UK partners and IJV managers	n	European partners and IJV managers
Overall satisfaction	24	0.574***	30	0.587***	28	0.550***
Profitability	19	0.729***	26	0.791***	25	0.684***
Growth of sales	19	0.349	25	0.408**	24	0.438**
Market share	18	0.437*	21	0.178	22	0.563***
Efficiency	19	0.414*	28	0.527***	27	0.304
Quality	19	0.348	26	0.440**	25	0.414**
Performance index	16	0.695***	21	0.621***	20	0.588***

Notes
* p < 0.1; ** p < 0.05; *** p < 0.01

Findings relating to H3b are also shown in Table 8.4. Correlations between subjective performance assessment of UK partners and IJV managers are positive and significant ($p < 0.05$ or better), for all measures except the individual performance measure of market share. The correlations between UK partners and IJV managers tend to be stronger and more significant than those between the two partners.

Correlations between subjective performance assessment of European partners and IJV managers are positive and significant ($p < 0.05$ or better) for all measures except the individual performance measure of efficiency. Again the correlations between European partners and IJV managers tend to be stronger and more significant than those between the two partners.

While marginally lower in strength than the similar set of correlations reported by Geringer and Hebert (1991), they are in line with and supportive of their findings. This set of findings provides a good deal of support for H3b.

Findings relating to H3c and H3d are shown in Table 8.5. There are positive, strong and significant ($p < 0.05$ or better) correlations between perceptions of satisfaction of performance and reported satisfaction of performance among all elements of the IJV. These findings provide strong support for H3c and H3d. It is particularly noticeable that the correlations between the IJV manager's perception of the partners' assessment of satisfaction are very strong and significant.

Hypothesis 4

Results relating to H4a are shown in Table 8.6. Measuring cultural difference by culture clusters and assuming that the Northern European cluster differs less from the UK national culture than the Latin European cluster, there is support for H4a. All of the correlations for the Northern European culture are of the correct sign and four of the seven correlations are significant ($p < 0.1$ or better). The significant correlations relate particularly to the global measures of performance: *overall performance, performance index* and the individual measure of profitability, evidencing relatively strong correlations. For three of the four significant correlations in the Northern European cluster, the size of the correlation exceeds that for the equivalent correlation in the grouped data (see Table 8.4). In contrast, the Latin European cluster correlations are not significant, and two of the seven correlations have a sign contrary to that hypothesized. These findings are in line with those of Geringer and Hebert (1991). Using culture clusters as a measure of cultural difference provides strong support for H4a.

No support is forthcoming for H4a, however, when cultural difference is measured by the Kogut–Singh index. Grouping the three partner nationalities with the lowest cultural distance on this measure (Italy, the Netherlands and

Table 8.5 Spearman rank order correlations between perception of performance satisfaction and reported performance satisfaction

UK Partner's:	perception of European partner's satisfaction and European partner's reported satisfaction	0.717*** (n=24)
	perception of IJV managers' satisfaction and IJV managers' reported satisfaction	0.549*** (n=30)
European partner's:	perception of UK partner's satisfaction and UK partner's reported satisfaction	0.718*** (n=23)
	perception of IJV managers' satisfaction and IJV managers' reported satisfaction	0.475** (n=28)
IJV manager's:	perception of UK partner's satisfaction and UK partner's reported satisfaction	0.880*** (n=28)
	perception of European partner's satisfaction and European partner's reported satisfaction	0.637*** (n=27)

Notes:
** $p < 0.05$; *** $p < 0.01$

Table 8.6 Spearman rank order correlations between parent firms' assessments of specific aspects of IJV performance by (i) culture clusters and (ii) Kogut–Singh index of cultural distance

Pooled data	(i) Culture clusters					(ii) Kogut–Singh measure of cultural distance			
	n	Northern European	n	Latin European	n	Nearest cultures	n	Furthest cultures
Overall performance	11	0.717**	13	0.249	15	0.246	9	0.889***
Profitability	9	0.725**	10	0.129	12	0.432	7	0.852**
Growth of sales	9	0.281	10	0.209	12	0.309	7	0.423
Market share	9	0.339	9	0.399	11	0.320	7	0.816**
Efficiency	9	0.603*	10	−0.074	12	0.442	7	0.626
Quality	9	0.509	10	−0.004	12	−0.369	7	0.842**
Performance index	7	0.791**	9	0.284	11	0.430	5	0.975***

Notes:
* $p < 0.1$; ** $p < 0.05$; *** $p < 0.01$
Culture clusters: Northern European = Germany, Holland, Norway, Sweden. Latin European = France, Italy, Spain.
Kogut–Singh measure: Nearest cultures = Italy, Holland, France. Furthest cultures = Germany, Norway, Spain, Sweden.

France) identified as the 'Nearest cultures', no correlations are significant, with one correlation having a sign contrary to that hypothesized. In contrast, for those remaining partners identified as the 'Furthest cultures', five of the seven correlations are positive, strong and significant ($p < 0.05$ or better). Moreover, the size of each of these significant correlations exceeds the size of the equivalent correlation for the grouped data (see Table 8.4). These findings are in stark contrast to the findings for the culture clusters and are entirely contrary to the expectations of H4a.

Results relating to H4b are shown in Table 8.7. For the Northern European culture cluster, four of the seven correlations between UK parents and IJV managers are positive, strong and significant ($p < 0.01$ or better); the remainder of the correlations are positive and non-significant. Each of the significant correlations exceeds in strength the equivalent correlation for the grouped data (see Table 8.4). For the Latin European culture cluster, two of the seven correlations are significant ($p < 0.05$), with the remainder positive and non-significant. The two significant correlations do not exceed in strength the equivalent correlation for the grouped data (see Table 8.4). Of the two matching pairs of significant correlations between the two culture clusters, the correlation from the Northern European culture exceeds that of the Latin European culture. Overall, the correlations from the Northern European cluster are stronger and at a higher level of significance than the correlations from the Latin European cluster, providing support for H4b.

Considering H4b in terms of the Kogut–Singh measure of cultural distance, for the Nearest cultures, three of the seven correlations between UK parents and IJV managers are positive, strong and significant ($p < 0.05$ or better); the remaining correlations are positive but non-significant. Two of these three significant correlations exceed in strength the equivalent correlation for the grouped data (see Table 8.4). For the Furthest cultures group, four of the seven correlations are positive, strong and significant (at $p < 0.01$ or better); the remainder of the correlations are positive and non-significant, except for one negative and non-significant correlation. Three of these four significant correlations exceed in strength the equivalent correlation for the grouped data (see Table 8.5). Of the two matching pairs of significant correlations between the two culture groups, one correlation is greater in the Nearest cultures group and one correlation is greater in the Furthest cultures group. From the findings of the study it is difficult to conclude that the set of correlations from the Nearest cultures group are stronger and more significant than those from the Furthest culture group. Consequently no real support for H4b is forthcoming from the set of correlations based on the Kogut–Singh measure of cultural distance.

For H4a there is a high degree of support from the data when culture difference is measured by way of culture clusters, but no real support when measuring cultural difference by way of the Kogut–Singh measure of cultural

Table 8.7 Spearman rank order correlations between UK parent firms and IJV managements' assessments of specific aspects of IJV performance by (i) culture clusters and (ii) Kogut–Singh index of cultural distance

Pooled data	(i) Culture clusters					(ii) Kogut–Singh measure of cultural distance			
	Northern European	n	Latin European	n		Nearest cultures	n	Furthest cultures	n
Overall performance	0.733***	14	0.537**	16	18	0.601***	12	0.521*	12
Profitability	0.802***	13	0.632**	13	15	0.562**	11	0.822***	11
Growth of sales	0.211	12	0.331	13	15	0.381	10	0.308	10
Market share	0.134	9	0.316	12	13	0.337	8	0.061	8
Efficiency	0.437	14	0.457	14	17	0.556**	11	0.438	11
Quality	0.663**	13	0.080	13	15	0.214	11	0.647**	11
Performance index	0.622*	9	0.285	12	13	0.224	8	0.671*	8

Notes:
* $p < 0.1$; ** $p < 0.05$; *** $p < 0.01$
Culture clusters: Northern European = Germany, Holland, Norway, Sweden. Latin European = France, Italy, Spain.
Kogut–Singh measure: Nearest cultures = Italy, Holland, France. Furthest cultures = Germany, Norway, Spain, Sweden.

154

distance. For H4b there is some degree of support from the data when culture difference is measured by way of culture clusters, but more limited support when measuring cultural difference by way of the Kogut–Singh measure of cultural distance. The methods of measuring cultural difference employed in this study are better grounded than the ones adopted by Geringer and Hebert (1991) or Glaister and Buckley (1998a). In Geringer and Hebert's study, for their Canadian sample, cultural similarity was measured dichotomously, with cultural similarity considered to exist only if all the IJV's parent firms were headquartered in either Canada or the United States. As Glaister and Buckley (1998b: 149) note, it is difficult to determine the extent of cultural similarity/dissimilarity in Geringer and Hebert's study because they do not report the partner nationality of the Canadian sample. The measure of cultural similarity adopted by Glaister and Buckley (1998a) was based on the perceptions of the UK respondents as to whether or not the national culture of the foreign partner was different from that of the national culture of the UK, and if it was perceived to be different, whether or not this difference had an important effect on the overall performance of the IJV.

Clearly, the manner of measuring cultural difference is debatable. Several studies have employed the Kogut–Singh measure for a variety of purposes (for example, Kogut and Singh, 1988; Erramilli, 1991; Erramilli and Rao, 1993; Contractor and Kundu, 1998). For this study the measure has produced results that are counterintuitive and which raise questions regarding efficacy in studies of this kind. For instance, for the partner nationalities in the sample, on the Kogut–Singh measure the least cultural distance is that between the UK and Italy. This appears to be surprising, as on the basis of most national cultural attributes, there would be a reasonable expectation that the national culture of the Netherlands or of Germany would be closer to that of the UK than the national culture of Italy. The computation across the four concepts of culture identified by Hofstede, may in aggregate produce a measure of cultural distance that is perhaps less meaningful than the individual comparison of each of these concepts as separate measures of cultural distance. Further, the actual measure of cultural distance in terms of the index produced provides little guide as to what is a small cultural distance and what is a large cultural distance. In the Nearest cultures group, the three partner nationalities in the Kogut–Singh measure have a measured cultural distance of 0.91 (Italy), 1.87 (Holland) and 2.27 (France). The measure of cultural distance for the remaining partner nationalities (Furthest cultures), range from 2.34 (Germany) to 2.50 (Sweden). There is clearly an issue of where the cut-off point should be for the Nearest cultures. In this study the three nationalities with the lowest measure of distance were chosen as the Nearest cultures. But this was an arbitrary decision. There is no guide in this measure in an absolute sense to what is near or what is distant – there is only a relative distance measure based on the comparison with other nationalities. So although the greatest distance occurs between the UK and Sweden, it is not clear whether a distance of 2.5 is actually a large measure of cultural distance. Clearly, more thought needs to be given to the Kogut–Singh index as to what this measure actually signifies in terms of cultural distance.

CONCLUSIONS

This study has replicated and extended a number of findings regarding performance assessment of IJVs. The data from the study largely confirms the hypotheses. Although the study adds weight to the view that IJV objective performance measures and IJV subjective performance measures are positively correlated, care should be taken over assuming that this finding will hold for *all* samples and for *all* subjective performance measures. There is growing evidence that while IJV objective performance measures and IJV subjective performance measures are positively correlated, they measure different phenomena. This should provoke research initiatives that identify and examine the phenomena they measure. For example, what are the environmental conditions under which IJVs operate and what are the strategic perspectives of the partners that encourage duration?

There is evidence from this study that the subjective performance assessment of one element of the IJV matches that of the other elements, and that each element of the IJV has a good perception of the performance evaluation of the other elements. These findings have implications for the kinds of data that it would be legitimate to collect in order to assess IJV performance. Research costs and research time scales can be reduced by obtaining assessment of performance from only one element of the IJV, on the reasonable assumption that this element will be able to provide a good approximation of the other elements' assessment of performance. This particularly relates to global or overall assessment of performance, such as *overall satisfaction* or the *performance index*, reported in this study, rather than items of individual measures of performance. Moreover, IJV managers would appear to be able to provide reasonably reliable data on each partner's assessment of performance and hence would act as a good data source. These conclusions support those of Geringer and Hebert (1991). The proviso is that such assessment is likely to be more accurate in those IJVs where the partners are from similar national cultures than from those IJVs where the national culture differences are great. This in turn leads to the question of how to determine national cultural distance between partners. The evidence of this study would indicate that for IJVs involving partners in Western Europe, it is preferable to measure cultural distance on the basis of culture clusters than on the basis of the Kogut–Singh index.

9. Culture and the management of IJVs

INTRODUCTION

A paradox of co-operative activity between firms is that while differences in culture can create a barrier to effective co-operation, at the same time cultural diversity provides an opportunity to use the knowledge embodied in each partner's culture as a valuable resource for the alliance (Child and Faulkner, 1998: 229). However, until the barriers are removed, mutual learning, which provides access to the respective partners' culturally embedded knowledge, cannot occur. Discovering ways of bridging the distinctive cultures which partners may bring to an alliance is viewed as a major management challenge, which cannot be avoided if successful venture performance is to be achieved.

While the concept of culture has been used extensively in the management literature, the phenomenon is somewhat slippery. 'Complex, intangible and subtle, culture has been notoriously difficult to conceptualize and scale' (Shenkar, 2001: 519). There are many different definitions of culture and different types of culture; however, when examining diversity between international joint venture (IJV) partners it is usual to distinguish between 'organization culture' and 'national culture' (Parkhe, 1991). Co-operative strategies, such as IJVs, bring into a working relationship people from different partner organizations. These partner organizations will have developed their own distinct cultures, which embody shared attitudes and norms of behaviour. These organizational cultures will encourage employees to regard their organization as different from other organizations. Where the co-operating organizations come from different countries, their employees will also have a sense of belonging to distinct national cultures. National cultural diversity may be reflected in 'different patterns of behaving and believing, and different cognitive blueprints for interpreting the world' (Parkhe, 1991: 583), which will tend to exaggerate the sense of difference between the partners. Faulkner and de Rond (2000: 28) note that although the demarcations between corporate culture and national culture conceptions appear somewhat vague, one argued point of difference is that national culture resides mostly in values (Hofstede, 1991) while corporate culture is located primarily in practices. However, there is some support for the conjecture that corporate culture can modify the behaviour and beliefs associated with national culture (Laurent, 1986; Weber et al.,

1996), although not necessarily in the way of reducing its impact, as national culture may play a stronger role in the face of a strong corporate culture (Schneider, 1988).

Corporate and national cultures are viewed as crucially important in selecting management methods, strategies and structures (Hampden-Turner and Trompenaars, 1993). Firms of different nationalities will tend to introduce distinctive management practices. Heterogeneity between cultures may be a source of weakness in IJVs in that the greater the distance between partners' organization and national cultures, the more difficult it will be for them to cooperate because cultural distance gives rise to differences in accepted management practices and policy orientations. In contrast, it is also argued that firms from different cultures are able to gain much from each other in terms of learning. It is likely that both these views have validity depending on specific circumstances. The extent to which differences in culture pose a problem to the management of international strategic alliances (IJVs) is the focus of this chapter.

The remainder of the chapter is set out in the following manner. The next section provides a brief review of the literature and develops the research questions of the study. Section three provides the findings and discussion. Conclusions are in the final section.

LITERATURE REVIEW AND DEVELOPMENT OF RESEARCH QUESTIONS

Faulkner and de Rond (2000: 29) note that

> the organizational culture literature views culture as a deep-seated, sense-making medium, allowing for the allocation of authority, power, status, and the selection of organization members, providing norms for handling interpersonal relationships and intimacy, and criteria for dispensing rewards and punishments, as well as ways to cope with unmanageable, unpredictable and stressful events.

Keesing (1974) describes a culture as providing its members with an implicit theory about how to behave in different situations and how to understand others' behaviours in those situations. Also, Gannon (2001) notes that members of different national cultures learn different implicit theories to help them interpret their worlds. Shenkar (2001: 527) notes that staffing is not only a means of control, but also a venue through which groups and individuals bring their cultural properties into a system. In an IJV, for instance, foreign parent expatriates bring with them both the national and corporate culture of the parent while third country nationals recruited by the foreign parent are likely to bring the parent firm's culture into the venture, but less of its national culture (Shenkar and Zeira, 1992).

Luostarinen (1980: 131–2) defines cultural distance as 'the sum of factors creating, on the one hand, a need for knowledge, and on the other hand, barriers to knowledge flow and hence also for other flows between the home and the target countries'. Where co-operative strategies run against powerful cultural beliefs they are not likely to be implemented successfully (Schein, 1985), and consequently alliances that fail often appear to do so because of poor cultural fit (Faulkner, 1995). 'Fit' in this context means the extent to which different cultures are brought into a workable relationship that permits the IJV to operate without undue misunderstanding and tension between the partners or between the employees that are attached to the IJV. Different cultures may or may not reach such a fit depending on the intentions, goodwill and skills of the employees of the partner organizations (Child and Faulkner, 1998: 244). Cultural fit in part determines the extent to which organizations are able to co-operate and realize anticipated synergies critical to the venture's success (Aulakh and Madhok, 2002). Saxton (1997: 447) notes that organizational learning theory suggests that similarities between partners may affect alliance performance because they facilitate the appropriability of tacit and articulated knowledge. A good cultural fit will maximize the potential of the IJV and help deflect threats to its ongoing viability arising from misunderstanding and antipathy. Cultural fit also provides a basis on which mutual trust can develop.

Child and Faulkner (1998: 233) point out that national cultural differences can present barriers to co-operation at the level of simple misunderstanding, for instance differences in language and the interpretation of behaviour, and at the more fundamental level of conflicts and values. Where the socially embedded values held by partners clash, this may give rise to serious problems concerning the priorities for the IJV and how it is to be managed. In a partner country where universalistic values predominate, for example, what is good and right can be defined and always applies. In contrast, in a partner country where particularistic values predominate it is valid to take into account specific circumstances and to make exceptions. This would be the case especially if personal relationships and obligations were involved (Trompenaars, 1993). One implication of this is that an IJV formed between partners from countries that contrast a great deal on the universalistic/particularistic dimension will find it more difficult to establish mutual trust on which a successful relationship should be based. Without mutual trust, the risk of cheating and non-compliance with partners is greater (Williamson, 1979; Buckley and Casson, 1988).

More generally, cultural distance can lead to many operational problems, in the worst case leading to a breakdown in the working relations between partners. Hofstede (1980) suggested that although some cultural gaps were not very disruptive or were even complementary, differences between two cultures in uncertainty avoidance were potentially very problematic for international co-operation because of correlated differences in tolerance towards risk, formalization, and so on. Barkema et al. (1997) argue that an uncertainty avoidance gap is likely to be detrimental to IJV operation because uncertainty is an inherent characteristic of operating in a foreign environment and because such a gap implies contrasting expectations regarding the predictability of partner behaviour, also a key issue in IJVs.

According to Dickson and Weaver (1997) individualism/collectivism (Hofstede, 1980) has emerged as the cultural dimension most often associated with co-operative behaviour (Wagner, 1995). People with individualistic orientations believe that the self is the basic unit of survival, value independence and self-sufficiency, give priority to personal goals, and place high value on self-direction, social justice and equality. People with collectivist orientations emphasize the importance of belonging to a stable, select in-group, value co-operation with the in-group, and expect the group to help provide for the welfare of group members (Hofstede, 1980; Hui and Trinadis, 1986). Where one partner manages and organizes according to individualistic values, then great importance will be placed on quick decisions, individual responsibility, expression of individual views and goals, competition between employees and individual incentives. In contrast, partners who manage according to collectivistic principles will place high value on such things as taking time to consult and secure consent before making decisions, group or team responsibility, sharing common superordinate goals, a high level of interpersonal and interdepartmental co-operation, and systems of rewards that do not single out individuals (Child and Faulkner, 1998: 235).

Differences in the cultural backgrounds of the partners generally have been perceived as a threat to the survival of IJVs (Brown et al., 1989; Harrigan, 1988b; Shenkar and Zeira, 1992). Wilkof et al. (1995) noted that cultural clash has caused many IJVs to fail due to the inability of the partners to work seamlessly. Woodcock and Geringer (1991) argued that cultural differences produce inefficient principal–agent contracts. Lane and Beamish (1990) argued that cultural compatibility between the partners is the most important factor in the endurance of an international alliance. Consistent with this view, various studies (for instance, Barkema et al., 1996, 1997) have found that the chances of survival of IJVs are lower when the cultural distance between the home country of the expanding firm and the host country is large. Li and Guisinger (1991) found that US affiliates whose partners came from culturally dissimilar countries were more likely to fail. Using Hofstede's (1980, 1991) dimensions of cultural distance (uncertainty avoidance, power distance, individualism, masculinity and long-term orientation), Barkema and

Vermeulen (1997) report that differences in uncertainty avoidance and long-term orientation in particular cause problems. They found that these differences have a negative effect on long-term survival and decrease the likelihood that firms enter a foreign country through an IJV rather than through a wholly owned subsidiary. Apparently, these differences, which translate into differences in how IJV partners perceive and adapt to opportunities and threats in their environment (Schneider, 1989; Schneider and De Meyer, 1991), are more difficult to resolve than differences along the other three dimensions. They conjecture that cultural differences regarding power distance, individualism and masculinity are more easily resolved because they are mainly reflected in different attitudes towards the management of personnel, which is something firms can make explicit agreements about before entering the partnership.

Despite claims that cultural difference is detrimental to IJV success, empirical work relating to the issue is mixed. For instance, Park and Ungson (1997) examine the effects of partner nationality, organizational dissimilarity, and economic motivation on the dissolution of JVs. They reported that cultural distance in general did not have an effect on dissolution, but US–Japanese JVs lasted longer than US–US JVs. Prior relationships between partners appeared to negate some complexities arising from cultural differences. Opportunistic threat and rivalry appeared to be a stronger indication of the dissolution of JVs than organizational variables. Luo (1997) reported that the link between partners' sociocultural distance and IJV performance was not significant. Saxton (1997) found that similarities between partners with respect to specific organizational characteristics, including culture and human resources, were negatively related to alliance outcomes, and that organizational process similarities were negatively related to initial satisfaction. Saxton's findings contradict the popular idea that 'culture clash' negatively influences alliance potential. For Saxton the negative relationship suggests that although similarities in strategic factors such as manufacturing activities and markets are important to alliance success, it is not as important for a company to pick a partner that thinks in the same way. Furthermore, Saxton (1997: 456) argues that 'It is also possible, perhaps even likely, that these relationships are not linear. A certain degree of similarity may be necessary and desirable for understanding a partner. Too much similarity though could limit the benefits because nothing novel is being brought to the relationship.' Aulakh and Madhok (2002) found corporate cultural congruence had a significant positive impact on IJV flexibility, but did not have a direct impact on alliance performance; they also reported no significant effect of national cultural congruence on IJV flexibility or performance. They comment that this is notable given that, ever since Hofstede's landmark study, national psychic distance has commanded the bulk of the attention in international business research rather than organizational culture. Aulakh and Madhok (2002) conjecture that it is possible that the impact of globalization has resulted in greater convergence among those business segments of countries that participate in international economic activity in a more substantive manner. They conclude that 'This suggests that it is more important for firms and their managers to pay attention to within-firm criteria underlying compatibility rather than extra-firm contextual ones' (Aulakh and Madhok, 2002: 41).

The assumption that differences in cultures produce lack of 'fit' has been questioned. Shenkar (2001: 524) notes that not every cultural gap is critical to performance, with different aspects of culture being differentially critical to operations (Tallman and Shenkar, 1994). Also, as previously noted, cultural differences may be complementary and provide synergistic effects on performance. The notion of cultural distance employed in the literature is also problematic. Shenkar (2001: 520) argues that the appeal of the cultural distance construct is illusory, in that 'It masks serious problems in conceptualization and measurement, from unsupported hidden assumptions to questionable methodological properties, undermining the validity of the construct and challenging its theoretical role and application.' More generally, Osborn and Hagedoorn (1997) argue that measurement of compatibility between partners and congruency in partner cultural factors is more illusive than its definition. Compatibility can be viewed from a number of perspectives, including organizational fit, strategic symmetry, resource complementarities and IJV task-based factors.

In summary, the literature indicates that from a conceptual perspective the impact of cultural difference on the successful management and operation of IJVs is ambiguous, as cultural difference has the potential both for disruption and synergy. Perhaps not surprisingly, the empirical evidence on the impact of cultural difference in IJVs, having produced mixed findings, is inconclusive. Inkpen (2001) concludes that more research is needed in this area. In order to shed new light on the issue this chapter addresses the following research questions.

1. *To what extent is cultural difference an important problem in managing the IJV?*
2. *Are national cultural differences or corporate cultural differences more important in contributing to different views on the management of the IJV?*

FINDINGS AND DISCUSSION

The research questions were first examined by investigating the qualitative data. Interviewees were asked the extent to which problems had been experienced in managing the IJV due to differences in culture. The interview responses were analysed and subsequently coded as cultural difference posing 'no problem', 'little problem', 'moderate problem' and 'major problem' to the management of the IJV. These coded responses are shown in Table 9.1a, with a numerical summary of the responses shown in Table 9.1b. Only a small proportion of the interviewees (5 per cent) considered that cultural difference had been a major problem to the management of the IJV, while over half of the interviewees (55 per cent) reported that cultural differences had been 'no problem' or 'little problem' in managing the IJV.

It is clear from Tables 9.1a and 9.1b that the IJV partners view cultural difference as somewhat less of a problem than do the IJV managers, with 65 per cent of the partners (60 per cent UK partners, 70 per cent European partners) reporting that cultural differences posed 'no problem' or 'little problem' to the management of the IJV, whereas only 35 per cent of IJV managers have this view. In contrast 65 per cent of the IJV managers reported that cultural differences were a 'moderate problem' or a 'major problem' to the management of the IJV, while only 32.5 per cent of the partners (40 per cent UK partners, 25 per cent European partners) have this view. It is perhaps not surprising that problems of managing the IJV due to cultural difference are observed rather more by the IJV managers than by the partners. The IJV managers will be more sharply exposed to cultural difference between the partners and will have to accommodate to the cultural differences between each partner.

The extent of agreement in responses for each IJV on the perception of the problems to the management of the IJV caused by cultural differences is shown in Table 9.1a. A disagreement is assumed to occur between partners if one partner has reported 'no problem' or 'little problem' while the other partner reported 'moderate problem' or 'major problem'. The table shows that in 14 cases (70 per cent) there is agreement of perceptions between partners, indicating that a clear majority agree with the impact of culture on the management of the IJV. Table 9.1a also compares the responses of each partner to those of the IJV managers, again assuming there was disagreement in perception if one partner has reported 'no problem' or 'little problem' while the IJV manager reported 'moderate problem' or 'major problem'. The comparison of UK partners and IJV managers shows there was agreement in perception in nine cases (45 per cent), while agreement between European partners and IJV managers occurred in 11 cases (55 per cent) indicating a somewhat wider divergence of view between the partners and the IJV managers than between the partners themselves. It should be noted, however, that in seven IJVs (35 per cent) there was agreement on the problems of managing the IJV due to cultural differences across the three elements of the IJV.

Respondents were also asked if there was a 'better understanding today concerning how the IJV should be managed compared to when it was first established'. In one of the relatively new IJVs the respondents considered it

Table 9.1a Problems in managing the IJV due to cultural differences

IJV	UK partners	European partners	IJV managers	Partners	UKPs & IJVMs	EPs & IJVMs
1	Little problem	Little problem	Moderate problem	Yes	No	No
2	No problem	Little problem	Little problem	Yes	Yes	Yes
3	No problem	Little problem	Moderate problem	Yes	No	No
4	Moderate problem	Moderate problem	Moderate problem	Yes	Yes	Yes
5	Moderate problem	Moderate problem	Major problem	Yes	Yes	Yes
6	No problem	Moderate problem	Moderate problem	No	No	Yes
7	No problem	Moderate problem	Moderate problem	No	No	Yes
8	Major problem	No problem	Major problem	No	Yes	No
9	No problem	Little problem	No problem	Yes	Yes	Yes
10	Moderate problem	Moderate problem	Moderate problem	Yes	Yes	Yes
11	No problem	No problem	Moderate problem	Yes	No	No
12	Moderate problem	Little problem	Little problem	No	No	Yes
13	Moderate problem	Little problem	Moderate problem	No	Yes	No
14	Little problem	No problem	Little problem	Yes	Yes	Yes
15	Moderate problem	Moderate problem	No problem	Yes	No	No
16	Little problem	No problem	Little problem	Yes	Yes	Yes
17	Moderate problem	No problem	No problem	No	No	Yes
18	Little problem	Little problem	Moderate problem	Yes	No	No
19	Little problem	Little problem	Moderate problem	Yes	No	No
20	Little problem	Little problem	Moderate problem	Yes	No	No

Notes:
UKPs = UK partners
EPs = European partners
IJVMs = IJV managers

Table 9.1b Problems in managing the IJV due to cultural differences: summary table

	UK partners	European partners	IJV managers	Total
No problem	6	5	3	14
Little problem	6	9	4	19
Moderate problem	7	6	11	24
Major problem	1	0	2	3
Total	20	20	20	60

too early to say, but in all of the other IJVs, with one exception the respondents reported that there was a better understanding concerning how the IJV should be managed. In the exception (IJV17), the UK partner reported that there were 'moderate problems' in managing the IJV due to cultural differences, while the European partner and the IJV manager reported 'no problem'. To the extent that cultural difference does pose problems for the management of IJVs, this appears not to prevent a better understanding developing in regard to how the IJV should be managed. Respondents were further asked whether there had been many disagreements between the partners concerning how the IJV should be managed. In only four IJVs (20 per cent) was there clear agreement between the partners and IJV managers that there had been many disagreements. In three of these IJVs the consensus view was that there had been moderate problems in managing the IJV due to cultural differences. These findings indicate that there is only weak evidence of an association between problems in managing the IJV due to cultural differences and the number of disagreements between partners over the management of the IJV. Overall, the findings lead to the view that the difference in culture does not appear to have led to many disagreements over the management of the IJV.

With respect to the first research question, the analysis of the interview responses underlying Table 9.1a shows that cultural differences in most cases have not been an important problem in managing the IJV. Respondents recognize cultural differences, but for the most part these differences have at worst posed 'little problem' to the management of the IJV. The lack of impact of cultural difference was summarized in a number of instances:

IJV1: UK partner: 'There's certainly been no cultural barriers and the odd issues which have arisen – which have come out of either misunderstandings or different ways of doing things – have largely been resolved.'

IJV3: IJV manager: Frankly speaking we had some differences, but it never interfered in our relationship – in the management of the joint venture.

IJV3: UK partner: I was surprised about that actually because I'd always thought of the French as being much more socialistic than we are and much less hard headed in terms of squeezing profit out of the business. But their cultural attitude is very, very similar to ours so we didn't have differences or problems.

Turning to the second research question regarding the relative importance of national culture differences or corporate cultural differences on the management of the IJV, it should be recognized that in some instances this distinction was often difficult to maintain. The manager of IJV5 observed this: 'It's difficult to separate national culture and corporate culture, I mean what you know about Italy is only by what you see through your business, and for sure other businesses will be different.'

The natural inclination appears to first associate cultural difference as applying at the national level and in several instances it was only with prompting that respondents began to discuss corporate culture differences, for instance the manager of IJV1 remarked:

> I think both parties have been recognising the differences as a national difference, not a company difference but it may very well be that there is a company culture that is involved, that we can't really distinguish. In our case, we were not that experienced that we could make that distinction and probably not [the UK partner] either, you really need to have more partnership with that nation.

However, this was not universally the case, particularly when differences in corporate culture were obvious:

IJV20: IJV manager: 'It wasn't culture of the people, it's culture of the companies. Curiously the cultural differences of two races are nil I would say.'

Differences in corporate culture were most apparent when private sector firms were in partnership with state owned firms (for example IJV2). Difference in firm size and orientation also caused corporate culture clashes, for example, when a large multinational company teamed up with a relatively small domestic company (IJV19). Other often mentioned corporate culture differences concerned the apparently more short-term financial perspectives of UK partner firms. This comes together in the comment from the IJV manager of IJV8: 'In [European partner] management of the business was dominated by views of market share, long-term position and sales, whereas in [UK partner] it was dominated by short-term perspective on cash and profit.'

Respondents were asked to make the distinction between national culture differences and corporate culture differences and to assess which kind of cultural difference had the greatest impact on the management of the IJV. After summarizing the responses, they were read and re-read in order to categorize the respondents' views. The précis of responses, categorized according to whether the respondents reported that the impact of cultural difference on the management of the IJV was the same for national culture and corporate culture (NC = CC), greater for national culture than corporate culture (NC > CC), or greater for corporate culture than national culture (CC > NC) are shown in Table 9.2a. A summary of the responses in Table 9.2a is provided in Table 9.2b, which shows that just over half (51 per cent) of respondents consider that national culture and corporate culture differences have the same impact on the management of the IJV, with UK partners taking this view slightly more often than European partners or IJV managers. Approximately an equal number of respondents considered that national culture differences were more important (25 per cent) as those who considered corporate culture differences more important (23.3 per cent) to the management of the IJV.

Columns five to seven of Table 9.2a show the extent of agreement on cultural difference between the partners and the partners and IJV managers. In eight cases (40 per cent) the IJV partners agree on the nature of the cultural difference impacting the management of the IJV. Agreement between UK partners and IJV managers occurs in nine cases (45 per cent) and agreement between European partners and IJV managers occurs in 10 cases (50 per cent). There is agreement on the relative importance of national culture and corporate culture both between partners and IJV managers in only four cases (20 per cent).

In summary, the findings from the interview data indicate that there was not a predominant view from respondents that either national cultural difference or corporate cultural difference had a bigger impact on management of the IJV.

We next report the findings from the quantitative data analysis. Respondents were asked the extent to which they had experienced a range of problems in managing the joint venture. The problems, ranked by the mean value of the response, are shown in Table 9.3. Of the six problems identified in managing the IJV, that of cultural differences is ranked second, indicating that this is perceived as a relatively important problem compared with most of the other identified problems. However, the mean of the variable at 3.07 is almost at the mid-point of the scale. This indicates that while cultural differences are perceived as problematic to an extent, overall they do not appear to constitute a major problem for the respondents in managing the sample of IJVs. The results reported in Table 9.3 are for the sample as a whole. Comparing the responses of the UK partners with those of the European partners, there were no significant differences in means between the two partner groups. With respect to the first research question, findings from the quantitative data show that cultural differences are not the most important problem in managing IJVs and of themselves do not constitute a major problem.

Respondents were further asked how far they thought (i) differences in national culture and (ii) differences in corporate culture had contributed to differing views on the management of the IJV. The mean responses are shown

Table 9.2a Relative importance of national culture and corporate culture differences for managing the IJV

JV	UK partner	European partner	IJV manager	Partners	UK partner & IJV manager	European partner & IJV manager
1	NC > CC	NC = CC	NC > CC	No	Yes	No
2	CC > NC	CC > NC	CC > NC	Yes	Yes	Yes
3	NC = CC	NC = CC	CC > NC	Yes	No	No
4	NC > CC	NC > CC	CC > NC	Yes	No	No
5	NC > CC	NC > CC	NC = CC	Yes	No	No
6	NC = CC	NC > CC	NC = CC	Yes	Yes	Yes
7	NC = CC	NC > CC	NC = CC	No	Yes	No
8	CC > NC	NC = CC	NC = CC	No	No	Yes
9	NC = CC	NC > CC	NC > CC	No	Yes	No
10	NC = CC	NC > CC	NC > CC	No	No	Yes
11	NC = CC	NC = CC	NC = CC	No	No	Yes
12	NC = CC	NC = CC	NC = CC	Yes	Yes	Yes
13	CC > NC	NC = CC	NC > CC	No	No	No
14	NC > CC	NC = CC	NC = CC	No	Yes	No
15	NC = CC	CC > NC	CC > NC	No	Yes	Yes
16	NC = CC	CC > NC	NC = CC	No	No	Yes
17	NC = CC	NC = CC	CC > NC	Yes	Yes	Yes
18	NC = CC	CC > NC	NC > CC	No	No	No
19	NC = CC	CC > NC	CC > NC	No	No	Yes
20	NC = CC	NC = CC	CC > NC	Yes	No	No

Notes:
NC: National culture
CC: Corporate culture
= Same importance
> More important

Table 9.2b Relative importance of national culture and corporate culture differences for managing the IJV: summary table

	UK partners	European partners	IJV managers	Total
NC = CC	13	9	9	31
NC > CC	4	6	5	15
CC > NC	3	5	6	14
Total	20	20	20	60

Table 9.3 Problems experienced in managing the IJV

	Rank	Mean	SD
Problems due to different practices of managers	1	3.00	1.03
Cultural differences	2	3.07	1.10
Differences between partners' objectives or priorities	3	3.19	1.07
Attitudes or behaviour of foreign partner managers	4	3.21	1.04
Human Resource Management problems	5	3.53	0.99
Language barriers	6	3.77	1.08

Notes:
1. The mean is the average on a scale of 1 (= 'major problem') to 5 (= 'no problem').
2. SD = standard deviation.

in Table 9.4. Respondents were of the view that differences in corporate culture contributed more to the differing views on the management of the IJV than did differences in national culture. However, the difference was marginal with no significant difference in the mean responses (t value = 1.192; p = 0.238), indicating there was no difference of view regarding the relative importance of national culture or corporate culture towards contributing to differing views on the management of the JV.

The results reported in Table 9.4 are for the full sample of respondents. In comparing the responses of the UK partners to the European partners, there is no significant difference between the partner groups regarding the extent to which differences in national culture have contributed to differing views on the management of the IJV (UK partners: mean = 3.31, SD = 1.49; European partners: mean = 2.64, SD = 0.84; *t*-value = 1.483, n.s.). In contrast there is a significant difference among the partner groups regarding the extent to which differences in corporate culture have contributed to differing views on the management of the IJV (UK partners: mean = 3.50, SD = 0.96; European partners: mean = 2.86, SD = 1.02; t-value = 1.766, p < 0.10). These findings indicate that UK partners have

Table 9.4 *Differences in culture contributing to differing views on management of the IJV*

Extent to which differences in:	Mean	SD
(i) *national culture* have contributed to differing views on the management of the IJV	2.98	1.19
(ii) *corporate culture* have contributed to differing views on the management of the IJV	3.18	1.09

Notes:
The mean is the average on a scale of 1 (= 'none') to 5 (= 'great deal').
SD = standard deviation.

a marginally greater perception of differences in culture contributing to differing views on the management of the IJV than do European partners, and this difference is significantly greater than that of European managers in the case of corporate culture.

In order to explore further the extent to which views regarding differences in culture were associated with respondents' experience of problems in managing the IJVs, the variables measuring the extent to which differences in national culture and corporate culture had contributed to differing views on the management of the IJV were correlated with the variables measuring the extent to which respondents experienced problems in managing the IJV. The correlation coefficients are shown in Table 9.5. The findings indicate that the more problems in managing IJVs have been experienced, the more differences in culture are perceived to contribute to differing views on the management of the IJV. This relationship is significantly stronger for differences in national culture compared to differences in corporate culture for Human Resource Management (HRM) problems, language problems and cultural differences per se. This is perhaps not surprising, as national cultural differences are obviously manifested through language differences and national legislation relating to HRM practices. This finding also indicates that unless prompted to make the distinction, respondents in considering cultural differences most readily think of national cultural differences. In contrast, the relationship is significantly stronger for differences in corporate culture compared to differences in national culture for differences between partners' objectives or priorities and attitudes or behaviour of partner managers. There is a similar strength of relationship between both national culture and corporate culture differences and problems due to different practices of managers. This latter finding, concerning the most pressing problem experienced by respondents, implies

Table 9.5 Spearman correlations between the extent culture differences contribute to different views on IJV management and problems experienced in managing the IJV

	Extent to which differences in:	
Problems in managing IJV	(i) **national culture** have contributed to differing views on the management of the IJV	(ii) **corporate culture** have contributed to differing views on the management of the IJV
Problems due to different practices of managers	0.393**	0.396***
Cultural differences	0.611***	0.361***
Differences between partners' objectives or priorities	0.215*	0.351***
Attitudes or behaviour of foreign partner managers	0.285**	0.455***
Human Resource Management problems	0.372***	0.150
Language barriers	0.344***	0.218*

Notes:
Problems in managing IJV measured on a scale of 1 (= 'major problem') to 5 (= 'no problem').
Differences in culture contributing to different views on managing IJV measured on a scale of 1 (= 'none') to 5 (= 'great deal').
The way these scales are measured produces negative correlation coefficients: for ease of understanding the relationships, the minus signs on the correlation coefficients have been removed.

that national culture differences and corporate culture differences are similarly related to problems arising from different practices of management. Overall these findings would indicate that while differences in culture do impact on problems of managing IJVs, there is little to show whether national culture differences or corporate culture differences are a more important problem in managing the IJV. Rather the effects of the two types of culture impact in different ways.

The respondents were further asked if there was a better understanding today concerning how the IJV should be managed compared to when it was first established. The mean response was 3.57 (on a scale of 1 = 'not at all' to 5 = 'very much') showing in general a better understanding. There is a significant positive correlation between this variable and the age of the IJV ($r = 0.279$; $p = 0.031$). It would appear that through time IJV parents and managers come to a better understanding concerning how the IJV should be managed compared to when it was first established, which implies that the effects of cultural differences are ameliorated over time.

Management Issues

Some clearly find it difficult to accommodate to other cultures. The IJV manager of one of the ventures reported: 'I mean my boss, Mr X, didn't like staying for lunch in France, can you believe, at board meetings, he would like to have just gone to the airport and disappeared, which is an absolute travesty professionally.'

It is clearly necessary to recognize and identify managers who have problems with coping with cultural difference and to be proactive in countering its potential negative impact. It is also necessary to identify where it is likely to impact most in the organization. The view of one partner was that the problems of coping with cultural differences would tend be more severe, the more junior the manager:

> IJV1: European partner: Let's say firstly we take the top management, that's more international, and if we go down to middle management, I don't think it's a problem there either, there are several used to this and can handle everything. But the more you get down into the management, the worse the problem because, maybe they're not so used to tackling those issues, and having slightly less experience and a slightly smaller area to look at.

This indicates that companies should deliberately attempt to alleviate the potential problems of cultural difference by engaging in training. This was recognized by several respondents who reported that their organizations engaged in such activity.

IJV 1: UK partner: We have actually set up a multi-cultural course and put a lot of people through it including the secretarial and support staff who maybe don't travel but do have a need to link backwards and forwards. So we've tried to look on the partnership as a real benefit for both sides, a real win–win. We've tried to translate that to the members who are party to the activity and then we've tried to plug them together and get them to understand each other's cultures and attitudes.

The JV manager in this IJV echoes this:

IJV 1: IJV manager: We've actually had cultural seminars to understand differences between the two parties and tried it.. if we can't bridge them to, let's anyway understand them and recognize where they are to be able to deal with them as they appear and not view them as something that is a factual difference but more a perception and where are you coming from.

IJV4: European partner: We go to great lengths to overcome the Anglo/French cultural problem in that we have inter-company games between the people in Belfast and the people in Paris, we mix them up together, they go off on Scottish games in the Highlands and they even race bath tubs in the sea off the coast of Cannes together. So we try to make them work together as an integrated group.

While such training will ultimately be beneficial to the management of the IJVs, it still remains that not all aspects of difference are negative, as was identified in the literature review, and acknowledged by at least one IJV manager:

IJV10: IJV manager: 'Those disagreements have resulted in quite good debate and possibly even a better result on occasions for having those disagreements ... having disagreements makes both parties think in a different way.'

Clearly, the dilemma of cultural difference posed for management is to work towards resolving problems caused by this difference while at the same time attempting to benefit from the difference.

CONCLUSIONS

The strategic logic and operational challenges facing IJVs are conditioned by the cultural differences between the partner firms. Shenkar (2001: 529) points out, however, that the key issue is not the cultural distance between organizations but the extent of 'friction', by which is meant 'the scale and essence of the interface between interacting cultures, and the "drag" produced by that interface for the operation of those systems'. Hence while cultural distance may exist, the extent to which the cultural difference is problematic is a function of the friction this causes. An implication of this perspective would appear to be that cultural difference might not produce friction if the interface between IJV partners is managed appropriately.

The findings from this study show that for this sample of IJVs, while cultural differences do exist, they are not severe enough to cause significant problems for the management of the IJVs. The impact and severity of cultural difference should not be exaggerated. In Shenkar's terms, while cultural difference might exist, it has not been responsible for noticeable friction between the IJVs. Where problems do exist it was not firmly established whether national culture differences or corporate cultural differences were the chief cause of problems in managing the IJV.

The findings of this study are based on IJVs between UK partners and partners from Western Europe. The findings therefore may not be generalizable to samples of IJVs with combinations of partners from different geographical locations. Indeed, were the cultural distances between the partners greater than those exhibited for this sample, then more severe management problems may have been reported. Future research should examine such possibilities.

10. Summary and conclusions

Chapter 1 identified five special issues in the analysis and operation of IJVs. This book has been a sustained attempt to shed light on these key issues. They are: motivation, partner selection, management, control and performance. In addition, our research suggests that learning and cultural differences are also crucial elements in the operation and performance of IJVs. Interrelations between these variables are also of great importance and will be highlighted in this final chapter. The conclusion encapsulates our findings on these issues in the order of the chapters of the book.

Our results, and our contribution to knowledge, must be taken within the specific circumstances of our empirical investigation. The sample was drawn from UK international equity joint ventures with Continental European partners in manufacturing industries (or industries closely related to manufacturing) formed between 1990 and 1996 (see Appendix 1). All generalizations must be tempered by reference to these specific circumstances. The sample of 20 IJVs had the virtue that all three elements of the IJV (the UK parent, the Continental European parent and the IJV management) were interviewed, providing triangulation of all findings. We can be confident of the robust nature of our results within this sample.

STRATEGIC MOTIVES

The firms in our sample exhibited a mix of motives including both market entry and other motives, of which meeting competition, reducing costs and sharing complementary assets were the most important. Motivation is important in performance measurement, because the true test of the success of any business venture is how far it has met its objectives. Our results show that performance measures are relatively invariant to motivation, and that they correlate strongly with financial criteria. In addition, partners that have different motives for the formation of IJVs do not adopt different performance criteria.

PARTNER SELECTION

Choice of partner is a complex and multifaceted phenomenon. Task-related selection criteria refer to the operation skills and resources that a venture requires for competitive success. Task-related selection criteria reflect resource complementarity. Partner-related criteria include favourable past relationships (which are more important than the number of ties between the partners) and trust between top management teams. Companies use status indicators such as financial stability and size in selection. Selection is a synthesis of task- and partner-related criteria.

MANAGEMENT CONTROL

The issue of how a joint venture is controlled – its governance – relates to how it is managed, organized and regulated by agreements and processes and how partners control and influence its evolution and performance over time. Our research concentrated on the mechanisms, extent and focus of control exercised by the partners over the IJV. In our sample, partner firms use an array of control mechanisms. The most used method of control is the formal control mechanism of the IJV board. Supporting mechanisms are sub-board level discussions, appointment of key personnel, personal relationships and financial controls (the latter especially for UK partners). Within a particular IJV, different partners may well use different control mechanisms. In our sample, the extent of partner control is independent of the equity share of the partner (this must be tempered by the observation that the majority of our cases have equally split equity shares between the partners). Partner firms tend to concentrate control on particular aspects of the IJV concerned with their key skills and competencies.

DECISION-MAKING AUTONOMY IN IJVs

Chapter 5 presents a pioneering study of autonomy in IJVs. Using perceptual measures, we show that there is broad agreement amongst the managers of the three elements of the IJV that there is a relatively high degree of autonomy afforded to the IJV management teams. This unanimity is somewhat misleading because disaggregation of this broad finding reveals that there are low levels of autonomy in strategic decisions but rather more in operational decisions, and that perceptions are rather less unanimous on the relationship between autonomy and performance. Over time, IJV management teams cannot presume that there will be a simple increase of autonomy in decision making as the IJV matures. The balance between operational and strategic decisions is difficult to draw and to hold over time as the venture develops – there are some indications that increases in autonomy are conditional on performance.

LEARNING TO MANAGE IJVs

It has been asserted that the ability to learn is a key intangible asset. As there are special factors in managing IJVs, so firms can learn how to cope with managing an IJV and become 'IJV experienced'. Learning takes place in selecting partners, interfacing with partners and managing IJVs. Our research suggests that attention be paid to the IJV formation process, managing boundary relationships and IJV operational management. These elements are linked and their influence on performance is nebulous and complex.

PARTNERING SKILLS AND CROSS-CULTURAL ISSUES

Our overall results show that there is nothing inevitable about the success and failure of IJVs and that it is management that makes the difference. Particular categories of management skill identified are: inter-partner skills, 'downward skills' of managing the IJV managers, 'upward skills' of IJV managers in dealing with the partners and the skills of managing the IJV itself. Cultural sensitivity plays a huge role in cross-partner and IJV dealings, as do qualities such as transparency, diplomacy and honesty. Shared objectives and vision among the managers helps to create solidarity across the various management teams involved. There is much to learn at the micro level by examining the results of this chapter in detail and in the case vignettes.

PERFORMANCE

Assessing the performance of an IJV is not straightforward. Given the multiplicity of motives, the fact that motives may differ between partners and the lack of an unequivocal measure where non-profit maximizing behaviour may be involved, this is unsurprising. Consequently, there has been a focus in the literature on the alignment between objective (often financial) and subjective performance measures. In this sample, objective and subjective performance measures of the IJVs are positively correlated. Further, there is evidence that the subjective assessments of performance of one element of the IJV match those of the other two elements and that each element has a good perception of the performance evaluation of the other elements.

CULTURAL DIFFERENCES AND THE MANAGEMENT OF IJVs

The impact of cultural distance on the ability to manage an IJV has been the subject of debate. For our sample of IJVs, while cultural differences do exist, they are not severe enough to cause significant problems for the management of the IJVs. Cultural differences have been responsible for little observable 'friction'. The selection of IJVs with partners from 'Western' Europe obviously minimizes national cultural differences in the sample. However, managers are aware of potential cultural misunderstandings as the quotes in the chapter show and the vignettes further illustrate.

SUMMARY

This study has examined the multiple issues surrounding the management and performance of international joint ventures on a single database using a sample of UK–continental European equity joint ventures and taking the viewpoint of all the elements of the IJV; UK parent, European parent and IJV management. It has identified and shed light on the key issues in the analysis and management of IJVs – motives, partner selection management, control and performance which had previously been identified in the literature. In addition, it has focused on the emerging issue of learning and the sensitive question of cultural differences in the mix of factors that surround the complexities of modern IJVs.

Appendix 1 Research methods and sample characteristics

SAMPLE/DATA SOURCES

The unit of measurement is the IJV, which in this study constitutes three elements: two parent firms and the IJV itself. The study involves IJVs voluntarily formed between partners from developed market economies. The research questions were examined using a sample of UK IJVs with partner firms from Western Europe, formed between January 1990 and December 1996. A list of qualifying IJVs was obtained from the *Financial Times* Mergers and Acquisitions (FT M&A) File. This is an online database providing comprehensive details on international bid activity including mergers, acquisitions, share swaps, buyouts and buy-ins as well as JVs. The information is researched and collated on a daily basis from an array of major international newspapers and magazines, as well as press releases and corporate and stock market sources. It was assumed that this source represented a good approximation to the population of qualifying IJVs and that any selection biases would be minimal.

Next the *FT* data were grouped for homogeneity across a number of key characteristics. First, we selected ventures with partners from Western Europe. This decision was driven by the need to keep the interview costs of the project relatively low. We selected only two partner IJVs because of difficulties associated with analysing multiple partner IJVs, which may demonstrate significant differences from IJVs with two partners (Geringer, 1991). IJVs with activities involving manufacturing or activities closely related to manufacturing were selected to minimize differences across industry sectors. Recognizing that data for very new IJVs might not be meaningful, it was decided to select only those IJVs that had been in existence for at least one year at the time of data collection. A sample size of 20 IJVs was decided upon in order to achieve the aims of depth and coverage within the cost and time constraints of the study. We randomly selected an IJV and attempted to gain permission to interview one of the elements of the IJV. Once one element agreed to be interviewed the other two elements usually readily agreed to an interview also. If it was not possible to obtain

180   *Strategic business alliances*

an interview we randomly selected another IJV. While randomly selected, the sample should be viewed more as a 'purposeful sample'. According to Patton (1990: 169) 'The logic and power of purposeful sampling lies in selecting *information-rich* cases for study in depth. Information-rich cases are those from which one can learn a great deal about issues of central importance to the purpose of the research, thus the term *purposeful sampling*.' Erlandson et al. (1993: 83–4) note that an aspect of purposeful sampling is sample size. 'The basic rule is, "There are no rules for sample size." In qualitative research one is looking more for quality than quantity, more for information richness than information volume.'

PROCEDURES OF ANALYSIS

To enhance the credibility of the findings, and interpretations based upon them, the study adopted the technique of triangulation. Triangulation was achieved through the use of multiple and different sources of information on each IJV (partners and IJV managers) and different data collection modes (interview and questionnaire).

A multi-method personal interview and self-administered questionnaire approach was used to obtain data from each of the three elements of the IJV system (that is UK partner, western European partner, IJV management). We also obtained and reviewed the annual reports and accounts of the parent firms. The personal interview schedule and self-administered questionnaire were developed from pilot interviews with two UK partners in IJVs with foreign firms that did not form part of the qualifying data set. In the design and conduct of the interviews, account was taken of the 'native category' issue. By 'native' in this context we mean self-generated and valid in the local context (Buckley and Chapman, 1998). There can be no guarantee that words and categories are congruent from one context to the next, so we did not assume that managers shared our 'objective' understanding of categories or words such as 'autonomy'. Qualitative results for answers to questions were obtained only after a full exploration of the issue under discussion. For instance, in the interview schedule, the word 'autonomy' is used only once in a prompt to the final question, after a full exploration of the issues surrounding decision making (Briggs, 1984).

The sample size of 20 IJVs therefore involves 60 elements of study: 20 UK parents, 20 foreign parents and 20 IJV managements, and correspondingly 60 in-depth interviews. An attempt was made to locate and interview the most senior manager in each element of the IJV who had the greatest knowledge of the venture. The 60 interviews were conducted over the period October 1997 to October 1998. The job category of the interviewees showed that they were all in senior management positions. Interviewees were all fluent in English so all interviews were conducted in English by two of the authors. Each personal interview lasted for approximately one hour. Interviews were usually conducted in the interviewee's office, which facilitated the consultation of relevant documents if the interviewee needed to check details of the IJV. The interviews elucidated perspectives on a number of aspects of IJV activity. One intention of the interviews was to secure the managers' 'native' understanding of the categories under discussion. Open-ended questions and probes were used to elicit each participant's views, as well as asking managers to rank a predetermined set of criteria for some dimensions of activity. However, the interviews were highly structured following a predetermined pattern across the topic areas of research. Where acceptable to respondents the interviews were tape-recorded. Only three respondents declined to be tape-recorded. For these three interviews copious notes were taken of the responses which were transcribed shortly after the interview. Tapes were transcribed by secretarial assistants. The accuracy of transcripts was checked by the interviewing authors against the original recordings.

Following completion of the interview, the interviewee was invited to identify three senior colleagues in the same element of the IJV who had a good understanding of the research issues and relevant knowledge of the venture. Three envelopes, each containing a covering letter, copy of a self-administered questionnaire and a return envelope were left with the interviewee to pass on to the identified colleagues. The covering letter outlined the purpose of the research and promised confidentiality to respondents. The questionnaires were available in English, French, German and Italian. A total of 180 questionnaires were distributed. After one written reminder, a total of 63 self-administered questionnaires were returned, representing a response rate of 35 per cent. The job category of the questionnaire respondents indicates that the respondents were also in senior management positions. All of the respondents had personal involvement in the IJV on which they reported. We are confident that the two groups of respondents (from interviews and self-administered questionnaires) were able to present an overall perspective for each IJV.

DATA ANALYSIS TECHNIQUES

Analysis proceeded by way of parallel mixed analysis of the qualitative (interview) and quantitative (self-administered questionnaire) data. Known as triangulation of data sources, parallel analysis of qualitative and quantitative data is probably the most widely used mixed data analysis strategy in the social and behavioural sciences (Tashakkori and Teddlie, 1998: 128).

The narrative data (audio tapes) were converted into partially processed data (transcripts) before coding and analysis. The themes of analysis were established a priori. The highly structured nature of the interviews facilitated coding during the analysis stage of the study. Data was coded using typical content analysis procedures (Lincoln and Guba, 1985; Taylor and Bogdan, 1984). The authors independently coded the interviews. Discrepancies were resolved through consensus between the researchers. Interpretation errors are a potential validity threat (Kirk and Miller, 1986). We have attempted to limit this possible hazard by analysing data from multiple respondents and the use of multiple coders. The qualitative data analysis also included an element of transformation of the qualitative data to a numerical form, for example, frequency counts of certain themes and responses. To facilitate coding, data retrieval and qualitative data analysis, the NUD*IST software was employed. The quantitative data was analysed through statistical procedures.

This study embodies mixed methods that combine qualitative and quantitative approaches in the data collection stage. Tashakkori and Teddlie (1998: 44) refer to this as an 'equal status mixed method design', i.e. the study is conducted using both qualitative and quantitative approaches about the phenomenon under study. The study follows a parallel/simultaneous mixed method design (Tashakkori and Teddlie, 1998: 47), that is the qualitative and quantitative data were collected at the same time and analysed in a complementary manner. Studies using this approach generate narrative and numerical data that answer similar questions. Instances of agreement and disagreement between the two data sources are analysed with respect to the research questions. The qualitative data can be used to make the quantitative data more meaningful and understandable, and vice versa. Tashakkori and Teddlie (1998: 95) note that 'an increasing number of researchers are collecting both quantitative and qualitative data in a single study'. Several studies in the strategy field, for example, have successfully combined interviewing and questionnaires (as reported in Snow and Thomas, 1994). Data derived from each of the elements of the IJV overcomes criticism in the prior literature levelled against IJV studies that only gather data from one, or at best two, of the IJV elements (Osland and Cavusgil, 1998).

The characteristics of the sample are shown in Table A1. The average age of the IJVs is 3.92 years (SD = 1.86 years).

Table A.2 shows a list of the JVs, the nationality of the partner, and the industry of the JV.

Table A1 *Characteristics of the sample*

Characteristic	No.	%	Characteristic	No.	%
Interview data			**Questionnaire data**		
Responses			**Responses**		
UK partners	20	33.3	UK partners	16	25.5
Foreign partners	20	33.3	Foreign partners	15	23.8
IJV managers	20	33.3	IJV managers	32	50.8
Total	*60*	*100*	*Total*	*63*	*100*
Nationality of partner			**Nationality of partner**		
France	8	40	France	23	36.5
Germany	1	5	Germany	4	6.3
Holland	3	15	Holland	7	11.1
Italy	2	10	Italy	13	20.6
Norway	1	5	Norway	2	3.2
Spain	2	10	Spain	4	6.3
Sweden	3	15	Sweden	10	15.9
Total	*20*	*100*	*Total*	*63*	*100*
Industry of IJV			**Industry of IJV**		
Agricultural production/distribution	2	10	Agricultural production/distribution	4	6.3
Aircraft ground handling	1	5	Aircraft ground handling	4	6.3
Aircraft parts manufacture	1	5	Aircraft parts manufacture	5	7.9
Chemicals production	2	10	Chemicals production	4	6.3
Defence manufacture	3	15	Defence manufacture	9	14.3
Electrical parts production	1	5	Electrical parts production	2	3.2
Explosives production	1	5	Explosives production	2	3.2
Film production	1	5	Film production	3	4.8
Food manufacture/distribution	1	5	Food manufacture/distribution	3	4.8
Motor parts production	2	10	Motor parts production	8	12.7
Motor vehicle production	1	5	Motor vehicle production	3	4.8
Steel processing and distribution	1	5	Steel processing and distribution	3	4.8
Telecommunications	1	5	Telecommunications	2	3.2
Textiles production	2	10	Textiles production	11	17.5
Total	*20*	*100*	*Total*	*63*	*100*

Table A2   JV number by partner nationality and industry

JV number	Partner nationality	Industry
1	Sweden	Defence manufacture
2	France	Aircraft parts manufacture
3	France	Chemicals production
4	France	Defence manufacture
5	Italy	Textiles production
6	Holland	Film production
7	Norway	Motor parts production
8	France	Defence manufacture
9	France	Chemicals production
10	Sweden	Defence manufacture
11	Sweden	Steel processing/distribution
12	France	Electrical parts production
13	Germany	Textiles production
14	France	Food distribution
15	Spain	Explosives production
16	Spain	Agribusiness
17	Italy	Motor parts production
18	Holland	Telecommunication
19	Holland	Agribusiness
20	France	Aircraft handling

Appendix 2   Case vignettes: outlines of the sample IJVs

IJV 1 | **Industry**
UK partner: | Aerospace and defence
European partner: | Aerospace and motors
Joint venture: | Military aircraft
European partner nationality: | Swedish
Year of formation: | 1995
Equity share: | 50:50

Motives of UK partner: Market entry – new market for product

Motives of European partner: Non-market entry – strategic issue to raise volume: sharing of R & D costs, exchange of complementary technology, and to increase competitiveness

Performance outcomes:
UK partner: Satisfied
European partner: Satisfied
Joint venture: Satisfied

IJV 2 | **Industry**
UK partner: | Aerospace
European partner: | Aerospace
Joint venture: | Aircraft landing gear
European partner nationality: | France
Year of formation: | 1995
Equity share: | 50:50

Motives of UK partner: Non-market entry: sharing of R & D costs, access to (French) government funding, improving position in market, reducing competition.

Motives of European partner:	Non-market entry: sharing of R & D costs, spreading risk of large project, faster payback on investment, reducing competition.
Performance outcomes:	JV terminated in 1998 (French partner bought out UK partner's shares)
UK partner:	Poor performance overall – lower returns than expected
European partner:	Very satisfied
Joint venture:	Satisfied
IJV 3	**Industry**
UK partner:	Chemicals production
European partner:	Chemicals production
Joint venture:	Chemicals services
European partner nationality:	France
Year of formation:	1991
Equity share:	50:50
Motives of UK partner:	Market entry: faster entry, presence in new markets
Motives of European partner:	Market entry: to facilitate international expansion starting in UK
Performance outcomes:	JV terminated in 1997 (UK partner bought out European partner's shares)
UK partner:	Satisfied
European partner:	Satisfied
Joint venture:	Satisfied
IJV 4	**Industry**
UK partner:	Defence manufacture
European partner:	Defence manufacture
Joint venture:	Defence manufacture
European partner nationality:	France
Year of formation:	1993
Equity share:	50:50
Motives of UK partner:	Market and non-market entry: sharing of R & D costs, faster payback on investment, product diversification, access to new market.

Motives of European partner:	Market entry: access to new market
Performance outcomes:	
UK partner:	Dissatisfied (with the partner's contribution)
European partner:	Very satisfied (returns better than forecast)
Joint venture:	Rather dissatisfied

IJV 5 — **Industry**

UK partner:	Textiles and chemicals
European partner:	Textiles
Joint venture:	Synthetic fibres
European partner nationality:	Italy
Year of formation:	1992
Equity share:	50:50
Motives of UK partner:	Non-market entry: obtain economies of scale
Motives of European partner:	Non-market entry: reduce competition, share R & D and production costs
Performance outcomes:	
UK partner:	Very satisfied (excellent financial performance)
European partner:	Satisfied
Joint venture:	Satisfied (but unresolved problems remain)

IJV 6 — **Industry**

UK partner:	Visual Entertainments
European partner:	Media
Joint venture:	Television production
European partner nationality:	Netherlands
Year of formation:	1997
Equity share:	50.1% (UK partner), 49.9% (European partner)
Motives of UK partner:	Market entry: faster entry, international expansion, new market
Motives of European Partner:	Market entry: faster entry, international expansion, new market

Performance outcomes:
UK partner: Very dissatisfied (big losses)
European partner: Dissatisfied (deteriorating market environment)
Joint venture: Very dissatisfied (poor profits)

IJV 7   **Industry**
UK partner: Car parts production
European partner: Car parts production
Joint venture: Car parts production
European partner nationality: Norway
Year of formation: 1995
Equity share: 50:50

Motives of UK partner: Non-market entry: access to R & D facilities and manufacturing sources
Motives of European partner: Market entry: faster entry, international expansion, new market

Performance outcomes: JV terminated in 1997 (both partners sold majority shares to 3rd party)
UK partner: Very dissatisfied (poor profits)
European partner: Very dissatisfied (poor profits)
Joint venture: Very dissatisfied (poor profits and conflicts)

IJV 8   **Industry**
UK partner: Defence manufacture
European partner: Defence manufacture
Joint venture: Defence electronics
European partner nationality: France
Year of formation: 1996
Equity share: 49.9 (UK partner), 50.1 (European partner)

Motives of UK partner: Non-market entry: cost-sharing
Motives of European partner: Non-market entry: share R & D costs, manufacturing facilities, product rationalization

Performance outcomes:
UK partner: Reasonably satisfied
European partner: Satisfied
Joint venture: Fairly satisfied

IJV 9

UK partner:	**Industry** Chemicals
European partner:	Petroleum and chemicals
Joint venture:	Chemicals production
European partner nationality:	France
Year of formation:	1990
Equity share:	50:50

Motives of UK partner: Market entry: faster entry
Motives of European partner: Market entry: international expansion

Performance outcomes:
UK partner: Dissatisfied
European partner: Satisfied
Joint venture: Satisfied

IJV 10

UK partner:	**Industry** Motor manufacturing
European partner:	Motor manufacturing
Joint venture:	Motor manufacturing
European partner nationality:	Swedish
Year of formation:	1994
Equity share:	51% UK partner, 49% European partner

Motives of UK partner: Market entry: facilitate international expansion, new market
Motives of European partner: Market and non-market entry: new market, increase competitiveness

Performance outcomes:
UK partner: Fairly satisfied
European partner: Fairly satisfied
Joint venture: Dissatisfied (low profits, low efficiency)

IJV 11

UK partner:	**Industry** Steel production
European partner:	Steel production
Joint venture:	Steel processing and distribution
European partner nationality:	Swedish
Year of formation:	1994

Equity share: 50:50

Motives of UK partner: Market entry: new market
Motives of European partner: Non-market entry: to reduce competition

Performance outcomes:
UK partner: Very satisfied
European partner: Very satisfied
Joint venture: Satisfied

IJV 12 **Industry**
UK partner: Electrical products
European partner: Electrical products
Joint venture: Electrical parts production
European partner nationality: France
Year of formation: 1991
Equity share: 49% (UK partner), 51% (European partner)

Motives of UK partner: Non-market entry: to obtain resources from partner
Motives of European partner: Non-market entry: low cost manufacturing facility

Performance outcomes:
UK partner: Very satisfied
European partner: Very satisfied
Joint venture: Satisfied

IJV 13 **Industry**
UK partner: Chemicals and textiles
European partner: Chemicals and textiles
Joint venture: Textiles
European partner nationality: Germany
Year of formation: 1994
Equity share: 72.5% (UK partner), 27.5% (European partner)

Motives of UK partner: Market and non-market entry: new market and resources from partner
Motives of European partner: Non-market entry: economies of scale, product diversification and exchange of technology

Performance outcomes:
UK partner: Very dissatisfied (deteriorating market conditions)
European partner: Fairly satisfied
Joint venture: Dissatisfied

IJV 14 **Industry**
UK partner: Dairy products
European partner: Dairy products
Joint venture: Dairy products distribution
European partner nationality: France
Year of formation: 1991
Equity share: 49% (UK partner), 51% (European partner)

Motives of UK partner: Market entry: to enable faster entry
Motives of European partner: Market entry: to enable faster entry

Performance outcomes:
UK partner: Satisfied
European partner: Very satisfied
Joint venture: Very satisfied

IJV 15 **Industry**
UK partner: Explosives
European partner: Explosives
Joint venture: Commercial explosives
European partner nationality: Spain
Year of formation: 1995
Equity share: 80% (UK partner), 20% (European partner)

Motives of UK partner: Market and non-market entry: faster entry and to overcome national regulations

Motives of European partner: Non-market entry: resources and technology of partner, to increase market share

Performance outcomes:
UK partner: Very dissatisfied (low profits, low market share)

European partner:	Very dissatisfied (low profits, low market share, low efficiency)
Joint venture:	Satisfied

IJV 16

	Industry
UK partner:	Agribusiness
European partner:	Fruit and vegetable grower
Joint venture:	Agricultural produce
European partner nationality:	Spain
Year of formation:	1996
Equity share:	51% (UK partner), 49% (European partner)
Motives of UK partner:	Non-market entry: share R & D costs, production facilities, faster payback on investment, reduce transport costs
Motives of European partner:	Non-market entry: spread risks, share R & D costs, economies of scale, product diversification
Performance outcomes:	
UK partner:	Satisfied
European partner:	Satisfied
Joint venture:	Satisfied

IJV 17

	Industry
UK partner:	Engineering components
European partner:	Engineering components
Joint venture:	Aluminium castings
European partner nationality:	Italy
Year of formation:	1996
Equity share:	50:50
Motives of UK partner:	Market entry: new market
Motives of European partner:	Non-market entry: resources of partner, increase competitiveness
Performance outcomes:	JV terminated in 1997 – UK partner bought out European partner
UK partner:	Dissatisfied (failed to meet plan)
European partner:	Dissatisfied (slow returns)
Joint venture:	Very dissatisfied

IJV 18
UK partner:	**Industry**
	Telecommunications
European partner:	Railways
Joint venture:	Telecommunications
European partner nationality:	Netherlands
Year of formation:	1997
Equity share:	50:50

Motives of UK partner: Non-market entry: to obtain licence
Motives of European partner: Market and non-market entry: new market, product diversification, partner expertise

Performance outcomes:
UK partner: Satisfied
European partner: Less than satisfied (higher than expected losses)
Joint venture: Dissatisfied

IJV 19
	Industry
UK partner:	Bioscience
European partner:	Sugar refining
Joint venture:	Agrochemicals
European partner nationality:	Netherlands
Year of formation:	1996
Equity share:	50:50

Motives of UK partner: Non-market entry: share R & D costs, economies of scale, complementary technology

Motives of European partner: Non-market entry: share R & D costs, economies of scale, complementary technology

Performance outcomes:
UK partner: Satisfied (good returns, desirable strategic direction)
European partner: Satisfied (good returns)
Joint venture: Less satisfied (concerns over the long term)

IJV 20
	Industry
UK partner:	Airport ground handling services
European partner:	Airline

Joint venture: Airport ground handling services
European partner nationality: France
Year of formation: 1996
Equity share: 49% (UK partner), 51% (European partner)

Motives of UK partner: Market entry: new market, faster entry, overcome regulations
Motives of European partner: Non-market entry: enhance position in market

Performance outcomes:
UK partner: Satisfactory (good efficiency and quality)
European partner: Satisfactory (good profits and sales growth)
Joint venture: Very satisfactory (committed staff)

References

Ali, M.Y. and A.B. Sim (1999), 'Assessing measures of performance of international joint ventures: Evidence from a developing country context', ANZIBA Annual Conference Proceedings, *International Business Dynamics of the New Millennium*, 30 September–2 October, pp. 23–33.

Anand, B.N. and T. Khanna (2000), 'Do firms learn to create value? The case of alliances', *Strategic Management Journal*, **21**, 295–315.

Anderson, E. (1990), 'Two firms, one frontier: On assessing joint venture performance'. *Sloan Management Review*, **31**(2), 19–30.

Argyris, C. and D. Schon (1978), *Organizational Learning*, London: Addison-Wesley.

Arino, A. (1997), 'Veracity and commitment: Co-operative behaviour in first-time collaborative ventures'. in P.W. Beamish and J.P. Killing (eds), *Co-operative Strategies: European Perspectives*, San Francisco: The New Lexington Press, pp. 22–56.

Arrow K.J. (1962), 'The economic implications of learning by doing', *Review of Economic Studies*, **29**, 155–73.

Arrow, K.J. (1985), 'The economics of agency', in J.W. Prath and R.J. Zeckhauser (eds), *Principals and Agents: The Structure of Business*. Harvard Business School Press: Boston, MA.

Attewell, P. (1990), 'What is skill?', *Work and Occupations*, **17**, 422–48.

Aulakh, P.S. and A. Madhok (2002), 'Co-operation and performance in international alliances: The critical role of flexibility', in Farok J. Contractor and Peter Lorange (eds), *Co-operative Strategies and Alliances*, Oxford: Elsevier, Chapter 2, pp. 25–48.

Barkema, Harry G. and Freek Vermeulen (1997), 'What differences in the cultural backgrounds of partners are detrimental for international joint ventures?', *Journal of International Business Studies*, 4th Quarter, 845–64.

Barkema, Harry G., John H.J. Bell and Johannes M. Pennings (1996), 'Foreign entry, cultural barriers, and learning', *Strategic Management Journal*, **17**, 151–66.

Barkema, Harry G., Oded Shenkar, Frank Vermeulen and John H.J. Bell (1997), 'Working abroad, working with others: How firms learn to operate international joint ventures', *Academy of Management Journal*, **40**(2), 426–42.

Barney, J.B. (1991), 'Firm resources and sustained competitive advantage', *Journal of Management*, **17**, 99–120.

Beamish, P.W. (1985), 'The characteristics of joint ventures in developed and developing countries', *Columbia Journal of World Business*, **20**(3), 13–19.

Beamish, P.W. (1988), *Multinational Joint Ventures in Developing Countries*, London: Routledge.

Beamish P.W. and J.C. Banks (1987), 'Equity joint venture and the theory of the multinational enterprise', *Journal of International Business Studies*, **19**(2), 1–16.

Beamish, P.W. and A. Delios (1997a), 'Incidence and propensity of alliance formation', in P.W. Beamish and J.P. Killing (eds), *Co-operative Strategies: Asian Pacific Perspectives,* San Francisco: The New Lexington Press, Chapter 4, pp. 91–114.

Beamish, P.W. and A. Delios (1997b), 'Improving joint venture performance through congruent measures of success', in Paul W. Beamish and J. Peter Killing (eds), *Co-operative Strategies: European Perspectives*, San Francisco: The New Lexington Press, Chapter 5, pp. 103–27.

Beamish, P.W. and Andrew Inkpen (1995), 'Keeping international joint ventures stable and profitable', *Long Range Planning*, **28**(3), 26–36.

Ben-Porath, Y. (1980), 'The F-connection: Families, friends, and firms and the organization of exchange', *Population and Development Review*, **6**, 1–30.

Blau, P.M. (1964), Exchange and Power in Social Life, New York: Wiley.

Bleeke, J., and D. Ernst (1993a), *Collaborating to Compete Using Strategic Alliances and Acquisitions in the Global Marketplace*, New York: Wiley.

Bleeke, J. and D. Ernst (1993b), 'The way to win in cross-border alliances', *Harvard Business Review* (Nov./Dec.), 129–35.

Blodgett, L.L. (1991a), 'Towards a resource-based theory of bargaining power in international joint ventures', *Journal of Global Marketing*, **5**(1/2), 35–54.

Blodgett, L.L. (1991b), 'Partner contributions as predictors of equity share in international joint ventures', *Journal of International Business Studies*, **22**, 63–78.

Blodgett, L.L. (1992), 'Factors in the instability of international joint ventures: An event history analysis', *Strategic Management Journal*, **13**, 475–81.

Blois, K.J. (1972), 'Vertical quasi-integration', *Journal of Industrial Economics*, **20**, 253–72.

Bourdieu, P. and L. Wacquant (1992), *An Invitation to Reflexive Sociology*, Chicago, IL: University of Chicago Press.

Briggs, C.L. (1984), 'Learning how to ask: Native metacommunicative competence and the incompetence of fieldworkers', *Language in Society*, **13**, 1–28.

Brooke, Michael Z. (1984), *Centralization and Autonomy: A Study in Organization Behaviour*, London: Holt, Rinehart and Winston.

Brown, L.T., A.M. Rugman and A. Verbeke (1989), 'Japanese joint ventures with western multinationals: Synthesising the economic and cultural explanations of failure', *Asia Pacific Journal of Management*, **6**(2), 225–42.

Buchel, B., C. Prange, G. Probst and C-C. Ruling (1998), *International Joint Venture Management: Learning to Co-operate and Co-operating to Learn*, Singapore: Wiley.

Buckley, P.J. (1996), 'The role of management in international business theory', *Management International Review*, **36**(1) (Special issue), 7–54.

Buckley, P.J. (1997), 'Cross border governance in multinational enterprises', in S. Thompson and M. Wright (eds), *Corporate Governance: Economic, Management and Financial Issues*, Oxford: Oxford University Press.

Buckley, P.J. and M.J. Carter (1999), ' Managing cross-border complementary knowledge', *International Studies of Management and Organisation*, **28**(1), Spring, 80–104.

Buckley, P.J. and M. Casson (1976), *The Future of the Multinational Enterprise*, London: Macmillan.

Buckley, P.J. and M. Casson (1988), 'A theory of co-operation in international business', in F.J. Contractor and P. Lorange (eds), *Co-operative Strategies in International Business*, Lexington, MA: Lexington Books.

Buckley, P.J. and M. Casson (1996), 'An economic model of international joint venture strategy', *Journal of International Business Studies*, **27**(5), 849–76.

Buckley, P.J. and M. Casson (1998a), 'Analyzing foreign market entry strategies: Extending the internalization approach', *Journal of International Business Studies*, **29**(3), 539–61.

Buckley, P.J. and M. Casson (1998b), 'Models of the multinational enterprise', *Journal of International Business Studies*, **29**(1), 21–44.
Buckley, P.J. and M. Chapman (1996), 'Wise before the event: The creation of corporate fulfilment', *Management International Review*, **36**(1) (Special issue), 95–110.
Buckley, P.J. and M. Chapman (1997), 'The perception and measurement of transaction costs', *Cambridge Journal of Economics*, **21**(2), March, 127–45.
Buckley, P.J. and M. Chapman (1998), 'The use of "native categories" in management research', *British Journal of Management*, **8**(4), 283–99.
Buckley, P.J. and S. Young (1993), 'The growth of global business: Implications and research agendas for the 1990s', in H. Cox, J. Clegg and G. Ietto-Gilles (eds), *The Growth of Global Business*, London: Routledge.
Burgers, W.P., C.W.L. Hill and W.C. Kim (1993), 'A theory of global strategic alliances: The case of the global auto industry', *Strategic Management Journal*, **14**(6), 419–32.
Burt, R.S. (1992), *Structural Holes*, Cambridge, MA: Harvard University Press.
Burton, F.N. and F.H. Saelens (1982), 'Partner choice and linkage characteristics of international joint ventures in Japan', *Management International Review*, **22**(2), 20–29.
Casson, M. (1994), 'Internationalization as a learning process: A model of corporate growth and diversification', in V.N. Balasubramanyam and D. Sapsford (eds), *The Economics of International Investment*, Aldershot, UK and Brookfield, US: Edward Elgar.
Chan, S., J. Kensinger, A. Keown and J. Martin (1997), 'Do strategic alliances create value?', *Journal of Financial Economics*, **46**, 199–221.
Child, J. and D.O. Faulkner (1998), *Strategies of Co-operation: Managing Alliances, Networks, and Joint Ventures*, Oxford: Oxford University Press.
Child, J. and L. Markoczy (1993), 'Host country managerial behaviour and learning in Chinese and Hungarian joint ventures', *Journal of Management Studies*, **30**, 611–31.
Child, J., Y. Yan and Y. Lu (1997), 'Ownership and control in Sino-foreign joint ventures', in Paul W. Beamish and J. Peter Killing (eds), *Co-operative Strategies: Asian Pacific Perspectives*, San Francisco: The New Lexington Press, Chapter 8, pp. 181–225.
Choi, C.J. and S.H. Lee (1997), 'A knowledge-based view of co-operative interorganizational relationships', in Paul W. Beamish and J. Peter Killing (eds) *Co-operative Strategies: European Perspectives*, San Francisco: The New Lexington Press, Chapter 2, pp. 33–58.
Chung, S., H. Singh and K. Lee (2000), 'Complementarity, status similarity and social capital as drivers of alliance formation', *Strategic Management Journal*, **21**, 1–22.
Coase, R.H. (1937), 'The nature of the firm', *Economica*, **4**, 386–405.
Cockburn, C. (1991) *Brothers: Male Dominance and Technological Change*, London: Pluto Press.
Cohen, W.M. and D.A. Levinthal (1990), 'Absorptive capacity: A new perspective on learning and innovation', *Administrative Science Quarterly*, **35**, 128–52.
Cohen, W.M. and D.A. Levinthal (1994), 'Fortune favors the prepared mind', *Management Science*, **40**, 227–51.
Coleman, J.S. (1990) *Foundations of Social Theory*, Cambridge, MA: Harvard University Press.
Contractor, F.J. and S.K. Kundu (1998), 'Modal choice in a world of alliances: Analysing organisational forms in the international hotel sector', *Journal of International Business Studies*, **29**(2), 325–58.

Contractor, F.J. and P. Lorange (1988), 'Why should firms co-operate? The strategic and economics basis for co-operative ventures', in F.J. Contractor and P. Lorange (eds) *Co-operative Strategies in International Business*, Lexington, MA: Lexington Books, pp. 3–30.

Dacin, M.T., M.A. Hitt and E. Levitas (1997), 'Selecting partners for successful international alliances: Examination of US and Korean firms', *Journal of World Business*, **32**(1), 3–16.

Dickson, P.H. and K.M. Weaver (1997), 'Environmental determinants and individual-level moderators of alliance use', *Academy of Management Journal*, **40**(2), 404–25.

Dodgson M. (1991), 'Technology learning, technology strategy and competitive pressures', *British Journal of Management*, **2**(3), 132–49.

Dodgson M. (1993), 'Organizational learning: A review of some literatures', *Organization Studies*, **14**(3), 375–94.

Doz, Y.L. (1988), 'Technology partnerships between larger and smaller firms: Some critical issues', in F.J. Contractor and P. Lorange (eds), *Co-operative Strategies in International Business*, Lexington, MA: Lexington Books, pp. 317–38.

Doz, Y. and G. Hamel (1998), *Alliance Advantage: The Art of Creating Value Through Partnering*, Boston, MA: Harvard Business School Press.

Dussauge, P. and B. Garrette (1995), 'Determinants of success in international strategic alliances: evidence from the global aerospace industry', *Journal of International Business Studies*, **26**(3), 505–30.

Dussauge, P., B. Garrette and W. Mitchell (2000), 'Learning from competing partners: Outcomes and durations of scale and link alliances in Europe, North America and Asia', *Strategic Management Journal*, **21**(2), 99–126.

Elg, U. (2000), 'Firms' home-market relationships: Their role when selecting international alliance partners', *Journal of International Business Studies*, **31**(1), 169–77.

Ellis, H.C. (1965), *The Transfer of Learning*, New York: Macmillan.

Erramilli, M.K. and C.P. Rao (1993), 'Service firms' international entry-mode choice: A modified transaction-cost analysis approach', *Journal of Marketing*, **57** (July), 19–38.

Erlandson, D.A., E.L. Harris, B.L. Skipper and S.D. Allen (1993), *Doing Naturalistic Inquiry: A Guide to Methods*, Newbury Park, CA: Sage.

Estes, W.K. (1970), *Learning Theory and Mental Development*, New York: Academic Press.

Farr, C.M. and W.A. Fischer (1992), 'Managing international high technology co-operative projects', *R&D Management*, **22**(1), 55–67.

Faulkner, D.O. (1995), *International Strategic Alliances: Co-operating to Compete*, Maidenhead: McGraw-Hill.

Faulkner, D.O. and M. de Rond (2000), 'Perspectives on co-operative strategy', in David O. Faulkner and Mark de Rond (eds), *Co-operative Strategy: Economic, Business and Organizational Issues*, Oxford: Oxford University Press, pp. 3–39.

Fiol, C. and M. Lyles (1985), 'Organizational learning', *Academy of Management Review*, **10** (4), 803–13.

Frayne, C.A. and J.M. Geringer (1990), 'The strategic use of human resource management practices as control mechanisms in international joint ventures', *Research in Personnel and Human Resources Management*, supplement 2, 53–69.

Gannon, M. (1993), 'Towards a composite theory of foreign market entry mode choice: The role of marketing strategy variables', *Journal of Strategic Marketing*, **1**(1), 41–54.

Gannon, M.J. (2001), *Understanding Global Cultures* (2nd edn), Thousand Oaks, CA: Sage Publications.

Garratt, R. (1987), *The Learning Organization*, London: Fontana.
Geringer, J.M. (1988), *Joint Venture Partner Selection: Strategies for Developed Countries*, Westport, CT: Quorom Books.
Geringer, J.M. (1990), *Trends and Traits of Canadian Joint Ventures*, Ottawa: Investment Canada.
Geringer, J.M. (1991), 'Strategic determinants of partner selection criteria in international joint ventures', *Journal of International Business*, **22**(1), 41–62.
Geringer, J.M. (1998), 'Assessing replication and extension. A commentary on Glaister and Buckley: Measures of performance in UK international alliances', *Organization Studies*, **19**(1), 119–38.
Geringer, J.M. and L. Hebert (1989), 'Control and performance of international joint ventures', *Journal of International Business Studies*, **20**(2), 235–54.
Geringer, J.M. and L. Hebert (1991), 'Measuring performance of international joint ventures', *Journal of International Business Studies*, **22**(2), 249–63.
Geringer, J. Michael and C. Patrick Woodcock (1995), 'Agency costs and the structure and performance of international joint ventures', *Group Decision and Negotiation*, **4**, 453–67.
Glaister, K.W. (1995), 'Dimensions of control in UK international joint ventures', *British Journal of Management*, **6**(2), 77–96.
Glaister K.W. (1996), 'Theoretical perspectives on strategic alliance formation', in P.E. Earl (ed.), *Management, Marketing, and the Competitive Process*, Cheltenham, UK and Brookfield, USA: Edward Elgar, Chapter 4, pp. 78–111.
Glaister, K.W. and P.J. Buckley (1994), 'UK international joint ventures: An analysis of patterns of activity and distribution', *British Journal of Management*, **5**(1), 33–51.
Glaister, K.W. and P.J. Buckley (1996), 'Strategic motives for international alliance formation', *Journal of Management Studies*, **33**(3), 301–32.
Glaister, K.W. and P.J. Buckley (1997), 'Task-related and partner-related selection criteria in UK international joint ventures', *British Journal of Management*, **8**, 199–222.
Glaister, K.W. and P.J. Buckley (1998a), 'Measures of performance in UK international alliances', *Organization Studies*, **19**(1), 89–118.
Glaister, K.W. and P.J. Buckley (1998b), 'Replication with extension: Response to Geringer', *Organization Studies*, **19**(1), 139–54.
Glaister, K.W., R. Husan and P.J. Buckley (1998), 'UK international joint ventures with the Triad: Evidence for the 1990s', *British Journal of Management*, **9**, 169–80.
Gomes-Casseres, Benjamin (1987), 'Joint venture instability: Is it a problem?', *Columbia Journal of World Business*, **22**(2), 97–107.
Gomes-Casseres, B. (1996), *The Alliance Revolution*, Cambridge, MA: Harvard University Press.
Grant, R.M. (1991), 'The resource-based theory of competitive advantage: Implications for strategic formulation', *California Management Review*, **33**(3), 113–35.
Grant, R.M. (1996), 'Towards a knowledge-based theory of the firm', *Strategic Management Journal*, **17** (Winter Special issue), 109–22.
Gulati, R. (1995a), 'Does familiarity breed trust?: The implications of repeated ties for contractual choice in alliances', *Academy of Management Journal*, **38**, 85–112.
Gulati, R. (1995b), 'Social structure and alliance formation: a longitudinal analysis', *Administrative Science Quarterly*, **40**, 619–52.
Hagedoorn, J. (1996), 'Trends and patterns in strategic technology partnering since the early seventies', *Review of Industrial Organization*, **11**, 601–16.

Hamel, G. (1991), 'Competition for competence and inter-partner learning with international strategic alliances', *Strategic Management Journal*, **12** (Special issue), 83–103.

Hamel, G., Y.L. Doz and C.K. Prahalad (1989), 'Collaborate with your competitors and win', *Harvard Business Review*, **67**(1), 137–9.

Hampden-Turner, C. and F. Trompenaars (1993), *The Seven Cultures of Capitalism*, London: Doubleday.

Harrigan, K.R. (1985), *Strategies for Joint Ventures*, Lexington, MA: Lexington Books.

Harrigan, K.R. (1986), *Managing for Joint Venture Success*, New York: Lexington Books.

Harrigan, K.R. (1988a), 'Joint ventures and competitive strategy', *Strategic Management Journal*, **9**(2), 141–58.

Harrigan, K.R. (1988b), 'Strategic alliances and partner asymmetries', in F.J. Contractor and P. Lorange (eds), *Co-operative Strategies in International Business*, New York: Lexington Books, pp. 205–26.

Hatfield, L., J.A. Pearce II, R.G. Sleeth and M.W. Pitts (1998), 'Toward validation of partner goal achievement as a measure of joint venture performance', *Journal of Managerial Issues*, **10**(3), 355–72.

Hergert, M. and D. Morris (1988), 'Trends in international collaborative agreements', in F.J. Contractor and P. Lorange (eds), *Co-operative Strategies in International Business*, Lexington, MA: Lexington Books.

Hill, C.W.L., P. Hwang and C.W. Kim (1990), 'An eclectic theory of the choice of international entry mode', *Strategic Management Journal*, **11**, 117–28.

Hirschman, A.O. (1970), *Exit, Voice and Loyalty*, Cambridge, MA: Harvard University Press.

Hofstede, G. (1980), *Culture's Consequences: International Differences in Work-Related Values*, Beverley Hills, CA: Sage.

Hofstede, G. (1991), *Cultures and Organisations: Software of the Mind*, Maidenhead: McGraw-Hill.

Hubbard, R. and D.E. Vetter (1996), 'An empirical comparison of published replication research in accounting, economics, finance, and marketing', *Journal of Business Research*, **35**, 153–64.

Huber G.P. (1991), 'Organizational learning: The contributing processes and the literature', *Organizational Science*, **2**(1), 88–115.

Hui, C.H. and H.C. Trinadis (1986), 'Individualism/collectivism and psychological needs: Their relationships in two cultures', *Journal of Cross-Cultural Psychology*, **1**, 225–48.

Inkpen, A. (1995), *The Management of International Joint Ventures: An Organisational Learning Perspective*, London: Routledge.

Inkpen, A.C. (2000), 'Learning through joint ventures: A framework of knowledge acquisition', *Journal of Management Studies*, **37**(7), 1019–43.

Inkpen, A.C. (2001), 'Strategic alliances', in M.A. Hitt, R.E. Freeman and J.S. Harrison (eds), *Handbook of Strategic Management*, Oxford: Blackwell, Chapter 14, pp. 409–32.

Inkpen, A.C. and P.W. Beamish (1997), 'Knowledge, bargaining power, and the instability of international joint ventures', *Academy of Management Review*, **22**(1), 177–202.

Inkpen, A.C. and J. Birkenshaw (1994), 'International joint ventures and performance: An interorganisational perspective', *International Business Review*, **3**(3): 201–17.

Jensen, M.C. and W.H. Meckling (1976), 'The theory of the firm: Managerial behaviour, agency costs and ownership structure', *Journal of Financial Economics*, **3**, 305–60.

Johnson, G. (1992), 'Managing strategic change: Strategy, culture and action', *Long Range Planning*, **25**(1), 28–36.

Kanter, R.M. (1989), *When Giants Learn to Dance*, London: Simon & Schuster.

Kanter, R.M. (1994), 'Collaborative advantage: The art of alliances', *Harvard Business Review*, July/Aug., 96–108.

Keesing, R. (1974), 'Theories of culture', *Annual Review of Anthropology*, **3**, 73–97.

Khanna, T., R. Gulati and N. Nohria (1998), 'The dynamics of learning alliances: Competition, co-operation, and relative scope', *Strategic Management Journal*, **19**(3), 193–210.

Killing, J.P. (1983) *Strategies for Joint Venture Success*, New York: Praeger.

Kirk, J. and M.L. Miller (1986), *Reliability and Validity in Qualitative Research*, Beverly Hills: Sage.

Kogut, B. (1988), 'Joint ventures: Theoretical and empirical perspectives', *Strategic Management Journal*, **9**(4), 319–32.

Kogut, B. (1991), 'Joint ventures and the option to expand and acquire', *Management Science*, **37**(1), 19–33.

Kogut, B. and H. Singh (1988), 'The effect of national culture on the choice of entry mode', *Journal of International Business Studies*, **19**(3), 411–32.

Kogut B. and U. Zander (1992), 'Knowledge of the firm, combinative capabilities, and the replication of knowledge', *Organization Science*, **3**(3), 383–97.

Koza, M and A.Y. Lewin (1998), 'The co-evolution of alliances', *Organization Science*, **9**, 255–64.

Kumar, S. and S. Seth (1994), 'The design of co-ordination and control mechanisms for managing joint venture–parent relationships', Working Paper, University of Houston.

Lane, H.W. and P.W. Beamish (1990), 'Cross-cultural co-operative behaviour in joint ventures in LDCs', *Management International Review*, **30** (Special issue), 87–102.

Lane, P. J., J.E. Salk and M.A. Lyles (2001), 'Absorptive capacity, learning, and performance in international joint ventures', *Strategic Management Journal*, **22**(12), 1139–61.

Laurent, A. (1986), 'The cross-cultural puzzle of international human resource management', *Human Resource Management*, **25**(1), 91–102.

Lecraw, D.J. (1984), 'Bargaining Power, Ownership, and Profitability of Transnational Corporations in Developing Countries', *Journal of International Business Studies*, Spring/Summer, 27–42.

Lecraw, D.J. (1983), 'Performance of transnational corporations in less developed countries', *Journal of International Business Studies*, **14**(1), 15–33.

Lei, D. and J.W. Slocum (1991), 'Global strategic alliances: payoffs and pitfalls', *Organizational Dynamics*, **19**(3), 44–62.

Levhari D. (1966), 'Extensions of Arrow's learning by doing', *Review of Economic Studies*, **33**, 117–32.

Lewis, J.D. (1990), *Partnerships for Profit: Structuring and Managing Strategic Alliances*, New York and London: The Free Press and Collier Macmillan, Chapter 16.

Li, J.T. and S. Guisinger (1991), 'Comparative business failures of foreign-controlled firms in the United States', *Journal of International Business Studies*, **22**(2), 209–24.

Lin, Julia L., Chwo-Ming J. Yu and Dah-Hsian W. Seeto (1997), 'Motivations, partners' contributions, and control of international joint ventures', in P.W. Beamish and J.P. Killing (eds), *Co-operative Strategies: Asian Pacific Perspectives*, Lexington, MA: Lexington Books, Chapter 5, pp. 115–34.

Lincoln, Y.S. and E.G. Guba (1985), *Naturalistic Inquiry*, Beverly Hill, CA: Sage.

Lorange, P. and J. Roos (1992), *Strategic Alliances: Formation Implementation and Evolution*, Cambridge, MA: Blackwell Business.

Luo, Y. (1997), 'Partner selection and venturing success: The case of joint ventures with firms in the People's Republic of China', *Organization Science*, 8, 648–62.

Luostarinen, R. (1980) *Internationalization of the Firm*, Helsinki: Helsinki School of Economics.

Lyles, M.A. (1987), 'Common mistakes of joint venture experienced firms', *Columbia Journal of World Business*, 22, 79–85.

Lyles M.A. (1988), 'Learning among joint venture sophisticated firms', in F.J. Contractor and P. Lorange (eds), *Co-operative Strategies in International Business*, Lexington, MA: Lexington Books, pp. 301–16.

Lyles, M.A. and I.S. Baird (1994), 'Performance of international joint ventures in two Eastern European countries: The case of Hungary and Poland', *Management International Review*, 34(4): 313–29.

Lyles, M.A. and R.K. Reger (1993), 'Managing for autonomy in joint ventures: A longitudinal study of upward influence', *Journal of Management Studies*, 30(3), 383–404.

Lyles M.A. and J.E. Salk (1997), 'Knowledge acquisition from foreign parents in international joint ventures', in P.W. Beamish and J.P. Killing (eds), *Cooperative Strategies: European Perspectives*, San Francisco: The New Lexington Press. pp. 325–55.

Lynn, L. and H. Rao (1995), 'Failures of intermediate forms: A study of the Suzuki Zaibatsu', *Organization Studies*, 16, 55–80.

Macaulay, S. (1963), 'Non-contractual relations in business: A preliminary study', *American Sociological Review*, 28, 55–67.

Madhok, A. (1995), 'Revisiting multinational firms' tolerance for joint ventures: A trust-based approach', *Journal of International Business Studies*, 26(1), 117–37.

Mariti, P. and R.H. Smiley (1983), 'Co-operative agreements and the organization of industry', *The Journal of Industrial Economics*, 31(4), 437–51.

McConnell, J. and T. Nantel (1985), 'Corporate combinations and common stock returns: The case of joint ventures', *Journal of Finance*, 40(2), 519–36.

Mohr, J. and R. Spekman (1994), 'Characteristics of partnership success: Partnership attributes, communication behaviour, and conflict resolution techniques', *Strategic Management Journal*, 15(2), 135–52.

Newburry W. and Y. Zeira (1999), 'Autonomy and effectiveness of equity international joint ventures (EIJVs): An analysis based on EIJVs in Hungary and Britain', *Journal of Management Studies*, 36(2), 263–88.

Nohria, N. and C. Garcia-Pont (1991), 'Global strategic linkages and industry structure', *Strategic Management Journal*, 12 (Summer Special issue), 105–24.

Nonaka, I. (1991), 'The knowledge creating company', *Harvard Business Review*, 69, 96–104.

Nonaka, I. (1994), 'A dynamic theory of organisational knowledge creation', *Organizational Science*, 5, 14–37.

Nooteboom B. (1999), *Inter-Firm Alliances: Analysis and Design*, London and New York: Routledge.

Nti, K.O. and R. Kumar (2000), 'Differential learning in alliances', in D.O. Faulkner and M. de Rond (eds), *Co-operative Strategy: Economic, Business and Organizational Issues*, Oxford: Oxford University Press. 119–34.

Nunnally, J. C. (1978), *Psychometric Theory* (2nd edn), New York: McGraw-Hill.

Olk, P. (2001), 'Measuring strategic alliance performance: A review and commentary on what have we used and how to proceed', paper given at the Conference on 'Co-operative Strategies and Alliances: What We Know 15 Years Later', Lausanne, Switzerland, 23–25 June.

Osborn, R. and Hagedoorn, J. (1997), 'The institutionalization and evolutionary dynamics of interorganizational alliances and network', *Academy of Management Journal*, **40**, 261–78.

Osland, G.E. and S.T. Cavusgil (1996), 'Performance issues in US–China joint ventures', *California Management Review*, **38**, 106–30.

Osland, G.E. and S.T. Cavusgil (1998), 'The use of multi-party perspectives in international joint venture research', *Management International Review*, **38**(3), 191–202.

Park, S.H. and G.R. Ungson (1997), 'The effect of national culture, organisational complementarity, and economic motivation on joint venture dissolution', *Academy of Management Journal*, **40**(2), 279–307.

Parkhe, A. (1991), 'Interfirm diversity, organisational learning, and longevity in global strategic alliances', *Journal of International Business*, **22**(4), 579–601.

Parkhe, A. (1993), ' "Messy" research, methodological predispositions, and theory development in international joint ventures', *Academy of Management Review*, **18**(2), 227–68.

Patton, M.Q. (1990), *Qualitative Evaluation and Research Methods*, Newbury Park, CA: Sage.

Payne, J. (1999), 'All things to all people: Changing perceptions of "skill" among Britain's policy makers since the 1950s and their implications', Skope Research Papers, No. 1, Oxford and Warwick.

Peteraf, M.A. (1993), 'The cornerstones of competitive advantage: A resource based view', *Strategic Management Journal*, **14**, 179–91.

Pfeffer, J. and P. Nowak (1976), 'Patterns of joint venture activity: Implications for anti-trust research', *Antitrust Bulletin*, **21**, 315–39.

Podolny, J.M. (1993), 'A status based model of market competition', *American Journal of Sociology*, **98**, 829–72.

Podolny, J.M. (1994), 'Market uncertainty and social character of economic exchange', *Administrative Science Quarterly*, **39**, 458–83.

Porter, M.E. and M.B. Fuller (1986), 'Coalitions and global strategy', in M.E. Porter (ed.), *Competition in Global Industries*, Boston, MA: Harvard Business School Press, Chapter 10, pp. 315–44.

Raub, W. and J. Weesie (1990), 'Reputation and efficiency in social interactions: An example of network effects', *American Journal of Sociology*, **96**, 626–54.

Ronen, S. and O. Shenkar (1985), 'Clustering countries on attitudinal dimensions: A review and synthesis', *Academy of Management Review*, **10**(3), 435–54.

Salk, J.E. (1992), *Shared-management joint ventures: Their development patterns, challenges, and possibilities,* Unpublished Ph.D. dissertation, Massachusetts Institute of Technology, Cambridge: Sloan School of Management.

Saxton, T. (1997), 'The effects of partner and relationship characteristics on alliance outcomes', *Academy of Management Journal*, **40**(2), 443–61.

Schaan, J-L. (1983), 'Parent control and joint venture success: The case of Mexico',

Unpublished doctoral dissertation, University of Western Ontario, London, Ontario, Canada.
Schaan, J-L. (1988), 'How to control a joint venture even as a minority shareholder', *Journal of General Management*, **14**, 4–16.
Schein, E.H. (1985), *Organisational Culture and Leadership*, San Francisco: Jossey-Bass.
Schelling, T.C. (1960), *The Strategy of Conflict*, Cambridge, MA: Harvard University Press.
Schneider S.C. (1988), 'National vs. corporate culture: Implications for human resource management', *Human Resource Management*, **27**, 231–246.
Schneider, S.C. (1989), 'Strategy formulation: The impact of national culture', *Organization Studies*, **10**, 149–68.
Schneider, S.C. and A. De Meyer (1991), 'Interpreting and responding to strategic issues: The impact of national culture', *Strategic Management Journal*, **12**, 307–20.
Senge P. (1990), 'The leaders's new work: Building learning organizations', *Sloan Management Review*, **32**(1), 7–23.
Shan W. and W. Hamilton (1991), 'Country-specific advantage and international co-operation', *Strategic Management Journal*, **12**(6), 419–32.
Shenkar, O. (2001), 'Cultural distance revisited: Towards a more rigorous conceptualization and measurement of cultural differences', *Journal of International Business Studies*, **32**(3), 519–35.
Shenkar, O. and Y. Zeira (1992), 'Role conflict and role ambiguity of chief executive officers in international joint ventures', *Journal of International Business Studies*, **23**, 55–75.
Sheshinski, E. (1967), 'Tests of the learning by doing hypothesis', *Review of Economics and Statistics*, **49**(4), 568–78.
Snow, C.C. and J.B. Thomas (1994), 'Field research methods in strategic management: Contributions to theory building and testing', *Journal of Management Studies*, **31**(4), 457–80.
Sorensen, H.B. and T. Reve (1998), 'Forming strategic alliances for asset development', *Scandinavian Journal of Management*, **14**(3), 151–65.
Spekman, R.E., L.A. Isabella, T.C. MacAvoy and T. Forbes III (1996), 'Creating strategic alliances which endure', *Long Range Planning*, **29**(3), 346–57.
Spender, J. (1994), 'Organizational knowledge, collective practice and Penrose rents', *International Business Review*, **3**, 353–68.
Stuart, T.E., H. Hoang and R.C. Hybels (1999), 'Interorganisational endorsements and the performance of entrepreneurial ventures', *Administrative Science Quarterly*, **44**, 315–49.
Stopford, J.M. and L.T. Wells (1972) *Managing the Multinational Enterprise*, New York: Basic Books.
Sutton, J. (1991), *Sunk Costs and Market Structure*, Cambridge, MA: MIT Press.
Tallman, S.B. and O. Shenkar (1994), 'A managerial decision model of international cooperative venture formation', *Journal of International Business Studies*, **25**(1), 91–114.
Tashakkori, A. and C. Teddlie (1998), *Mixed methodology: combining qualitative and quantitative approaches*, Thousand Oaks, CA: Sage.
Taylor, S.J. and R. Bogdan (1984), *Introduction to Qualitative Research Methods* (2nd edn), New York: Wiley.
Teece, D.J. (1986), 'Profiting from technological innovation: Implications for integration, collaboration, licensing and public policy', *Research Policy*, **15**, 285–305.

Tomlinson, J.W.C. (1970) *The Joint Venture process in International Business: India and Pakistan*, Cambridge, MA: MIT Press.
Trompenaars, F. (1993), *Riding the Waves of Culture: Understanding Cultural Diversity in Business*, London: The Economist Books.
Tsang, E.W.K. (1998), 'Motives for strategic alliance: A resource-based perspective', *Scandinavian Journal of Management*, **14**(3), 207–21.
Tsang, E.W.K. (1999), 'A preliminary typology of learning in international strategic alliances', *Journal of World Business*, **34**(3), 211–29.
Tsang, E.W.K. (2000), 'Transaction cost and resource-based explanations of joint ventures: A comparison and synthesis', *Organization Studies*, **21**(1), 215–42.
Tsang, E.W.K. and K-M. Kwan (1999), 'Replication and theory development in organizational science: A critical realist perspective', *Academy of Management Review*, **24**(4), 759–80.
Wagner, J.A. (1995), 'Studies of individualism/collectivism: Effects on co-operation in groups', *Academy of Management Journal*, **16**, 43–70.
Weber, Y., O. Shenkar and A. Raveh (1996), 'National and corporate cultural fit in mergers/acquisitions: An exploratory study', *Management Science*, **42**(8), 1215–27.
Wernerfelt, B. (1984), 'A resource-based view of the firm', *Strategic Management Journal*, **5**, 171–80.
Wilkof, M.V., D.W. Brown and J.W. Selsky (1995), 'When stories are different: The influence of corporate culture mismatches in interorganizational relations', *Journal of Applied Behavioral Science*, **30**, 373–88.
Williamson, O.E. (1975), *Markets and Hierarchies: Analysis and Antitrust Implications*, New York: Free Press.
Williamson, O.E. (1979), 'Transaction-cost economics: The governance of contractual relations', *Journal of Law and Economics*, **22**, 3–61.
Williamson, O.E. (1985) *The Economic Institutions of Capitalism: Firms, Markets, Relational Contracting*, New York: Free Press.
Williamson, O.E. (1996), *The Politics and Economics of Redistribution and Inefficiency: The Mechanisms of Governance*, Oxford: Oxford University Press.
Woodcock C.P. and M.J. Geringer (1991), 'An exploratory study of agency costs related to the control and structure of multi-partner, international joint ventures', *Academy of Management Best Papers Proceedings*, 115–18.
Yan, A. and B. Gray (1994a), 'Bargaining power, management control, and performance in United States–China joint ventures: A comparative case study', *Academy of Management Journal*, **37**(6), 1478–517.
Yan, A. and B. Gray (1994b), 'An empirical investigation of a negotiations model in American–Chinese joint ventures', Paper given to the Conference on 'Management Issues for China in the 1990s', March, St John's College, Cambridge, England.
Yan, A. and B. Gray (1996), 'Linking management control and interpartner relationships with performance in US–Chinese joint ventures', in J. Child and Y. Lu (eds), *Management Issues in China: International Enterprises*, London: Routledge, pp. 106–27.
Yeung, H.W. (1997), 'Co-operative strategies and Chinese business networks: A study of Hong Kong transnational corporations in the ASEAN region', in P.W. Beamish and J.P. Killing (eds), *Co-operative Strategies: Asian Perspectives*, San Francisco: The New Lexington Press, pp. 215–41.
Young, S., J. Hamill, C. Wheeler and J.R. Davies (1989) *International Market Entry and Development: Strategies and Management*, Hemel Hempstead: Harvester Wheatsheaf.

Zahra, S. and G. Elhagrasey (1994), 'Strategic management of international joint ventures', *European Management Journal*, **12**(1), 83–93.
Zucker, L.G. (1986), 'Production of trust: Institutional sources of economic structure: 1840–1920', *Research in Organizational Behavior*, **8**, 53–111.
Zukin, S. and P. DiMaggio (1990), *Structures of Capital: The Social Organization of the Economy*, Cambridge, MA: Cambridge University Press.

Index

absorptive capacity 104
age 94–6
Ali, M.Y. 140, 141, 146, 147
analysis 8–9
   procedures 180–81
analytical matrix 136
Anand, B.N. 101, 103, 104, 105, 119
Anderson, E. 20, 140, 141
Argyris, C. 100
Arino, A. 121
Aristotelian method 8
Arrow, K.J. 78, 100
Attewell, P. 120
Aulakh, P.S. 159, 161–2
autonomy
   decision-making 176
   see also decision-making autonomy

Baird, I.S. 80, 140
Bangladesh 140
Banks, J.C. 117
Barkema, H.G. 160–61
Barney, J.B. 32, 77
Beamish, P.W. 1, 20, 31, 53, 80, 101, 117, 160
   performance assessment 138, 139, 140
Ben-Porath, Y. 34
Birkenshaw, J. 80, 140
Blau, P.M. 37
Bleeke, J. 1, 31, 79
Blodgett, L.L. 31, 139
Blois, K.J. 10, 13
board of directors 55
Bogdan, R. 182
boundary relationships 110–14
Bourdieu, P. 31
Briggs, C.L. 82, 180
Brown, L.T. 31, 160
Buchel, B. 2, 19, 20, 34, 57, 102, 103
   decision-making autonomy 77, 79, 81, 86

Buckley, P.J. 54, 117, 159, 180
   decision-making autonomy 77, 78, 82
   knowledge of international joint ventures 1, 2–3, 5, 8–9, 10, 11, 13
   partner selection 35, 38, 47–8
   partnering skills and cross-cultural issues 120, 121
   performance assessment 138, 140, 143, 146, 147, 155
   strategic motives and performance 18, 19, 20, 21, 23
Burgers, W.P. 33
Burt, R.S. 34, 35
Burton, F.N. 31
business
   institutions 2–3
   plan 89–90
   practice 2–3

Canada 143, 155
Carter, M.J. 8
case vignettes 185–94
Casson, M. 35, 77, 117, 121, 159
   knowledge of international joint ventures 2–3, 5, 7, 8–9, 10, 11
Cavusgil, S.T. 182
Chan, S. 101
Chapman, M. 8, 13, 78, 82, 120, 180
Child, J. 11
   culture and management 157, 159, 160
   decision-making autonomy 80, 86
   management 100, 101, 102, 112
   management control 54, 55, 57, 58, 59
   partner selection 31, 32, 35
China 58, 59, 121
Choi, C.J. 100
Chung, S. 31, 33, 34, 35, 36
Coase, R.H. 77
Cockburn, C. 120
Cohen, W.M. 104

Coleman, J.S. 31, 36
collaborative experience, prior 33–4, 44–7
commitment 122, 135–6
communication 113
competencies 133–4
conceptual innovations 8–9
Contractor, F.J. 19, 77, 138, 155
contracts 58
control 4–5, 11–12
   dimensions 54–9
   extent 4, 54
   focus 4, 54
   mechanisms 4, 54
   see also management control
corporate learning alliances 9
credibility 127
Cronbach's alpha 144
cross-cultural issues 177
   see also partnering skills and cross-cultural issues
culture/cultural
   awareness 128–30, 132
   differences 131–2, 177–8
   and management 157–74
      findings 162–73
      literature review and research questions 158–62
      management issues 172–3
   see also performance assessment: subjective and objective methods and culture

Dacin, M.T. 31, 37
data analysis techniques 145, 181–4
De Meyer, A. 161
de Rond, M. 51, 157, 158
decision-making autonomy 77–99, 176
   and age 94–6
   dynamics 96–7
   empirical evidence 79–82
   governance 78–9
   in operational decisions and strategic decisions 84–9
   and parameters of business plan 89–90
   perceptions of autonomy 82–4
   and performance 90–4
decisions, operational 84–9
decisions, strategic 84–9

Delios, A. 1, 31, 101, 138
Dickson, P.H. 160
DiMaggio, P. 37
diplomacy 123–6
Dodgson, M. 100
Doz, Y. 1, 53, 102
   partner selection 32, 33
   partnering skills and cross-cultural issues 124, 126
   strategic motives and performance 19, 28–9
duration 141–2, 143
Dussauge, P. 80, 102, 140
dynamics 96–7

East Asia 121
Eisenhardt 77
Elg, U. 35
Elhagrasey, G. 31
Ellis, H.C. 104
empathy 128–30
empirical evidence 79–82
Eramilli, M.K. 155
Erlandson, D.A. 180
Ernst, D. 1, 31, 79
Estes, W.K. 104
Europe 16, 19, 175
   cultural differences and management 178
   culture and management 163–70, 172–4
   decision-making autonomy 82–3, 91–5
   management 101, 104–7, 111, 116–17
   management control 53, 63–5, 67–74, 75
   partner selection 38, 39–41, 42–51
   partnering skills and cross-cultural issues 123
   performance assessment 139, 144, 150, 151, 152, 156
   procedures of analysis 180
   sample/data sources 179
   strategic motives and performance 21–2, 25, 26–7, 30
exit strategy 110
experience
   importance 134–5
   prior collaborative 33–4, 44–7

Farr, C.M. 31
Faulkner, D.O. 11, 128, 157
  culture and management 158, 159, 160
  decision-making autonomy 80, 86
  management 100, 102, 112, 117
  management control 54, 57, 58, 59
  partner selection 31, 32, 35, 51
Fiol, C. 100
Fischer, W.A. 31
flexibility 123–6
formation process 108–10
France 25, 74–5, 144–5, 153, 155, 166, 183–4
Frayne, C.A. 57
Fuller, M.B. 10, 18, 31

Gannon, M. 19, 158
Garcia-Pont, C. 31, 33
Garratt, R. 100
Garrette, B. 80, 140
Geringer, J.M. 11–12, 15, 80, 160, 179
  management control 53, 54, 57, 59
  partner selection 31–2, 38, 47
  performance assessment 138, 139, 140, 141–3, 145–6, 147, 148, 150, 155, 156
  strategic motives and performance 20, 21
Germany 144, 145, 155, 183, 184
Glaister, K.W. 1, 101
  decision-making autonomy 77, 79
  management control 54, 58, 59
  partner selection 38, 47–8
  performance assessment 138, 140, 143, 146, 147, 155
  strategic motives and performance 18, 19, 20, 21, 23
Gomes-Casseres, B. 1, 3, 9, 139
governance 78–9
Grant, R.M. 5, 32, 77
Gray, B. 58, 59, 81
guanxi 121, 122
Guba, E.G. 182
Guisinger, S. 160
Gulati, R. 31, 33, 34, 105, 110

Hagedoorn, J. 11, 162
Hamel, G. 33, 54, 77, 101, 103
Hamilton, W. 33

Hampden-Turner, C. 158
Harrigan, K.R. 1, 18, 54, 57, 81, 139, 160
  partner selection 31, 33
Hatfield, L. 140, 141, 145, 146, 147, 148
heads of functions 55
Hebert, L. 11–12, 20, 21, 80
  management control 53, 54, 59
  performance assessment 140, 141–3, 145–6, 147, 148, 150, 155, 156
Hergert, M. 1
Hill, C.W.L. 18
Hirschman, A.O. 8
Hofstede, G. 144, 155, 157, 160, 161
Hubbard, R. 139
Huber, G.P. 100
Hui, C.H. 160
Human Resource Management 79, 170
hypotheses development 139–43

implementation issues 114
influence, levels of 122–3
Inkpen, A.C. 80, 100, 101, 139, 140, 162
innovations, conceptual 8–9
interface 130–1
  parent 131–2
  partner 136–7
interrelationships 13–14
interview data 21–2, 23–5
Italy 144, 145, 150, 155, 183, 184

Japan 19, 30, 121, 161
Jensen, M.C. 78
Johnson, G. 134

Kanter, R.M. 31
kappa coefficients 82
Keesing, R. 158
Khanna, T. 101, 102, 103, 104, 105, 119
Killing, J.P. 20, 55, 57, 80, 81, 114, 140
Kirk, J. 182
Kogut, B. 5, 18, 33, 101, 139
Kogut-Singh index 17, 144–5, 150, 152, 153, 154, 155, 156
Korea 121
Koza, M. 102
Kumar, R. 102, 104

Kumar, S. 54
Kundu, S.K. 155
Kwan, K.-M. 139

Lane, H.W. 160
Lane, P.J. 102
Laurent, A. 157
'learning from strategic alliance experience' 103
'learning the other partner's skills' 103
'learning to learn' 104
Lecraw, D.J. 57, 139
Lee, S.H. 100
Lei, D. 9, 31
Levhari, D. 100
Levinthal, D.A. 104
Lewin, A.Y. 102
Lewis, J.D. 121
Li, J.T. 160
Likert-type scales 21, 38, 143
Lin, J. 53
Lincoln, Y.S. 182
Lorange, P. 18, 19, 31, 33, 36, 77, 81, 138
Luo, Y. 161
Luostarinen, R. 159
Lyles, M.A. 57, 79, 80, 100, 101, 104, 140
Lynn, L. 100

Macaulay, S. 36
McConnell, J. 101
Madhok, A. 117, 128, 159, 161–2
majority equity shareholding 55
management 4, 11, 100–19, 177–8
   analytic matrix 122–3
   boundary relationships 110–14
   control 53–76, 176
      extent 55–8, 65–70
      focus 58–9, 70–5
      mechanisms 54–5, 59–64
   formation process 108–10
   general 55
   implications 136–7
   operational 114–17
   research propositions 117–19
   top 34–5, 47
   see also culture and managment
Mann-Whitney test 28, 42, 47

Mariti, P. 18
market-based reasons 9
Markoczy, L. 101
Marshall, A. 7, 13–14
Meckling, W.H. 78
methodology 13–14
Mexico 59
Miller, M.L. 182
Mohr, J. 35
Morris, D. 1
motives 3–4, 9–10
   see also strategic motives
multinational enterprises 29

Nantel, T. 101
native category 13
negotiating skills 128
Netherlands 89, 135, 144, 145, 150, 155, 183, 184
Newburry, W. 78, 79, 80, 98, 115
Nohria, N. 31, 33
Nonaka, I. 100
non-contractual support 58
Nooteboom, B. 117
Norway 144, 145, 183, 184
Nowak, P. 32
Nti, K.O. 102, 104
NUD*IST software 182
Nunnally, J.C. 144

objective methods see performance assessment: subjective and objective methods and culture
Okham's razor 8
Olk, P. 138, 140
operating culture 116
operational decision making 84–9, 115
operational management 114–17
Osborn, R. 162
Osland, G.E. 182

parent interface 131–2
Park, S.H. 161
Parkhe, A. 1, 2, 5, 31, 103, 138, 139, 157
partner/partnering 10–11
   choice 4
   differences 37–8, 50
   interface 136–7
   selection 31–52, 108, 175–6

criteria 33–8, 44–9
  task-related criteria 32–3, 38–43
skills 177
skills and cross-cultural issues 130–7
  analytical matrix 136
  commitment 135–6
  competencies 133–4
  concept of skills 120
  experience, importance of 134–5
  inter-partner skills 123–30
    clear vision 126–7
    credibility 127
    flexibility and diplomacy 123–6
    negotiating skills 128
    trust, empathy and cultural awareness 128–30
  interface 130–1
  management, analytic matrix of 122–3
  managerial implications 136–7
  parent interface 131–2
  skills 120–2
Patton, M.Q. 180
Payne, J. 120
performance 5, 13, 90–4, 177
  assessment: subjective and objective methods and culture 138–56
  hypothesis 1 145–7
  hypothesis 2 147–8
  hypothesis 3 148–50
  hypothesis 4 150–6
  issues and hypotheses development 139–43
  variables, measurement of 143–5
  index 144
  overall 143
  see also strategic motives and performance
Peteraf, M.A. 32
Pfeffer, J. 32
Platonic method 8
Podolny, J.M. 36
Porter, M.E. 10, 18, 31

questionnaire data 22–3, 25–8

Rao, C.P. 155
Rao, H. 100
Raub, W. 36

Reger, R.K. 79
regression analysis 145, 147–8
relationships, boundary 110–14
research methods 179–84
research propositions 117–19
Resource Based Theory 3
resource complementarity 38–43
respondents, single and multiple 141–2
Reve, T. 31
Ronen, S. 144
Roos, J. 31, 33, 36, 81

Saelens, F.H. 31
Salk, J.E. 101, 114
sample/data sources 179–80
satisfaction 146, 147, 148, 151, 156
Saxton, T. 159, 161
Schaan, J.-L. 20, 57, 58, 59, 80, 140
Schein, E.H. 159
Schelling, T.C. 35, 122
Schneider, S.C. 158, 161
Schon, D. 100
Schoonhoven 77
selection 136–7
  task-related 32–3, 38–43
  see also partner/partnering
Senge, P. 100
Seth, S. 54
Shan, W. 33
shared strategic vision 108
Shenkar, O. 144, 157, 158, 159, 160, 162, 173–4
Sheshinski, E. 100
Sim, A.B. 140, 141, 146, 147
skills 122
  see also partner/partnering skills
Slocum, J.W. 9, 31
Smiley, R.H. 18
Snow, C.C. 182
social capital 33–4
Sorensen, H.B. 31
Spain 144, 145, 183, 184
Spearman rank order correlation 145, 146, 149, 151, 152, 154, 171
special issues 3–8
Spekman, R. 33, 35
Spender, J. 100
status indicators 36–7, 48–9
Stopford, J.M. 57
strategic decisions 84–9

strategic motives 175
strategic motives and performance 18–30
　motives 21–3
　motives for formation 18–19
　performance 19–21, 23–8
Stuart, T.E. 36, 37
subjective methods *see* performance assessment: subjective and objective methods and culture
sunk costs 14
supply-based alliances 9
survival 141–2, 143
Sutton, J. 14
Sweden 144, 145, 155, 156, 183, 184

Tallman, S.B. 162
Tashakkori, A. 182
task-related selection criteria 32–3, 38–43
Taylor, S.J. 182
Teddlie, C. 182
Teece, D.J. 33
telecommunications 89
Thomas, J.B. 182
Tomlinson, J.W.C. 57
top management, trust between 34–5, 47
training 136–7
Trinadis, H.C. 160
Trompenaars, F. 158, 159
trust 34–5, 47, 112, 128–30
Tsang, E.W.K. 32, 102, 103, 139

Ungson, G.R. 161
United Kingdom 16, 19, 175, 178
　culture and management 163–9, 173–4
　data analysis techniques 183
　decision-making autonomy 79, 80, 82–3, 89, 91–5
　management 101, 105–8, 116–17
　management control 53, 58, 63–5, 67–74, 75, 176
　partner selection 37, 38, 39–41, 42–51

partnering skills and cross-cultural issues 124, 127, 128, 130, 132–3, 135, 136
performance assessment 139–40, 143, 144, 145, 150, 151, 153, 154, 155, 156
procedures of analysis 180
sample/data sources 179
strategic motives and performance 21–2, 23, 25, 26–7, 30
United States 19, 30, 58, 104
　culture and management 160, 161
　investment banks 33
　performance assessment 140, 144, 155
upward management skills 132–3

variables, measurement of 143–5
veracity 122
Vermeulen, F. 160–1
Vetter, D.E. 139
vision, clear 126–7

Wacquant, L. 31
Wagner, J.A. 160
Weaver, K.M. 160
Weber, Y. 157
Weesie, J. 36
Wells, L.T. 57
Wernerfelt, B. 32, 77
Wilkof, M.V. 160
Williamson, O.E. 5, 8, 33, 77, 117, 159
Woodcock, C.P. 139, 160

Yan, A. 58, 59, 81
Yeung, H.W. 121
Young, S. 1, 18, 118

Zahra, S. 31
Zander, U. 101
Zeira, Y. 78, 79, 80, 98, 115, 159, 160
Zucker, L.G. 35
Zukin, S. 37